Teach Yourself VISUALLY™

PowerPoint® 2016

Barbara Boyd With Ray Anthony

Visual

A Wiley Brand

Teach Yourself VISUALLY™ PowerPoint® 2016

Published by
John Wiley & Sons, Inc.
10475 Crosspoint Boulevard
Indianapolis, IN 46256

www.wiley.com

Published simultaneously in Canada

Wiley publishes in a variety of print and electronic formats and by print-on-demand. Some material included with standard print versions of this book may not be included in e-books or in print-on-demand. If this book refers to media such as a CD or DVD that is not included in the version you purchased, you may download this material at http://booksupport.wiley.com. For more information about Wiley products, visit www.wiley.com.

Library of Congress Control Number: 2015946004

ISBN: 978-1-119-07470-0 (pbk); ISBN: 978-1-119-07496-0 (ePDF); ISBN: 978-1-119-07467-0 (ePub)

Manufactured in the United States of America

10 9 8 7 6 5 4 3 2

Trademark Acknowledgments

Contact Us

For general information on our other products and services please contact our Customer Care Department within the U.S. at 877-762-2974, outside the U.S. at 317-572-3993 or fax 317-572-4002.

For technical support please visit www.wiley.com/techsupport.

Credits

Acquisitions Editor
Aaron Black

Project Editor
Maureen S. Tullis

Copy Editor
Scott D. Tullis

Technical Editor
Vince Averello

**Manager, Content Development
& Assembly**
Mary Beth Wakefield

**Vice President, Professional
Technology Strategy**
Barry Pruett

Editorial Assistant
Jessie Phelps

Production Editor
Barath Kumar Rajasekaran

Proofreading
Debbye Butler

About the Authors

Barbara Boyd is the author of *Innovative Presentations For Dummies* with Ray Anthony and was a contributor to *Killer Presentations with Your iPad*, written by Ray Anthony and Bob LeVitus. She is also the author of *iPhone All-In-One For Dummies* and *Macs All-In One For Dummies*, both with Joe Hutsko. She writes about technology, food, travel, and country life in Italy. When not writing, she divides her time between Rome and an olive farm in Calabria.

Ray Anthony is a dynamic keynote speaker and a national leading authority in advanced presentation engineering, training, consulting, and executive coaching. He founded and is president of the Anthony Innovation Group in The Woodlands, Texas. Ray's clients include numerous Fortune 500 companies, the CIA, NASA, and the military. An expert in business creativity and innovation, he has a passion for helping people use creativity in ways that will boost their careers, bring prosperity to their organizations, and enrich their lives.

Authors' Acknowledgments

This book, like any, is a collaborative effort. Our thanks go to Acquisitions Editor Aaron Black for asking us to write this book, and to the executive and support staff at Wiley who do all the invisible background work to make these books happen. A special thank you goes to Project Editor Maureen Tullis and the editing team at T-Squared Consulting, who coached us through learning the new-to-us style of the Teach Yourself Visually series and, without complaint and with much patience, put up with changes at the eleventh hour. Thank you to Technical Editor Vince Averello for keeping us on our technical toes and doing an accurate, detailed job. Last but not least, a shout out to our literary agent Carole Jelen — we wouldn't have written this book without her guidance and support.

How to Use This Book

Who This Book Is For

This book is for the reader who has never used this particular software application but is familiar with the workings of PCs in general and specifically the Windows operating system. It is also for readers who want to expand their knowledge about PowerPoint 2016.

The Conventions in This Book

1 Steps

This book uses a step-by-step format to guide you easily through each task. Numbered steps are actions you must do; bulleted steps clarify a point, step, or optional feature; and indented steps give you the result.

2 Notes

Notes give additional information — special conditions that may occur during an operation, a situation that you want to avoid, or a cross reference to a related area of the book.

3 Icons and Buttons

Icons and buttons show you exactly what you need to click to perform a step.

4 Tips

Tips offer additional information, including warnings and shortcuts.

5 Bold

Bold type shows command names, options, and text or numbers you must type.

6 Italics

Italic type introduces and defines a new term.

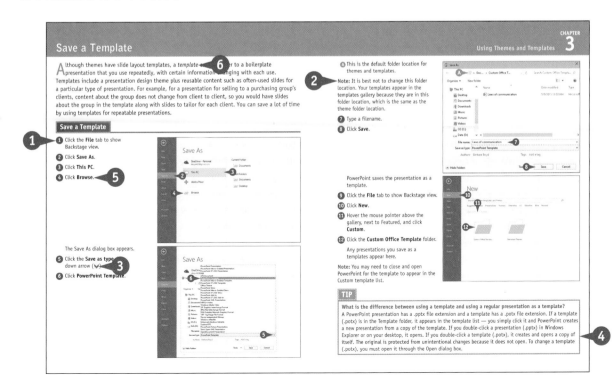

Table of Contents

Chapter 3   Using Themes and Templates

Chapter 4   Writing and Formatting Text

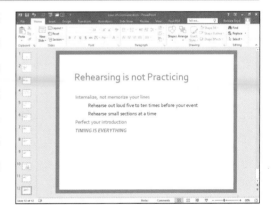

Table of Contents

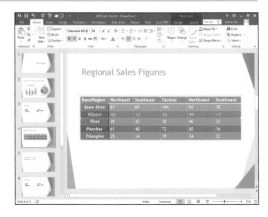

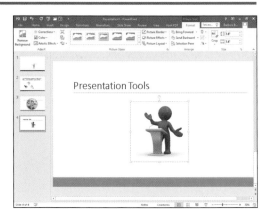

Chapter 7 — Incorporating Media

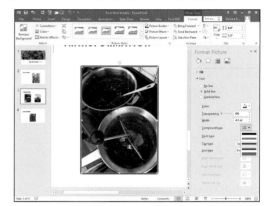

Chapter 8 — Enhancing Slides with Action

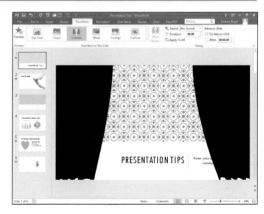

Table of Contents

Chapter 9   Organizing Slides

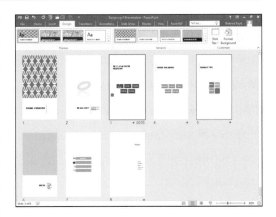

Chapter 10   Working with Outlines

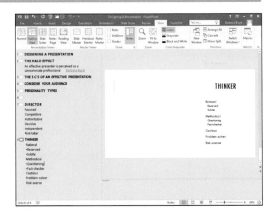

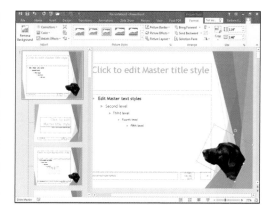

Chapter 12 Finalizing a Slide Show

Table of Contents

Chapter 13 · Presenting a Slide Show

Chapter 14 · Sharing a Presentation

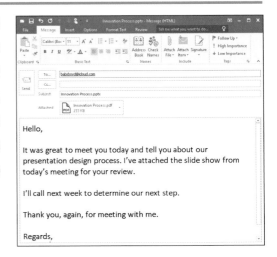

Chapter 15 — Printing Presentations

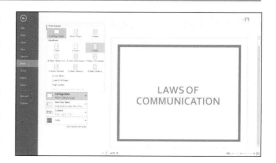

Chapter 16 — Changing PowerPoint Options

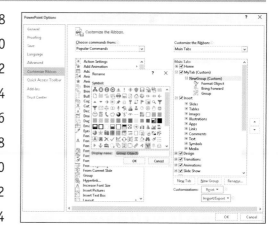

Table of Contents

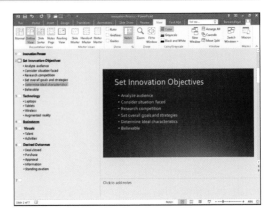

CHAPTER 1

Starting with PowerPoint Basics

Whether you want to convey ideas to your staff, convince a new client to hire you, or give a Technology, Entertainment, Design (TED) talk, PowerPoint provides the tools for creating visuals to support your words and help your audience remember you. This chapter covers PowerPoint basics, then explains the parts of the PowerPoint window, different views, and more.

DESIGNING A PRESENTATION

Introducing PowerPoint

With PowerPoint, you can create a compelling, professional-looking slide show. The PowerPoint program provides tools you can use to build presentations that include graphics, charts, video, sound, animations, and an assortment of ways to transition from slide to slide. It provides various views to create, organize, view, and display your presentation. Many tasks start in Backstage view. To access this view, click the **File** tab on the Ribbon. For more on creating presentations, see Chapter 2.

Choose a Slide Theme and Layout

A slide *theme* applies preset design elements such as colors, background graphics, and text styles to a slide. A particular slide *layout* applied to a slide determines what type of information that slide includes. For example, a Title Slide layout has a title and subtitle. A Title and Content layout includes a title, plus a placeholder that holds a list of bullet points, a table, or other graphic elements. For more on themes and layouts, see Chapter 3.

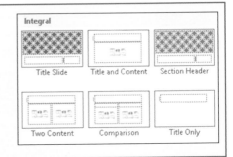

Add Content and Media

You can create original text, charts, graphs, and graphics in PowerPoint or import a media file, such as a photo, logo, or video, created in another app. Normal view displays all the elements of your slide. The Slides pane shows miniature versions of all your slides, whereas the Outline pane displays only the text of each slide. You can insert text boxes that enable you to add slide text that does not appear in the presentation outline. For more on content and media, see Chapters 4 to 7. For more on adding animation, see Chapter 8.

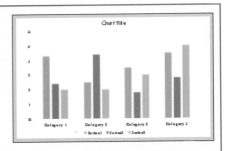

Organize Slides

After creating several slides, you may need to reorganize them to create the proper sequence for your presentation. You can reorder slides in Slide Sorter view. This view shows slide thumbnails that you can move, delete, duplicate, or hide. You can also perform these actions on the Slides pane in Normal view. For more on organizing slides, see Chapter 9.

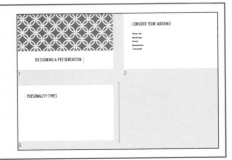

Build an Outline

You can type text in outline form to build slides for your presentation. In the Outline pane in Normal view, an icon represents each slide, and each slide contains a slide title next to the icon. Second-level lines of text on the outline appear as bullet points on the slide. These bullets convey the main points you want to make about each topic. For more on building outlines, see Chapter 10.

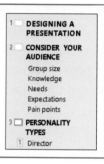

Work with Masters

A set of slide themes and layouts combines to create a set of *master* slides. Masters enable you to change design elements and add content that you want to appear in a particular location on all slides that use that template. This saves you from having to add repeating content, such as your company logo, to each slide. For example, you can set up the master so an identical footer appears on every slide. For more on working with masters, see Chapter 11.

Set Up Your Show and PowerPoint Options

You can add audio, animations, and transitions to your slides. You can record a narration that plays when you give your presentation. Use animation to move an element on-screen, such as a ball bouncing onto the screen. Transitions control how a new slide appears on-screen — for example, a slide can fade in over the previous slide. For more on setting up a show, see Chapter 12. For more on customizing PowerPoint to fit your needs, see Chapter 16.

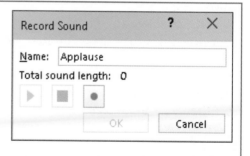

Present or Share a Slide Show

After you add the content, choose slide designs, and add special effects, you are ready to run your slide show presentation. Tools appear on-screen during the slide

show — they help you control your presentation and even enable you to make annotations on your slides as you present them. Presenter view shows your notes and provides a timer to ensure that your presentation is flawless. For more on presenting, sharing, or printing a slide show, see Chapters 13, 14, and 15. For more on designing a presentation, see Chapter 16.

Explore the PowerPoint Start Screen

You start PowerPoint from the Windows 10 Start screen so that you can begin designing a presentation. When you open PowerPoint 2016, the Start screen appears automatically. From the Start screen, you can start a new presentation or open an existing one. The Start screen lists recently opened presentations and enables you to create a presentation from templates on your computer, or search for PowerPoint templates on the Internet, which is explained in Chapter 3.

Explore the PowerPoint Start Screen

1 Press the **Windows** button (⊞).

The Start menu appears.

2 Hover the mouse pointer slightly above the toolbar to hide it.

The All Apps button appears in the lower left corner.

3 Click the **All apps** button.

A scrollable pane on the left displays an alphabetical list of all apps on your computer.

4 Position the mouse pointer to the right of the apps list.

A scroll bar appears.

5 Scroll down to find PowerPoint 2016.

If you do not see it, scroll to and click **Microsoft Office 2016**, and look for PowerPoint 2016.

6 Click PowerPoint 2016.

PowerPoint opens and displays the Start screen.

Ⓐ You can open a recently opened presentation here.

Ⓑ You can open a file from your computer, an external drive, or cloud service here.

Ⓒ You can create a new presentation by clicking a template.

Ⓓ You can use the search box to look for a template on the Internet.

⑦ Click one of the themes.

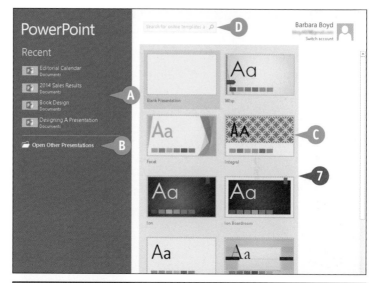

The theme preview dialog box opens.

Ⓔ Click the arrows (◀ or ▶) to view the theme's layouts.

Ⓕ You can preview different theme designs here.

Ⓖ Click the arrows (◀ or ▶) to view the previous or next theme.

Ⓗ Click **Create** to start a new presentation.

Ⓘ You can click the **Close** button (✕) to cancel the preview dialog box.

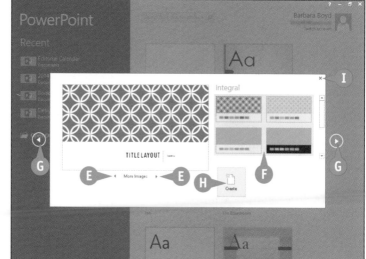

TIP

Is there a quicker way to open PowerPoint?

Yes, you can add the PowerPoint app icon to the taskbar for one-click access to the program:

① Follow Steps 1 to 5 in this section.

② Right-click **PowerPoint 2016**.

③ Click Pin to taskbar.

The app icon appears on the taskbar.

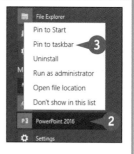

Create a Presentation in Backstage View

You can create a new presentation from the PowerPoint Start screen, or from the File tab on the Ribbon (also known as *Backstage view*). You can create a new presentation from scratch or by using a theme and templates. Creating a presentation from scratch enables you to design freely without preconceived notions, whereas working from a template saves time and promotes ideas by starting you off with a certain look and color scheme. You can find templates on your computer, as well as on the Internet for free or for a fee.

Create a Presentation in Backstage View

1 Click the **File** tab to show the Backstage view.

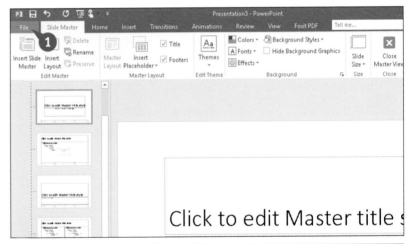

2 Click **New**.

   Templates available on your computer appear.

Ⓐ Click here to choose a blank presentation.

Ⓑ You can hover the mouse pointer over a template and click the **Pushpin** button (📌), which pins a theme to this list (📌 changes to 📌).

3 Click the presentation theme of your choice.

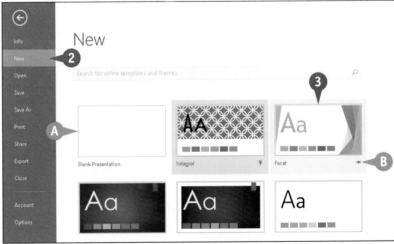

This example uses the Facet theme.

④ Click a color scheme.

The preview changes to reflect your preferences.

⑤ Click **Create**.

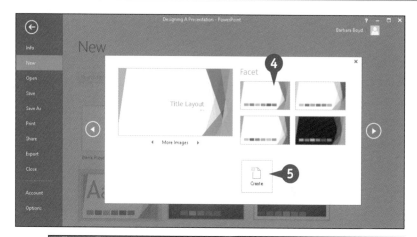

PowerPoint creates a presentation from the template.

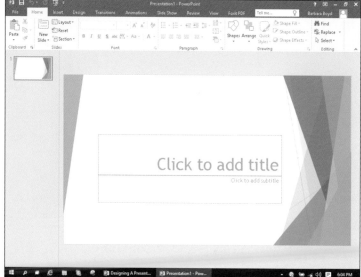

Is there another way to create a blank presentation?

Yes. When you launch PowerPoint from the Windows 10 Start screen, the Start screen has an option to create a blank template. Simply click the **Blank Presentation** option.

Can I get templates from the Internet?

Yes. You can find many templates online, a lot of them free. Click the **File** tab, and then click **New**. At the top of the screen, click in the **Search online templates and themes** text box to start the process. See Chapter 3 to learn more about finding templates online.

Save a Presentation

After you create a presentation, you should save it for future use. Saving a PowerPoint file works much like saving any other Microsoft Office program file: You need to specify the location in which to save the file and give the file a name. By default, PowerPoint saves your presentation every ten minutes. If you want to save a presentation that has previously been saved, you can click the **Save** icon in the upper left corner of the PowerPoint window to quickly save it.

Save a Presentation

1. Click the **File** tab to show the Backstage view as shown in the section "Create a Presentation in Backstage View."

2. Click **Save As**.

3. Click **This PC**.

4. Click **Browse**.

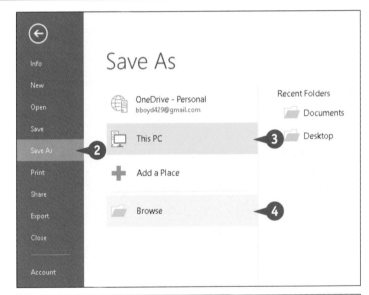

The Save As dialog box appears.

5. Click the folder where you want to save your file.

   This example saves to the Documents folder.

6. Click in the **File name** text box to select the text and then type a filename.

   A. You can click and drag the scroll bar to find more folder locations.

   B. You can click **New folder** to create a new folder.

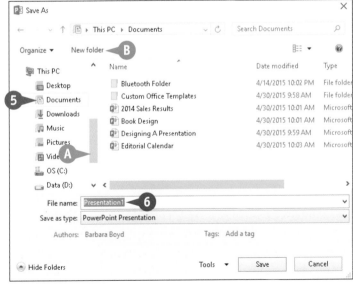

In this example, the filename is Presentation Tips.

⑦ Click the **Save as Type** drop-down arrow (∨) to change the file type from the default.

Note: If you choose a format other than the default PowerPoint format, you may see a prompt about an issue such as version compatibility. Respond to the prompt to continue saving.

⑧ Click **Save**.

PowerPoint saves the presentation and the Save As dialog box closes.

ⓒ The new filename appears in the title bar.

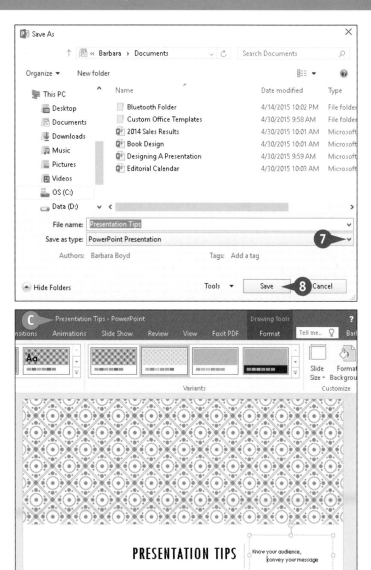

Can I change how often PowerPoint automatically saves my presentation?
Yes. By default, the AutoRecover feature is set to save information every 10 minutes, but you can use the PowerPoint Options dialog box to change the frequency your work is saved. See Chapter 16 to learn how to change PowerPoint options.

Is there a quicker way to reach Save As in Backstage view?
Yes. You can click the **Save** icon (🖫) on the Quick Access Toolbar or press Ctrl + S. To save a copy of your presentation under a new name, click the **File** tab, click **Save As**, and then specify a new filename and save location.

Explore Normal View

PowerPoint offers several views that you can use to work on different aspects of your presentation. Having different views is important because certain views are better for performing certain tasks. For example, arranging slides is easiest in Slide Sorter view.

You will usually work in Normal view, where you can create, position, and format objects on each slide. In Outline view, you can enter presentation text in outline form and the text automatically appears on the slide. In Slide Show view, you can preview your presentation as your audience will see it.

Ⓐ Navigation Buttons

You can change views by clicking the View tab on the Ribbon and then clicking the command buttons for the view you want to use, or by clicking the command buttons on the status bar. These buttons include Normal view (▣), Slide Sorter view (▦), Reading view (▤), and Slide Show view (�).

Ⓑ Slides Thumbnail Pane

The Thumbnails pane contains thumbnails of each slide. The thumbnails are numbered by the order in which they appear in the slide show. If you have more slides than fit in the pane, a scroll bar appears so you can scroll up and down through your show. You can click and drag the thumbnails to change the order of slides and you can delete slides from this pane.

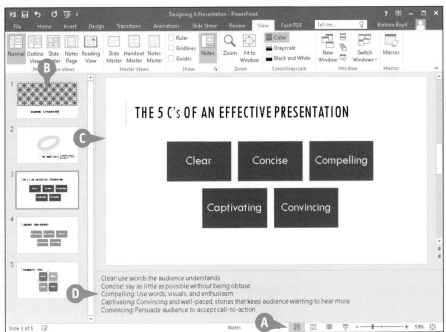

Ⓒ Slide Pane

The Slide pane is the largest pane in Normal view and shows a slide and all its contents. Here you can create and manipulate slide objects such as graphics and animations, and type text directly onto the slide. Drag the scroll bar on the right up or down to move to the previous or next slide.

Ⓓ Notes Pane

The Notes pane appears below the Slide pane. You can type speaker notes associated with each individual slide. Position the mouse pointer on the line between the two panes until the pointer becomes a resizing tool, then click and drag to resize the Notes pane. You can refer to your notes while presenting without your audience seeing them.

Navigate PowerPoint Views

In addition to Normal view, you can use Slide Sorter view to organize slides, Notes Page view to create detailed speaker notes, and Slide Show view or Reading view to display your presentation. Each view has certain tasks that are easier to perform in that particular view.

Outline View

Outline view has a pane that enables you to enter text into your slides in a familiar outline format. In this view, the Outline pane replaces the Slides Thumbnail pane. Top-level headings in the outline are slide titles, and entries at the second level appear as bullet points, but text in text boxes does not appear. The outline is a great reference if you need to write a paper to accompany your presentation.

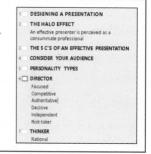

Slide Sorter View

Slide Sorter view is the best view to change the order of slides, delete slides, or duplicate slides. In Slide Sorter view, you can click and drag a slide to move it. If you double-click a slide, PowerPoint changes to Normal or Outline view — whichever you last used — and displays that slide in the Slide pane.

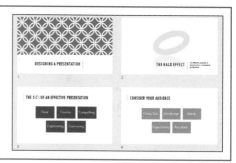

Reading View

You can click Slide Show view (⌨) to present your show. Slides appear one at a time at full screen size. Reading view (📖) is very similar to Slide Show view, but gives you more navigation flexibility because the status bar remains at the bottom of the screen and the title bar remains at the top. To exit either view, press Esc.

Notes Page View

In Notes Page view, you can display each slide and the associated speaker notes as one full page. You can also type notes on the page while viewing your slide. From the View tab, click Notes Page to work with this view.

Navigate Slides

Slide show presentations generally contain many slides. As a result, PowerPoint provides different ways to navigate the slides so that you can choose one that is most efficient and effective for what you are doing. The way you work on your project determines the way you choose to navigate. You can use the various scroll bar buttons to navigate slides in Normal view, click a slide in the Slides Thumbnail pane to select a slide, or view slide thumbnails in Slide Sorter view.

Navigate Slides

Navigate Using the Scroll Bar

1 Click the **View** tab.

2 Click **Normal**.

3 Click and drag the scroll bar to scroll through slides.

4 Click the **Next Slide** button (⯆) to display the next slide.

5 Click the **Previous Slide** button (⯅) to display the previous slide.

Navigate Using the Slide Thumbnail Pane

1 Click and drag the scroll bar to move through the slides.

2 Click a slide thumbnail.

The selected slide appears in the Slide pane.

Navigate Using the Outline View

① Click Outline View.

② Click and drag the scroll bar to move through the slides.

③ Click a slide icon (▢).

The selected slide appears in the Slide pane.

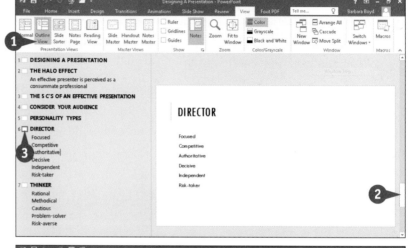

Navigate in Slide Sorter View

① Click Slide Sorter.

Slide Sorter view appears.

② Click and drag the scroll bar to move through the slides.

③ Click a slide.

PowerPoint selects the slide.

Note: Double-click a slide to view it in Normal view.

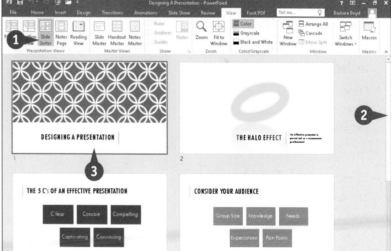

TIPS

Why are there no scroll bars in the Slide Thumbnails or Outline View panes?

If PowerPoint can display all slides in the presentation without scrolling down or up, it does not display a scroll bar. The fact that there is not a scroll bar means you are viewing all the slides in the presentation.

Is there a way to see more slides in Slide Sorter view so I can easily find the one I want?

Yes. You can click and drag the Zoom slider in the lower right corner of the PowerPoint window to make the slides smaller, which shows more slides. You can also click the **Zoom In** (➕) or **Zoom Out** (➖) buttons at each end of the slider.

Work with Ribbon Groups, Commands, and Galleries

You can find all the commands that you need to design and present your slide show on the *Ribbon,* the user interface at the top of the PowerPoint window. If you work with other Microsoft Office apps, you are probably familiar with the Ribbon, but knowing the location of PowerPoint commands means you can work more efficiently.

Related commands are grouped on the Ribbon tabs. Commands are further arranged into groups on the tab, with the group names shown at the bottom of the group. Some command buttons include down arrows that display menus or galleries of commands.

Work with Ribbon Groups, Commands, and Galleries

1 Click any tab on the Ribbon.

This example selects the Insert tab.

The commands for the particular tab you clicked appear on the Ribbon.

2 Click the button or check box for any command.

This example selects SmartArt.

The SmartArt dialog box appears.

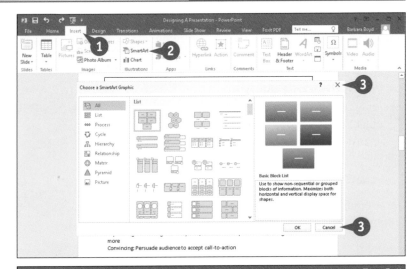

3 Click **Cancel** or the **Close** button (**X**) to cancel the command.

4 Click the down arrow (⬇) next to any button to display a gallery.

Note: Clicking a down arrow (⬇) displays a menu or gallery.

5 Click the choice you want from the menu or gallery that appears.

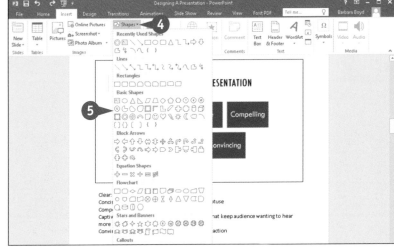

6 Click a dialog box launcher (▣).

Note: A dialog box launcher (▣) displays a dialog box when you click it.

In this example, the Font dialog box appears.

7 Click **OK** to accept any selections you have made in the dialog box.

The presentation reflects any changes you made.

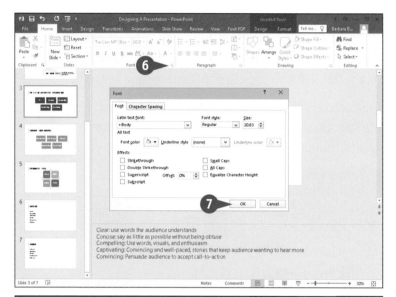

A For some Ribbon commands, such as those on a contextual tab, you must first select an object on the slide before choosing a command.

B Note that the Drawing Tools Format tab does not appear until you click an object such as a text box.

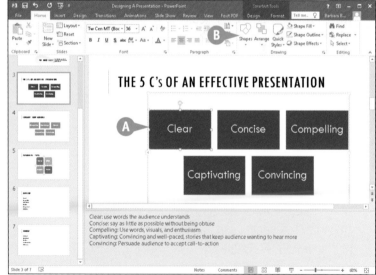

TIPS

How do I learn what a particular Ribbon button does?

Position the mouse pointer over the button and a *ScreenTip* appears, showing the name, any available shortcut key, and a brief description of the button. By default, ScreenTip features are enabled, but you can disable them in the PowerPoint Options dialog box (described in Chapter 16).

Can I use keyboard commands rather than the mouse or trackpad?

Yes. The *KeyTips* features enable you to use keyboard shortcuts to select and execute Ribbon commands. Press and release Alt; letters or numbers appear next to the Quick Access Toolbar and Ribbon commands. Press the letter or number for the command you want to use. Press Esc to abort using KeyTips.

Using the Quick Access Toolbar

The *Quick Access Toolbar* appears above the File tab at the top of the PowerPoint application window. For your convenience, it contains command buttons for the most commonly used PowerPoint commands. When you first open PowerPoint, the Save, Undo, Redo, Slide Show, and Customize Quick Access Toolbar buttons are present.

You can click the command buttons on the Quick Access Toolbar to execute these commands quickly. You can also easily add (or remove) some of these commonly used commands to (or from) the Quick Access Toolbar. You can even add your personal favorite commands to it.

Using the Quick Access Toolbar

1 Click the down arrow (▼) on the right side of the Quick Access Toolbar to access the drop-down menu.

A Note the check mark appearing next to commands on the Quick Access Toolbar.

B Click **More Commands** to see all available commands (see Chapter 16 for more information).

2 Click one of the commands from the drop-down menu.

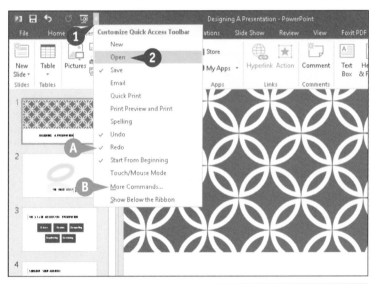

C The selected command appears as an icon on the Quick Access Toolbar and a check mark appears next to it in the drop-down menu.

You can click a button on the Quick Access Toolbar to execute a command.

Note: Right-click a command on the Ribbon and click **Add to Quick Access Toolbar** to quickly add that command to the Quick Access Toolbar.

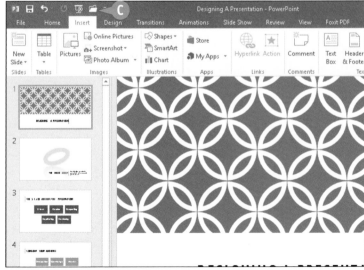

Arrange Presentation Windows

Sometimes you need to view multiple presentations on-screen at once — for example, when you want to compare their contents or copy a slide from one presentation to another. You can arrange PowerPoint in such a way that you can see multiple open presentations at the same time. This handy feature is found on the View tab.

Unless you have a really big monitor, you should limit the number of open presentations to three or four. Otherwise, you cannot see enough of each presentation to make this feature useful.

Arrange Presentation Windows

① Open two or more presentations.

② Click the **View** tab.

③ Click **Cascade** (⧉).

The presentation windows move so they overlap.

Ⓐ You can click **Switch Windows** and then click a presentation in the menu to make that presentation active.

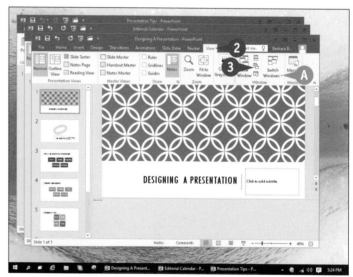

④ Click **Arrange All** (▤).

The presentation windows appear side by side.

Ⓑ You can drag a window's title bar to move the window.

⑤ Click the **Maximize** button (▢) on one of the windows.

The window appears full screen again.

Ⓒ If you do not see the Window buttons on the Ribbon, click the down arrow on the Window tab to see the gallery of commands.

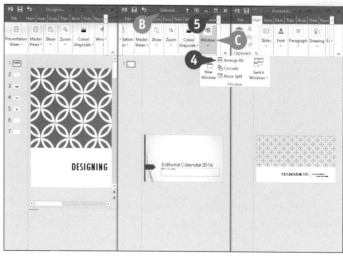

Close a Presentation

When you finish working with a presentation, you can close it. Closing the presentation gives you a less cluttered workspace on your computer and frees valuable computer memory to process other work that you need to do. If you share the file with others on a network, closing it allows them to access the file without worrying about sharing violations.

When you close a file with unsaved changes, PowerPoint prompts you to save the presentation to avoid accidentally losing your work. For more on saving a presentation, see the section "Save a Presentation" in this chapter.

Close a Presentation

1 Click the **Close** button (✕).

Ⓐ You can click the **Search** (♀) button on the taskbar and type a keyword from your presentation in the text field. A list of files that contain that keyword appears and you can click one to view it.

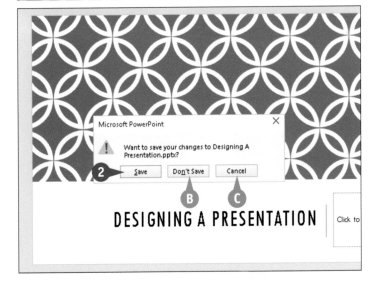

A message may appear, asking if you want to save changes.

2 Click **Save**.

Ⓑ If you do not want to save the changes to your presentation, click **Don't Save**.

Ⓒ To abort closing the presentation, click **Cancel**.

The file closes, but PowerPoint remains open.

Note: You can also close the presentation, and PowerPoint, by pressing [Alt]+[F4].

Using Help

Microsoft Office PowerPoint Help offers two ways to get help. If you are connected to the Internet, it provides help articles and videos from Microsoft Office Online. You find answers to your questions by typing keywords. If an Internet connection is not available, type your keyword in the Tell Me field on the Ribbon; PowerPoint shows you where to find the task you seek on the Ribbon.

Using Help

1 Click the **Help** button (?).

2 In the PowerPoint Help window, type a keyword in the search text box.

3 Click the **Search** button (🔍) to show a list of online articles and videos.

Ⓐ You can click an article, which may have steps, to answer your question.

4 Click a video to view a solution to your problem.

Ⓑ You can click to **Pause** (⏸), adjust the **Volume** (🔊), turn on **Closed Captioning** (CC), **Share** (📤) the video, see more **Info** (ⓘ) such as the name or creation date, adjust **Video Quality** (HQ), or see the **Full Screen** (⛶) of the video within the Help window.

5 Hover the pointer in the upper right corner to reveal the button to close (✕) the window.

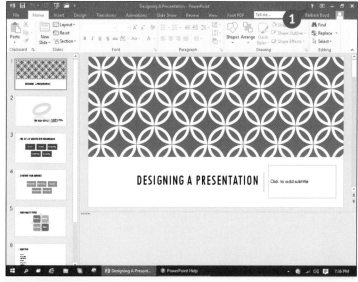

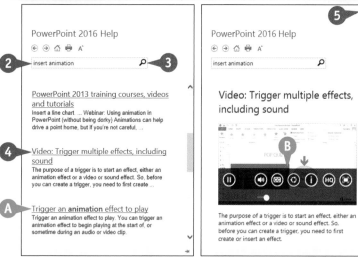

CHAPTER 2

Creating a Presentation

As you plan your presentation, consider how to arrange information on each slide to support and convey your message. PowerPoint comes with preset layouts that contain different arrangements of various types of information such as text, charts, or images. Your presentation will probably comprise a variety of slide layouts, which saves you the time and trouble of designing slides from scratch.

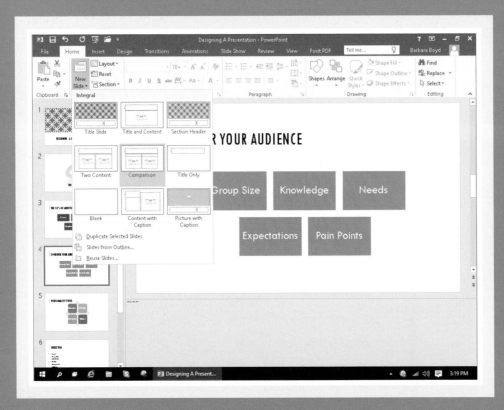

Understanding Slide Structure

You use PowerPoint to build a presentation slide by slide. Those slides, whether shown as a slide show that accompanies a speech or as a self-running video at a kiosk or on a website, make up your presentation. A *template* contains several preset slide layouts that consist of different combinations and arrangements of placeholders. *Placeholders* are rectangular objects on slides that you replace with your own text, graphics, charts, tables, SmartArt, and multimedia while maintaining the preset layout. Slides may contain one or more placeholders, and your presentation may contain diverse layouts. Different types of slide layouts serve different functions in your presentation.

Title Slide

The Title slide typically appears first and includes the presentation title or topic, and a subtitle or image. The subtitle might be the presenter's name or the name of the presenting company, or it might be the date and location of the presentation. There is usually just one title slide in a presentation, though they are sometimes used at the beginning of slide sections.

Title and Content Slide

A Title and Content slide is perhaps the most frequently used slide layout. It includes a title plus a placeholder where you can add one of several types of content: bulleted lists, tables, charts, clip art, pictures, SmartArt graphics (diagrams), or media clips (sound or video).

Choose an Appropriate Layout

PowerPoint provides preset slide layouts for your convenience. Choose layouts that best present your concepts and the associated data or graphics and support each part of your presentation. A diagram with key words helps your audience pick up on the salient points of your presentation, and a single memorable image displayed while you relate a story can have more impact than six items on a bulleted list.

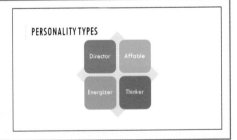

Additional Slide Elements

You can add elements that automatically repeat on each slide — for example, your name, your company's logo, the name of the event, or the slide number. This not only saves you work but gives your presentation a consistent look.

Understanding Layouts and Placeholders

Many presentation slides combine a slide title, graphic elements, and slide text in the form of a bulleted list or table. The slide layout you select determines where the title, graphics, and text appear. Titles, bulleted lists, and other text usually exist in text placeholders. Content placeholders can also contain graphic elements, tables, charts, pictures, and SmartArt. The layout of a slide is established by the placement of placeholders on the slide; however, you can resize or move placeholders.

Slide Layout Gallery

Clicking the down arrow (▼) of the New Slide button on the Ribbon opens the Slide Layout gallery. You will find a New Slide button on both the Home and Insert tabs. You can use the gallery to insert a slide with a particular layout.

Placeholders

Each slide layout has an arrangement of placeholders. Text placeholders accept only text. Content placeholders accept either text or a graphic element. A content placeholder contains icons that help you insert graphics. You can move placeholders to design slides that suit your particular needs.

Types of Slide Layouts

The Slide Layout gallery enables you to choose a layout for a slide. Some layouts hold only text, such as the Title Slide, Section Header, and Title Only layouts. Other layouts include a title, plus content placeholders. The options vary between *themes* — the design you choose when you create a new presentation — and may include: Two Content, Comparison, Content with Caption, Picture with Caption, Quote with Caption, Name Card, True or False, and Blank. Each layout includes placeholders to position your information.

Slide Layouts Remain Flexible

You can adjust a layout to meet your particular needs. Handles appear on placeholder borders — dragging any handle resizes the placeholder. To move a placeholder, click its border and then drag it to another location. If a placeholder does not contain any content, it is not visible when you print or show your presentation. You can also insert text, graphics, or media without a placeholder or replace an existing layout with a different one. Each task is explained in this chapter.

Using Layouts with Content Placeholders

Content placeholders appear on most of the slide layouts that you will use. You can use content placeholders to build your presentation effectively and efficiently. Content placeholders are convenient containers that enable you to place text or graphics on a slide. Placeholders are easy to move and simple to change, and enable you to insert text or one of six types of graphical objects onto the slide. You can use text to convey ideas, and graphics to make your presentation more aesthetically dynamic and visually appealing.

Ⓐ Bulleted List

Click the bullet to add text or a list of items. Press Enter at the end of each item.

Ⓑ Tables

Click the **Insert Table** icon (⬜) to create a table. You can specify the number of columns and rows in the table.

Ⓒ Charts

Click the **Insert Chart** icon (▮▮) to generate a chart using a chart type that you specify and data that you type into a spreadsheet.

Ⓓ SmartArt

Click the **Insert a SmartArt Graphic** icon (⬜) to insert a diagram using one of the many diagram styles PowerPoint provides.

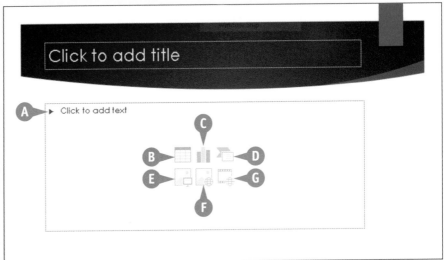

Ⓔ Pictures

Click the **Insert** Pictures icon (⬜) to insert a picture file such as a bitmap or JPEG that you have stored on your computer or other storage media.

Ⓕ Online Pictures

Click the **Insert Online Picture** icon (⬜) to select an image from the built-in clip art collection, or to import clip art from Microsoft Office Online.

Ⓖ Videos

Click the **Insert Video** icon (⬜) to insert a video file that plays during the slide show. You can specify that it plays on command or automatically.

CHAPTER
2

Add a Slide

When you open a new presentation, PowerPoint creates a blank Title slide. To build your presentation, you can add as many slides as you want — just select one from the slide templates in the Slide Layout gallery. The various slide layouts enable you to give your presentation diversity and to accomplish different objectives such as comparing two lists or showing data in chart form. PowerPoint inserts slides after the currently selected slide. With some exceptions, if you click the main part of the New Slide button, PowerPoint inserts a slide with the same layout as the selected slide.

Add a Slide

1 With a presentation open, click the **Home** tab.

2 Click the slide that appears before where you want to add the new slide.

3 Click the **New Slide** down arrow ( ).

The Slide Layout gallery appears.

4 Click the desired slide layout from the gallery.

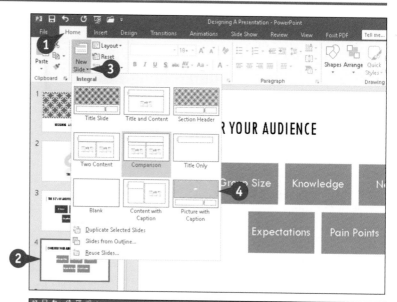

A A new slide appears after the slide you clicked in Step **2** with the specified layout.

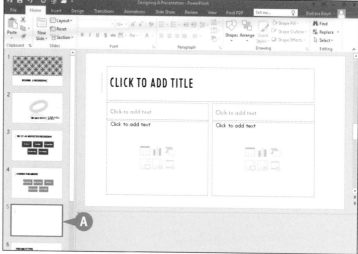

Change a Slide Layout

If you decide a slide's original layout no longer works, you can apply a different slide layout in Normal view or Slide Sorter view. This enables you to change the layout without designing the slide again. If the configuration of the new layout does not include an element from the original layout — such as a chart that you have set up — PowerPoint keeps that additional element on the slide, even with the new layout.

Change a Slide Layout

1 Select the slide whose layout you want to change.

Note: To learn how to select a slide, see Chapter 1.

2 Click the **Home** tab.

3 Click the Layout down arrow ( ).

The Slide Layout gallery appears.

4 Click a slide layout from the gallery.

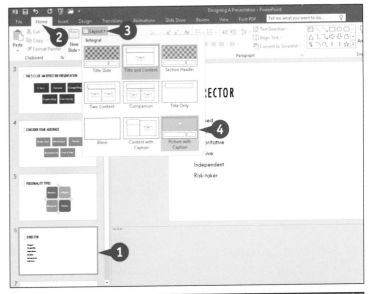

The slide changes to the selected layout.

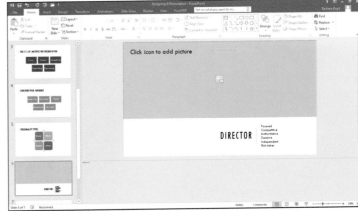

Make a Duplicate Slide

If you need to make two slides very similar, you can design the first one, duplicate it using the Duplicate Slide feature, and then make minor changes to the new slide. For example, if a slide at the beginning of a presentation lists key topics, you can duplicate it, make minor changes, and use it as a summary. Or you may want to make a duplicate slide in one presentation, modify it while looking at both slides, and then move it. Duplicating a slide can save time and ensure accuracy of the information on the slide.

Make a Duplicate Slide

1 In Normal, Outline, or Slide Sorter view, select the slide(s) you want to duplicate.

Note: To select multiple slides, click the first slide, and then press **Ctrl** while clicking additional slides.

2 Click the **Home** tab.

3 Click the New Slide down arrow (▾).

4 Click Duplicate Selected Slides.

Ⓐ PowerPoint duplicates the selected slide(s).

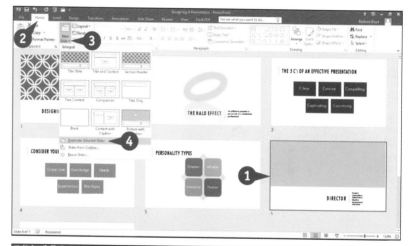

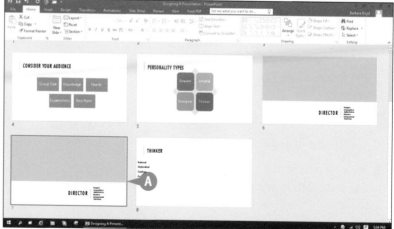

Insert a Slide from Another File

You can insert a slide from one presentation file into another. This can be a great timesaver when you have created a slide with a highly detailed chart, table, or diagram in another presentation. Or you may want to use a favorite slide in several presentations. For example, a slide showing sales growth may go into a presentation for the sales team, a different one for management, and yet another presentation for potential customers. Importing the slide from the other presentation saves you the trouble of reentering data and reformatting the object on the slide.

Insert a Slide from Another File

① Select the slide after which you want to insert the new slide.

Note: You can also perform this task in Slide Sorter view. See Chapter 1 to learn how to switch views.

② Click the **Home** tab.

③ Click the **New Slide** down arrow (▼).

The Slide Layout gallery appears.

④ Click Reuse Slides.

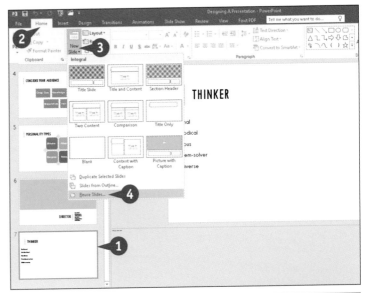

The Reuse Slides task pane appears.

⑤ Click Open a PowerPoint File.

The Browse dialog box opens.

⑥ Click the folder that contains the presentation file you want to view.

⑦ Click the presentation file that contains the slide you want to insert.

⑧ Click **Open**.

The slides of the selected presentation appear in the Reuse Slides task pane.

9 Drag the scroll bar to find the slide you want to insert.

10 Click the slide.

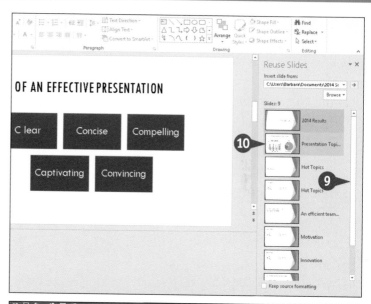

A PowerPoint inserts the slide you clicked after the slide you originally selected.

You can click the Close button (✕) to close the Reuse Slides task pane.

Note: If you have two presentations open, you can drag slides from one to another.

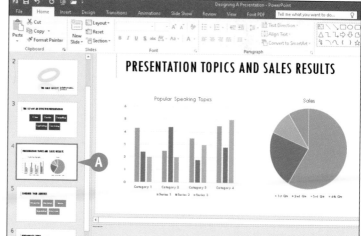

TIP

Is there an easy way to import slides from multiple presentations?
Yes. Repeat Steps **1** to **8** and then follow these steps:

1 Click the **Browse** down arrow (▼) in the Reuse Slides task pane.

2 Click Browse File.

The Browse dialog box appears so that you can open a different presentation file in the Reuse Slides task pane.

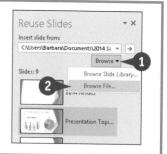

Delete a Slide in Normal or Slide Sorter View

As you build your presentation, you may decide you do not need a particular slide. In this case, you can simply delete that slide. It is common to use an existing presentation as the basis for other presentations. In that situation, you may need to delete several slides that are irrelevant or out of date. You can either hide or delete slides. If you are confident that you do not need a slide, delete it to keep your presentation uncluttered.

Delete a Slide in Normal or Slide Sorter View

Delete a Slide in Normal View

1 Click the **Normal** View button (image) in the status bar.

Note: For more on Normal view, see Chapter 1.

2 In the Slide Thumbnails pane, right-click the slide you want to delete.

The submenu appears.

3 Click Delete Slide.

PowerPoint deletes the slide.

Note: You can also click the slide and then press Delete.

A Click the Undo button (image) on the Quick Access Toolbar if you decide you need the slide and want it back in the presentation.

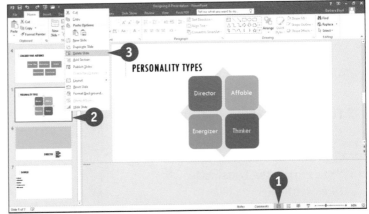

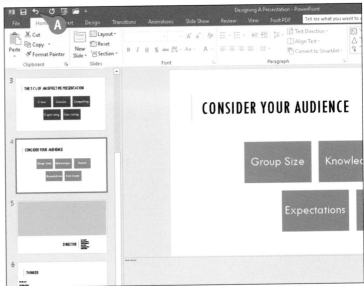

Delete a Slide in Slide Sorter View

1 Select the slide(s) you want to delete in Slide Sorter view.

Note: To select multiple slides, click the first slide and then press Ctrl while clicking additional slides.

2 Right-click any selected slide.

The shortcut menu appears.

3 Click Delete Slide.

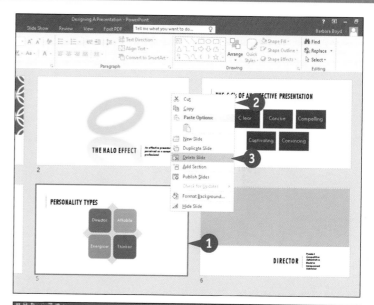

PowerPoint deletes the selected slide(s) from the presentation.

Note: You can also delete a slide by selecting it and then pressing Delete.

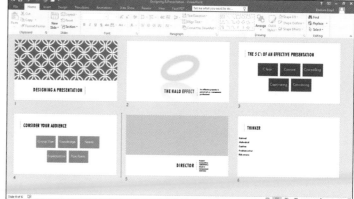

TIP

Is there a rule of thumb to help me decide how many slides my presentation should have?

Yes — and no. A loose rule is to prepare one slide per minute of presentation time. However, presentation styles have changed, especially with the possibility of video within a presentation and live audience interaction. As a general, leave 5 to 10 minutes for questions and prepare one slide for every 1 to 2 minutes. For example, if you have 30 minutes to speak, subtract 10 minutes for questions and then prepare 10 to 20 slides for the remaining 20 minutes. Each slide should cover a new topic or expand on the previous one.

CHAPTER 3

Using Themes and Templates

PowerPoint's preset themes, templates, and layouts make it easy to create presentations with a consistent look and feel. You can use built-in themes or choose from hundreds of themes online. Although you can design your own slide templates by applying backgrounds and graphics as well as formatting elements on master slides manually, people most commonly use themes and templates to develop presentations.

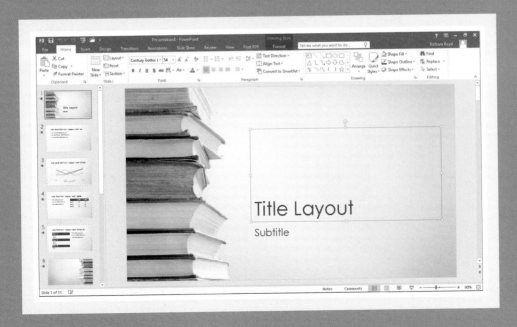

Understanding Themes

A theme is the look, color, and graphics that the slides in your presentation have in common. The colors and style you choose support the mood of your presentation — professional, entertaining, fun, sober. A consistent style throughout your presentation leads your audience from one point to the next and helps them remember what you say.

You can use a theme from the PowerPoint program, get one from Microsoft Office Online or another online source, or use a theme from an existing presentation. You can also create a blank presentation, and then apply a background and graphics to create your own theme — and then save the theme to use again.

Theme Elements

When you create a new presentation, PowerPoint prompts you to choose a theme. When you choose a specific non-blank theme, PowerPoint applies a set of colors, fonts, and placeholders to the slides. All these elements vary from theme to theme. Themes may include a background color, background graphics, and effects for background graphics, and most themes offer color scheme variations.

Apply Themes

It is easy to apply a theme to a single slide, a section, or the entire presentation. Generally it is better to use one theme for an entire presentation so that the slides have a consistent look and feel. However, you can also choose to apply a different theme to a particular slide for emphasis.

Modify Themes

Although PowerPoint provides professionally designed slide themes, you can tailor existing themes to meet your specific needs. You can change the background, background color, or the color scheme of the entire theme. After you design a theme you really like, you can save it to the Theme gallery to use again.

Themes and Masters

Slide masters determine where placeholders and objects appear on each slide layout. Each theme has a master slide for the Title slide, a master slide for the Title and Content slide, and so on. After you apply a theme, you can modify the masters. Any changes you make to the master slides automatically appear in your presentation slides. You can also change the fonts on the master slides. Chapter 11 explains all you need to know about masters.

Explore the Anatomy of a Theme

Themes control several aspects of your slide design. The theme determines the locations of placeholders in slide layouts, the color scheme, the slide background, and any graphics that may be part of the theme. These characteristics vary from theme to theme. For example, the title may be on the top of slides in one theme and on the bottom of slides in another. These variations give each theme its own flavor and personality.

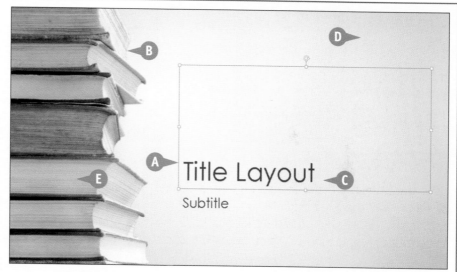

Ⓐ Placeholder Position

Placeholder positions vary from theme to theme. Each theme has a set of slide masters that control where placeholders appear on each slide layout.

Ⓑ Graphic Elements

Some themes include graphic elements that are typically part of the background. To avoid accidentally changing them, you can modify them on the slide masters, but not on individual slides.

Ⓒ Color Scheme

Themes control the colors applied to slide text, the background, and objects such as tables, charts, and SmartArt graphics. Themes often have multiple color scheme options. You can change colors on individual slides or apply a color change to your entire presentation.

Ⓓ Background

Themes specify the background applied to slides. The background might be a solid color, a gradient, or a pattern, and may include graphics. Backgrounds may be different on different layouts.

Ⓔ Effects

Effects give a dimensional appearance to graphics by adding shadows, transparency, 3-D, and more. A theme may apply a particular style of effect to graphics.

Search for Themes and Templates Online

The larger your choice of PowerPoint themes and templates, the greater the chance you will find one that suits your needs. Fortunately, there are literally thousands of PowerPoint theme templates available online. You can search for them by using the PowerPoint search feature, or an Internet search engine.

The PowerPoint search feature enables you to search by a keyword and shows you online presentation templates associated with that keyword. The search feature shows you a preview of the template and the name of who provided it, and then downloads the template for you! Remember to download files only from websites that you trust.

Search for Themes and Templates Online

1 Click the **File** tab on the Ribbon to show Backstage view.

2 Click **New**.

Templates available on your computer appear.

A You can search by clicking one of the suggested searches.

3 Type a keyword in the Search text box.

This example uses Books.

4 Click **Search** (🔍) or press Enter.

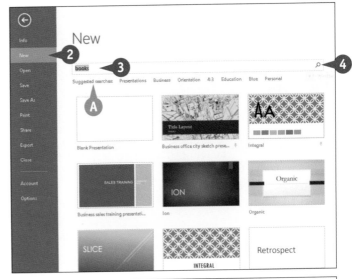

PowerPoint shows online templates that match the search text.

B Click the **Pushpin** button (📌) to pin a template to your list of templates (📌 changes to 📌).

5 Click the template of your choice.

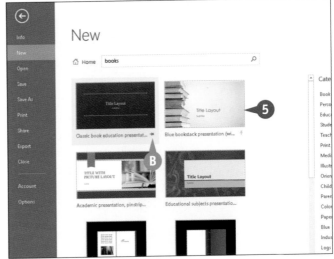

A dialog box appears, showing a preview of the template.

C You can click **Back** (◀) or **Forward** (▶) to view other slides from this template.

D You can click **Back** (◉) or **Forward** (◉) to view other templates from the list.

6 Click **Create**.

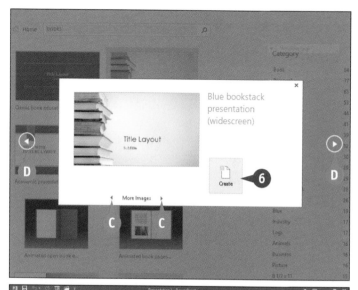

PowerPoint creates a presentation from the template.

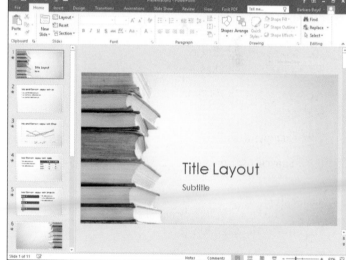

TIPS

Do templates come in different sizes?
Yes. Templates come in two slide sizes. The commonly used 16:9 aspect ratio is for widescreen — indicated as *widescreen* in the theme name — and the 4:3 aspect ratio is for older monitors. Your choice of template may require you to change the aspect ratio. See Chapter 9 to learn about changing aspect ratios.

Is there a difference between themes and templates online?
Yes. Themes contain sets of templates with a color scheme and stylized graphics. You also find individual templates for a single slide or for special effects such as animation.

Apply a Theme to Selected Slides

You can apply a different theme to a single slide in either Normal or Slide Sorter view. You may want to apply a different theme to one or more slides to make them stand out. If you decide to use more than one theme in the same presentation, you will normally want their designs to be complementary. You can apply a theme to multiple slides you select manually or apply a new theme to all slides that use the same theme.

Apply a Theme to Selected Slides

Apply One Theme to Slides

1. Click the **Slide Sorter** button (⊞) on the status bar.

2. Select a slide or slides.

Note: To select multiple slides, click the first slide and then press **Ctrl** while clicking additional slides.

3. Click the **Design** tab.

4. Click the **Themes** down arrow (▼).

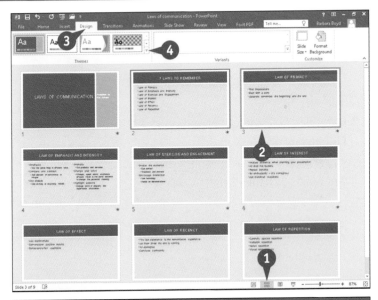

The gallery of themes appears.

5. Right-click a theme.

The shortcut menu appears.

6. Click **Apply to Selected Slides**.

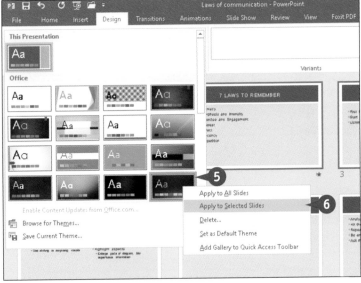

40

Ⓐ PowerPoint applies the theme to the slide(s) you selected.

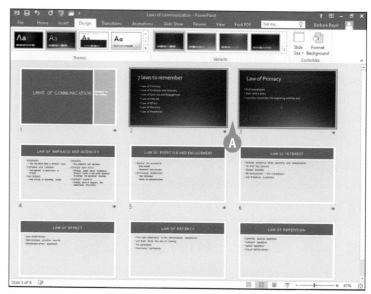

Apply a New Theme to Slides Using the Same Theme

1 Click the **Slide Sorter** button (▤) on the status bar.

2 Select a slide that uses the theme you want to change throughout.

3 Click the **Design** tab.

4 Click the **Themes** ▾ (not shown).

The gallery of themes appears.

5 Right-click a theme.

The shortcut menu appears.

6 Click **Apply to Matching Slides**.

Your chosen theme is applied to all slides that have the same theme as the currently selected slide.

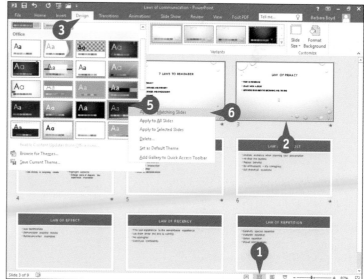

TIPS

If I change a few slides to a different theme, can I use the slide master features for those slides?

Yes. When you apply a theme to a presentation, PowerPoint creates a set of master slides for that theme. You get a set of slide masters for every theme in your presentation — any of which you can modify. In Chapter 11, you learn about using slide masters.

Is there an easy way to use more than one theme in the same presentation?

Yes. One way to select complementary themes is to apply variants of the same theme to different slides. When you click a theme on the Design tab, variants appear to the right. Select the slides you want to change and click a variant to apply it.

Apply a Theme to All Slides

You can apply one theme to all the slides in a presentation. A consistent appearance makes your presentation look professional and helps the audience focus on your message instead of a mishmash of colors, fonts, and graphics. Whereas the slide layouts may vary, the theme supplies common colors, fonts, graphics, and more, so your audience focuses on content rather than formatting. In designing a presentation, you may decide the selected theme does not strike the proper mood for the presentation. No problem, just apply a different theme. You can change the theme in either Normal or Slide Sorter view.

Apply a Theme to All Slides

1 In Slide Sorter view, click the **Design** tab.

2 Click the **Themes** ⏷ (not shown).

The gallery of themes appears.

3 Click a theme.

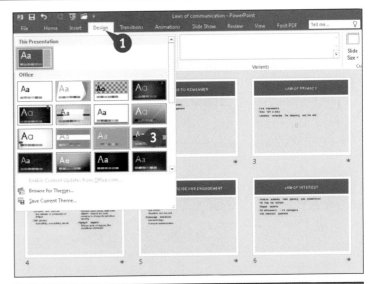

PowerPoint applies the theme to all slides in the presentation.

Note: You can also right-click a thumbnail in the gallery and then click **Apply to All Slides**.

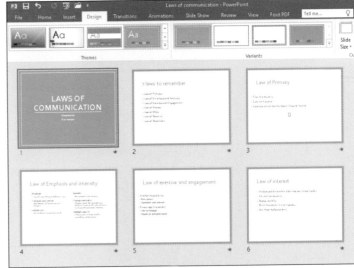

Add a Section with a Different Theme

It is common to change topics during a presentation. For example, a person teaching a class about Microsoft Office changes topics when moving from teaching PowerPoint to teaching Excel. If you change topics, you might want to alter the mood to one that is more appropriate for the new topic. You can apply themes to sections of a presentation. Doing so gives each section a look and feel consistent with the others, yet makes it obvious that that particular section of your presentation is dedicated to a specific topic. You can change the theme in either Normal or Slide Sorter view.

Add a Section with a Different Theme

1 In Slide Sorter view, click the slide where you want to begin your section.

2 Click the **Home** tab.

3 Click **Section**.

4 Click **Add Section** in the drop-down menu.

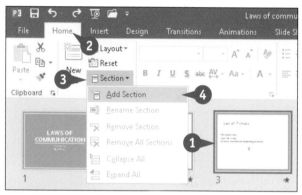

A The slides including and after the one you selected are placed in an Untitled Section.

Note: Right-click **Untitled Section** to rename the section to something more descriptive.

5 Perform Steps **1** to **3** from the previous section.

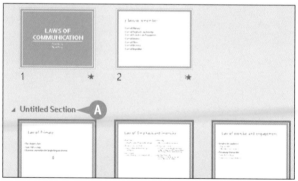

B PowerPoint applies the theme to all slides in the section.

C Click a Variant in the Ribbon to apply a different color scheme to the theme.

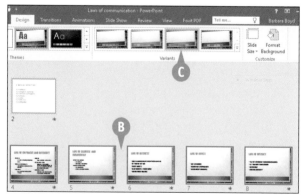

Change Theme Colors

Each theme includes at least one color scheme, and some themes have variant color themes. You can add variety or emphasize certain slides by changing the color scheme of only those particular slides. You can also change the color scheme of an entire presentation or a section of a presentation. When you alter the color scheme, the other aspects of the theme, such as placeholder position and background objects, stay the same — only the colors change. You can change the color scheme in Normal view or Slide Sorter view.

Change Theme Colors

Apply to Selected Slides

1 In Slide Sorter view, click a slide or slides.

Note: To select multiple slides, click the first slide and then press **Ctrl** while clicking additional slides.

2 Click the **Design** tab.

3 Right-click a color scheme from the Variants gallery.

4 Click **Apply to Selected Slides**.

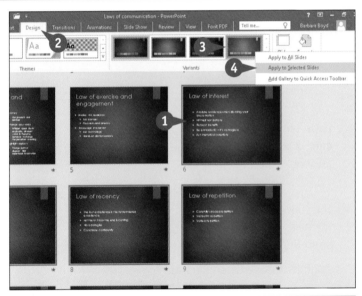

PowerPoint applies the color scheme to the slides you selected.

5 Select a slide designed with the theme you want to change.

6 Right-click a color scheme from the Variants gallery.

7 Click **Apply to Matching Slides**.

PowerPoint applies the color scheme to all slides whose theme matches the selected slide.

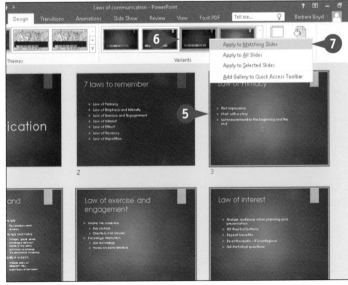

Apply to All Slides

1 Right-click a color scheme from the Variants gallery.

2 Click **Apply to All Slides**.

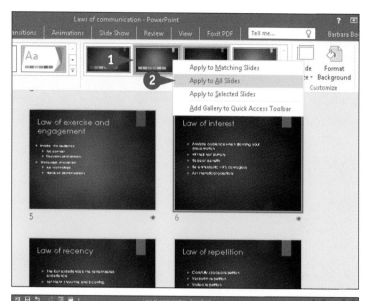

PowerPoint applies the selected color scheme to all slides in the presentation.

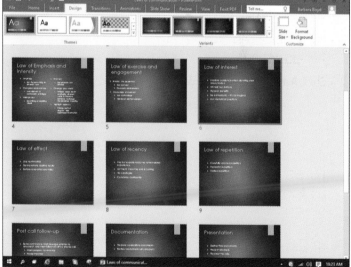

TIP

Is changing the background color of the theme different than changing the color scheme (variant) of the theme?

Yes. When you apply a variant of a theme, it changes the colors of the background plus all the geometric shapes on the slide, including charts and tables; when you format the background — explained in the next section — and change its color, it affects only the background and not the geometric shapes. Objects such as pictures and clip art are not affected by either type of change. You can change the background and foreground of objects such as clip art and pictures by formatting them.

Modify the Background

A theme applies a background on which all slide elements sit. You can make the background a color or plain white, or you can even use a texture or digital image as a background. For example, you can use a photo of a new product as a slide background for a presentation introducing the product. You can change the background for one slide, for a theme, or throughout the presentation and you can do this in Normal or Slide Sorter view. Be careful with your choice of background — a complicated background can make a presentation hard to read or distracting.

Modify the Background

1 Select the slide(s) you want to modify in Slide Sorter view.

Note: To select multiple slides, click the first slide and then press **Ctrl** while clicking additional slides.

2 Click the **Design** tab.

3 Click **Format Background**.

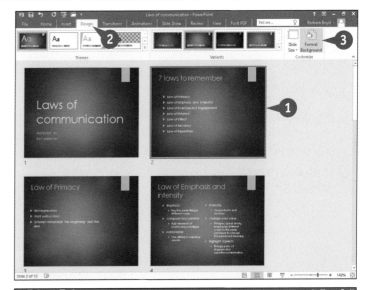

The Format Background pane appears.

4 Click **Solid fill** (◯ changes to ◉).

5 Click the **Color** button ( ).

6 Click a color.

Ⓐ You can click **Apply to All** to apply the color to all slides.

Ⓑ PowerPoint applies the background color to the selected slides.

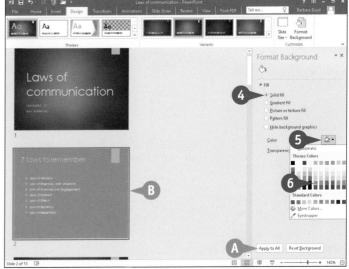

7 Click **Gradient fill** (⚪ changes to ◉).

PowerPoint applies a preset gradient to the background.

C You can adjust gradient options to change the direction and gradient type.

D You fine-tune the gradient by adjusting its characteristics, such as brightness and transparency.

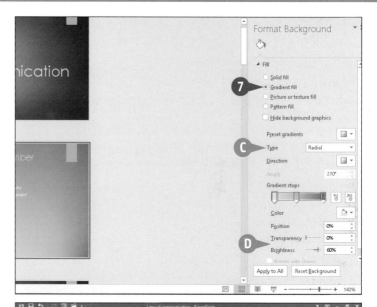

8 Click **Pattern fill** (⚪ changes to ◉).

9 Click a pattern from the gallery.

E PowerPoint applies the background pattern to the selected slides.

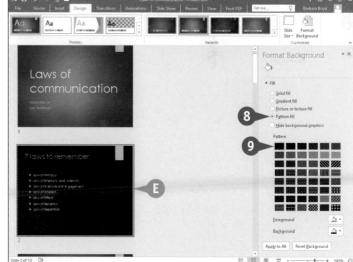

Why does PowerPoint give me a pattern as soon as I click the Pattern Fill option?
PowerPoint applies a preset pattern when you click the **Pattern fill** option. You can either select a different pattern version, or you can click the **Solid fill** option to get rid of the pattern.

Apply a Texture or Picture Background

If you really want to make a slide more dramatic, you can push design limits by using either a texture or a digital picture as a background. For example, you can use a digital photo of a landscape and sunrise for a slide introducing a new idea. Typically, you would not do this for an entire set of slides because a complicated background makes a slide difficult to read and can be hard on the audience's eyes. You can add a picture to the background of a slide in either Slide Sorter or Normal view.

Apply a Texture or Picture Background

1. Repeat Steps **1** to **3** from the previous section and click **Picture or texture fill** (○ changes to ⦿).

2. Click the **Texture** button (▣▾).

   The Texture gallery opens.

3. Click a texture you want to apply to the chosen slides.

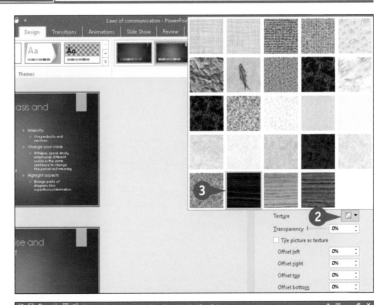

Ⓐ The slide(s) fills with the texture you chose.

4. To apply an image from a file on your computer, click **File**.

The Insert Picture dialog box appears.

5 Click the folder that contains the picture file you want to insert.

6 Click the image file.

7 Click **Insert**.

B The Insert Picture dialog box closes and the picture becomes the background on your selected slide.

8 Click the **Picture** icon (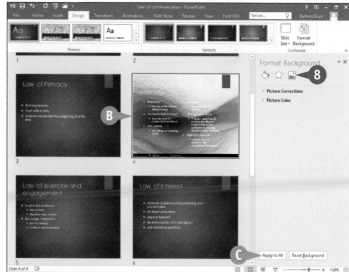) to apply color corrections to the picture.

C You can click **Apply to All** to apply the background to all slides in the presentation.

TIP

How can I remove a texture or picture from the background?
With the Format Background pane open, follow these steps:

1 Click the **Fill** icon (⬧).

2 Click **Solid fill** (○ changes to ◉).

3 Click the **Color** button (▦▾).

4 Click **Automatic**.

PowerPoint removes the background.

Note: You can also click **Reset Background**.

Save Your Own Theme

If you spent a lot of time creating your own theme, you may want to use it again. For example, say you designed a theme from scratch or modified an existing theme, where you applied a color scheme and background that really works and possibly some graphics. If you do not want to do all this work again, you can save the results as a theme. This enables you to quickly apply that combination of color, background, and graphics to other presentations.

Save Your Own Theme

1 Click the **Design** tab.

2 Click the **Themes** ▼ (not shown).

The gallery of themes appears.

Ⓐ If you save your theme in the PowerPoint theme default folder, it will appear under Custom.

3 Click **Save Current Theme**.

The Save Current Theme dialog box appears.

4 Type a filename.

Ⓑ This is the default folder location for themes.

Note: Do not change the folder location. Your themes appear in the Themes gallery because they are in this folder location.

5 Click **Save**.

PowerPoint saves the theme and adds it to the Custom section of the gallery.

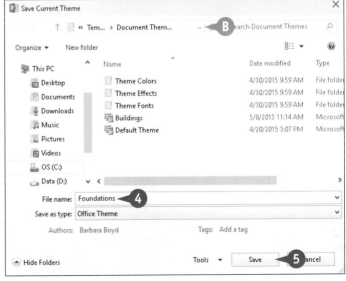

50

Make a Theme the Default for New Presentations

When you click **New** in Backstage view, the first presentation on the Themes gallery is Blank Presentation. If you have a theme that you use often — for example, a custom theme that contains your company logo, color scheme, and font styles — you can make that theme the *default theme*. When you click the default theme in the Themes gallery, a new presentation is automatically created without showing the theme preview. This gives you a fast start in creating a new presentation. If the default theme is not right for any particular presentation, you can always choose one you prefer.

Make a Theme the Default for New Presentations

1 Click the **Design** tab.

2 Click the **Themes** ☰ (not shown).

The gallery of themes appears.

3 Right-click the theme you want to set as the default.

4 Click **Set as Default Theme**.

5 Click the **File** tab to show Backstage view.

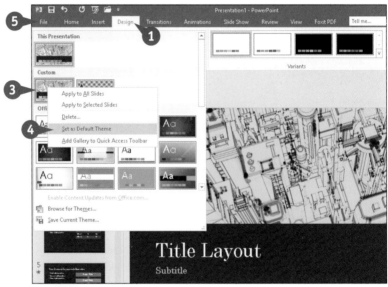

6 Click **New**.

Ⓐ The selected theme appears as the default theme.

Note: The default theme appears when you open PowerPoint from the Windows Start menu, too.

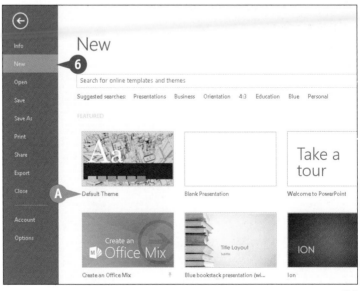

Save a Template

Although themes have slide layout templates, a *template* can also refer to a boilerplate presentation that you use repeatedly, with certain information changing with each use. Templates include a presentation design theme plus reusable content such as often-used slides for a particular type of presentation. For example, for a presentation for selling to a purchasing group's clients, content about the group does not change from client to client, so you would have slides about the group in the template along with slides to tailor for each client. You can save a lot of time by using templates for repeatable presentations.

Save a Template

1 Click the **File** tab to show Backstage view.

2 Click **Save As**.

3 Click **This PC**.

4 Click **Browse**.

The Save As dialog box appears.

5 Click the **Save as type** drop-down arrow (⌄).

6 Click **PowerPoint Template**.

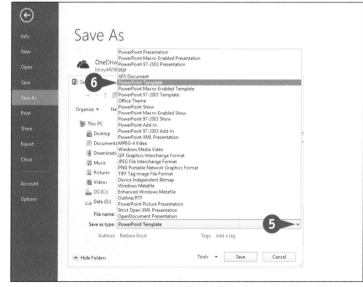

A This is the default folder location for themes and templates.

Note: It is best not to change this folder location. Your templates appear in the templates gallery because they are in this folder location, which is the same as the theme folder location.

7 Type a filename.

8 Click **Save**.

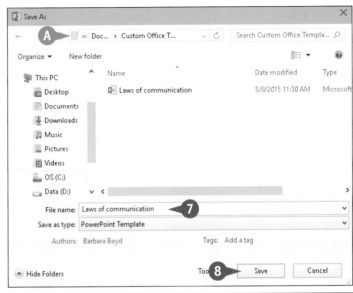

PowerPoint saves the presentation as a template.

9 Click the **File** tab to show Backstage view.

10 Click **New**.

11 Hover the mouse pointer above the gallery, next to Featured, and click **Custom**.

12 Click the **Custom Office Template** folder.

Any presentations you save as templates appear here.

Note: You may need to close and open PowerPoint for the template to appear in the Custom template list.

TIP

What is the difference between using a template and using a regular presentation as a template?
A PowerPoint presentation has a .pptx file extension and a template has a .potx file extension. If a template (.potx) is in the Template folder, it appears in the template list — you simply click it and PowerPoint creates a new presentation from a copy of the template. If you double-click a presentation (.pptx) in Windows Explorer or on your desktop, it opens. If you double-click a template (.potx), it creates and opens a copy of itself. The original is protected from unintentional changes because it does not open. To change a template (.potx), you must open it through the Open dialog box.

CHAPTER 4

Writing and Formatting Text

Although a picture speaks a thousand words, sometimes you will want to put actual words on the slides you create. Legible formatting makes text easier to read, making your slides more effective. PowerPoint gives you the tools to change the font, size, color, and style of your text. Carefully chosen text formatting can completely change the look, feel, and mood of a presentation.

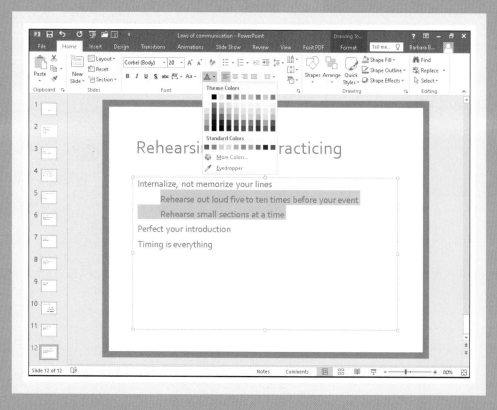

Type and Edit Text on a Slide

The text you type into placeholders on your slides should support your spoken presentation — you do not want your audience reading your slides but rather listening to your words and relying on your visual presentation to remember your message. Several types of placeholders can hold text: title, content (bulleted list), subtitle, section header, caption, quote, and name card. You simply click the placeholder and then start typing. You can also go back and edit text you have already typed. Bullet points are discussion points, not detailed sentences; remember to keep them short.

Type and Edit Text on a Slide

Enter Text

1 With a presentation in Normal view, add a Title and Content Slide.

Note: To learn how to insert a new slide, see Chapter 2.

2 Click the title placeholder.

The insertion point appears and the "Click to add title" text disappears.

3 Type your text.

4 Click outside the placeholder.

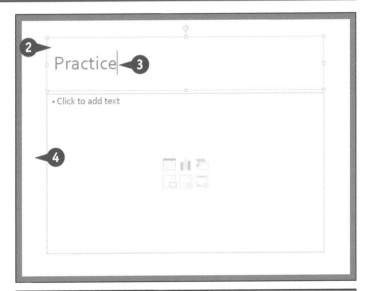

A PowerPoint adds the text.

5 Click the content placeholder.

6 Type your text.

7 Press Enter.

B The insertion point moves to the next line.

8 Repeat Steps **6** and **7** for all bullet points for that slide.

PowerPoint adds the text.

Edit Text

1 Click anywhere within a title, subtitle, or text placeholder.

2 Click the existing text where you want to change it.

The insertion point appears where you clicked. You can press `Backspace` to delete text to the left, or press `Delete` to delete text to the right of the insertion point.

3 Press `Backspace`.

This example deletes the extra "r" in "yourself."

4 Type any text you want to add.

C A new bullet was inserted between the first and third in the example.

5 Click and drag over one or more words.

Note: To select a single word, double-click in the middle of it.

6 Press `Delete`.

PowerPoint deletes the selected text.

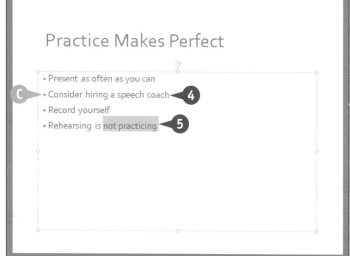

TIPS

Will the placeholder wording "Click to add text" appear if I print or run my presentation?

That is simply an instruction to let you know that this placeholder currently has no text entered in it. The words and the placeholder neither print nor appear when you present the slide show. When you click the placeholder to type, the words disappear.

When I type text in Outline view, where does it appear?

Text that you type in the Outline tab appears on the current slide. The top-level heading in a slide corresponds to the title placeholder on the slide. Second-level entries become the bullet items in the text placeholder. Third-level entries are bullet items, and so on. See Chapter 10.

Format Text Color and Style

Color adds flair to any presentation. You can use text color to emphasize your words or to make your text more readable. Choose text colors that contrast with the background so your audience can easily read the text during the slide show. You can select colors from a standard palette or work with custom colors. Use text colors along with text styles such as bold or shadow to add emphasis to the words in your presentation.

Format Text Color and Style

1 Click a placeholder to select it.

2 Click and drag over one or more words.

3 Click the **Home** tab.

4 Click the **Font Color** down arrow (▼).

A color palette appears.

5 Select a color from the palette.

Ⓐ For a custom color, click **More Colors**.

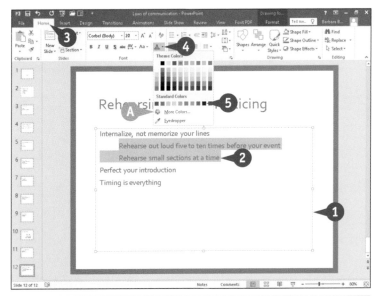

Ⓑ The text you selected changes to the color you chose.

6 Click and drag over one or more other words.

7 Click the dialog box launcher button (🗔) in the Font group.

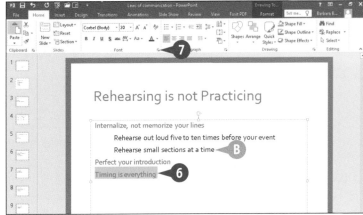

58

The Font dialog box appears.

8 Click the **Font style** drop-down arrow (▾).

9 Click a style from the list.

10 Click an effect to apply to your text (☐ changes to ☑).

11 Click **OK**.

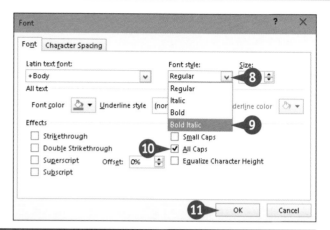

C PowerPoint changes the text to the style that you selected.

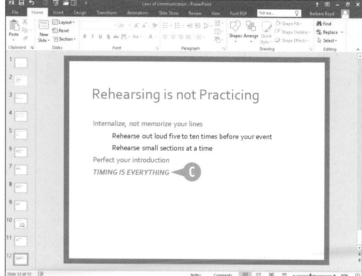

What is the difference between the Home tab Font buttons and the Font dialog box?

The Font dialog box enables you to apply several formats at one time from a single location. All options are there, including some specialized attributes, which you do not see in the Font group on the Home tab. You do, however, see the fonts in their true form in the Home tab Fonts group.

What are superscript and subscript?

These formats either raise (superscript) or lower (subscript) the selected text a set distance from the regular text. Superscript and subscript are often used for footnote or scientific notation, such as 4^2 representing 4 to the second power, or f_x to represent a function of x.

Format Text Font and Size

The font you choose for text portrays a certain look and feel. Some fonts are playful, and others more formal. Fonts are divided into four main types: serif fonts, with cross strokes on the letter ends; sans serif fonts, which do not have cross strokes on the letter ends; script fonts, which look like handwriting; and decorative fonts such as Algerian, which are heavily stylized. Font size is important because your audience should be able to read all the text in your presentation without straining their eyes.

Format Text Font and Size

1 Click a placeholder to select it.

2 Click and drag over one or more words.

3 Click the **Home** tab.

4 Click the dialog box launcher button (⌐) in the Font group.

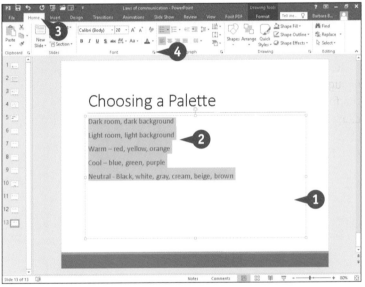

The Font dialog box appears.

5 Click the **Latin** text font drop-down arrow (∨).

6 Click the desired font.

number in the
type a new

the spinner
ze text box to
se the font

size.

8 Click **OK**.

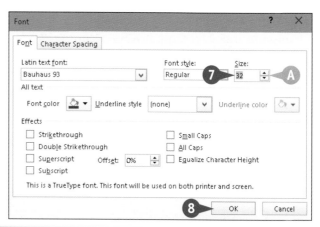

B PowerPoint applies the new
formatting to the text.

Note: If the placeholder is not wide
enough to accommodate the size of
the font with the number of
characters in one line, then the
auto-formatting feature makes the
text two lines.

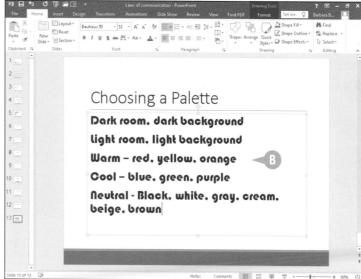

**What does the Character Spacing tab in the Font
dialog box do?**

The Character Spacing tab enables you to *kern* the font or
adjust the character spacing of the text. You can kern the
font and specify above which font size you want to start
kerning. If your text runs to the next line by a word, try
using condensed spacing to keep the phrase on one line.

**Are there limitations on how large or small
text can be?**

No. You can type font sizes from 1 to 4000.
However, remember to keep the text readable
for the viewer. A very small text size is difficult
to see; a huge text size can make text look
rough or pixelated.

Cut, Copy, and Paste Text

When you edit your presentation, you can move text by using the Cut, Copy, and Paste features. Using these features assures accuracy and saves time because you avoid typing the text manually. *Cut* removes text from its original location. *Copy* duplicates the text, leaving the original in place. *Paste* places either cut or copied text into another location. You can also cut, copy, and paste objects like placeholders and pictures. If you change your mind or make a mistake, you can use the Undo feature to reverse the commands you made.

Cut, Copy, and Paste Text

1 Click the **Home** tab.

2 Click the dialog box launcher button (⌐) in the Clipboard group.

The Clipboard task pane appears.

3 Click a text placeholder to select it.

4 Click and drag to select text.

5 Click the **Cut** button (✂).

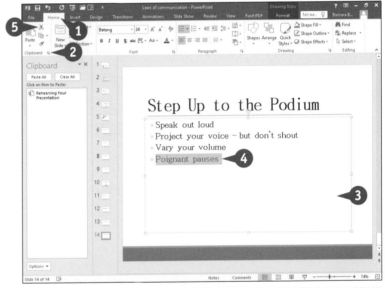

Ⓐ PowerPoint removes the selected text and places it on the Windows Clipboard.

6 Click and drag to select different text.

7 Click the **Copy** button (📋).

Note: If you do not open the Clipboard Task Pane, it holds only your most recent copied or cut text.

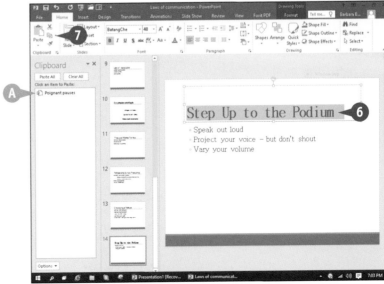

B PowerPoint copies the selected text to the Clipboard.

8 Select the slide where you want to paste the text.

Note: For more information on navigating slides, see Chapter 1.

9 Click within the placeholder to position the insertion point where you want to paste the text.

The insertion point appears in the placeholder.

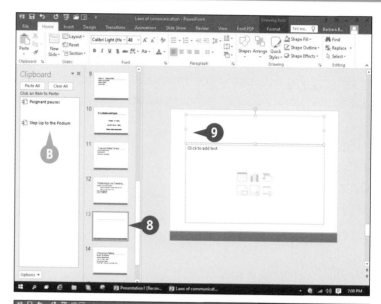

10 To paste an item that you copied, click it in the Clipboard.

C PowerPoint pastes the cut or copied text into the placeholder.

D You can also click **Paste** to paste the most recently copied item, which is always the first item on the Clipboard.

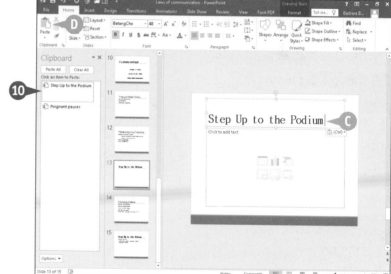

Is there an easier and faster way to cut, copy, and paste?

Yes. You can perform these commands by using keystrokes. Select the text, placeholder, or object and then press `Ctrl`+`X` to cut, `Ctrl`+`C` to copy, and `Ctrl`+`V` to paste. Use these keystrokes to perform these commands with text, objects, and even files throughout Microsoft Windows.

The text that I copied in Word appears on the Clipboard. Can I delete it?

Yes. Position your mouse pointer over the item that you want to delete and then click the down arrow (▼). Click **Delete** on the drop-down list that appears, and the item disappears from the Clipboard.

Format Bulleted Lists

Bulleted lists, although used sparingly in popular presentations such as Technology, Entertainment, Design (TED) talks or scientific speeches, are still the heart of many presentations. They summarize key points the presenter wants to make. You can format bulleted lists with different styles of bullets. For example, you can use check marks as bullets in a list of points for a project. You can use pictures and symbols as bullet points and dictate the size of bullet points as well.

Format Bulleted Lists

1 Click the border of a placeholder containing a bulleted list.

2 Click the **Home** tab.

3 Click the **Bullets** down arrow (▼).

4 Click a bullet style from the gallery.

Ⓐ The bullets change to the new style.

5 Click the **Bullets** down arrow (▼).

6 Click **Bullets and Numbering** at the bottom of the gallery.

Note: To change the bullet for one line, place the insertion point within the text of a placeholder. To change all bullets, click the placeholder border, then change the bullet style.

The Bullets and Numbering dialog box appears.

Ⓑ You can change the bullet color.

Ⓒ You can click **Customize** to use a symbol as a bullet.

7 Click **Picture**.

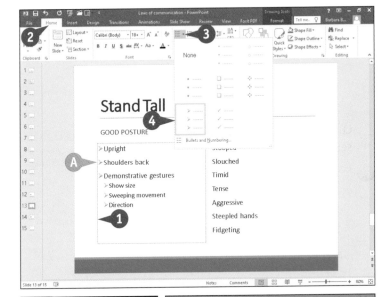

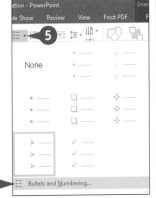

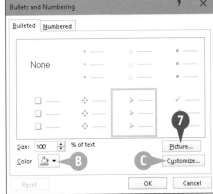

The Insert Pictures dialog box appears.

D You can use a picture from your computer.

8 Type a keyword into the **Bing Image Search** text box.

9 Click the **Search** button ($\mathcal{P}$).

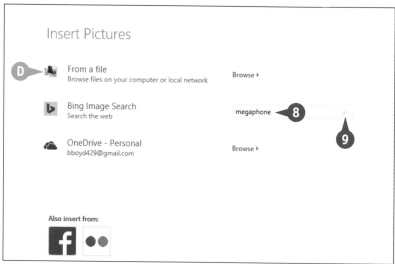

10 Click a picture from the selection.

11 Click **Insert**.

E The picture appears as a bullet.

Note: Bing finds Creative Commons images; consult the source before using for commercial purposes.

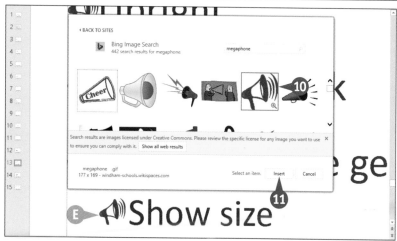

How can I make the bullets larger?
The Bullets and Numbering dialog box includes a size setting. This setting is expressed in percentage of the text size. If you increase the text size, the bullet size increases proportionally. Double-click in the **Size** text box, type the size you want, and then click **OK** to apply the sizing.

Can I apply a new bullet style to every bullet in the presentation without having to change each individually?
Yes. You can use the master slides to make formatting changes that apply to every slide in the presentation. Chapter 11 covers master slides in detail.

Using the Spelling Check Feature

You should check the contents of your presentation for spelling accuracy because good presentations do not have spelling errors. Not all of us are spelling bee winners, but your audience will definitely notice spelling errors. Fortunately, PowerPoint offers a spelling check feature to improve your spelling accuracy without using a dictionary. You can check the spelling of all the words throughout your presentation to ensure it is as professional as possible.

Using the Spelling Check Feature

1 Click the **Review** tab.

2 Click **Spelling**.

Note: You can also press **F7** to start the spelling check.

A The Spelling task pane appears, displaying the first questionable word and suggested spellings.

Note: If your presentation does not have spelling errors, a dialog appears that reads "Spell Check Complete."

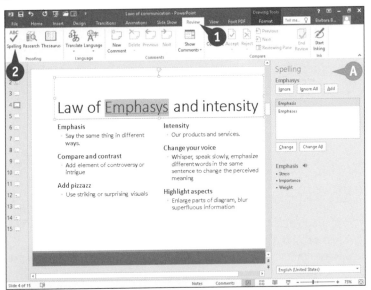

3 Click a suggestion from the **Suggestions** list.

4 Click **Change** to replace the misspelling.

B You can click **Change All** to replace all instances of the misspelled word.

C You can click **Ignore** to leave the spelling as is.

D You can click **Ignore All** to leave all instances of this spelling as they are.

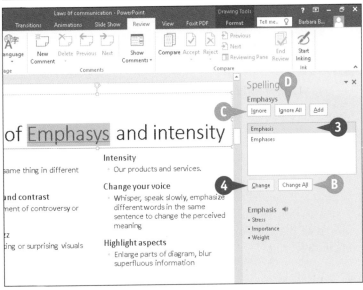

E The spelling check proceeds to the next questionable word.

5 Repeat Steps **3** and **4** until the spell check is complete.

Note: If none of the suggestions is the word you intended to type, click the misspelled word and edit as explained in previous sections.

A dialog box appears notifying you when the spelling check is complete.

6 Click **OK**.

The Spelling task pane closes and any changes are reflected in the presentation.

F If PowerPoint options are set to check spelling as you type, red wavy lines may appear under possibly misspelled words after you type them.

G You can right-click the word and then click an option in the shortcut menu that appears.

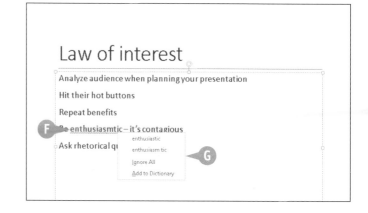

Is it possible to check spelling for a specific word?

Yes. Select the word before you run the spelling check. The spelling check starts with the word you select. After taking the appropriate action, simply click the **Close** button (✕) in the Spelling pane.

Is there a way to get PowerPoint to stop flagging a particular word as misspelled?

Yes. In the Spelling pane, click **Add**. This adds the word to your custom dictionary, so it recognizes the spelling as legitimate in the future. Keep in mind that your custom dictionary affects all Microsoft programs, so the word you add will be viewed as a legitimate spelling in all Microsoft programs.

Using the Research Feature

As you type text in a presentation, you may need to check definitions or facts. PowerPoint gives you the convenience of researching a topic without a dictionary, thesaurus, or any other references; you can research the topic without leaving PowerPoint! If your computer has an Internet connection, you can use the Research feature to search reference books and research sites for relevant information on your topic. PowerPoint finds relevant references so you can open them with a click of your mouse button.

Using the Research Feature

1 Click the **Review** tab.

2 Click and drag across the text you want to research.

3 Click **Research**.

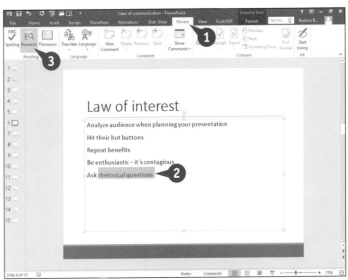

The Research task pane appears with the selected text in the Search For text box.

4 Click the **Search** button (➡ changes to ⏹).

You can click the **Stop** button (⏹) to cancel the search.

A The search results appear.

B If you want to change the search topic, type it in the **Search for** text box and click the **Search** button (➡).

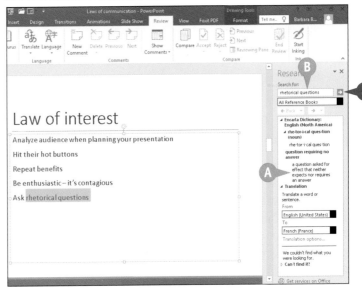

5 Click the **Search for** down arrow
(▼) to change where the Research
feature looks for information.

6 Click to select a research site from
the drop-down list.

PowerPoint changes the search
results to reflect your change.

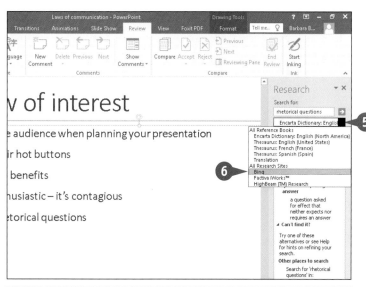

C Click the **Expand** icon (▷) to
expand a listing (▷ changes
to ◢).

D Click the **Collapse** icon (◢) to
collapse a listing (◢ changes
to ▷).

E Click **Next** to see the next listings.

7 Click a link.

Additional information appears or
a website opens, depending on the
type of link it is.

8 Click the **Close** button (✕) to
close the Research task pane.

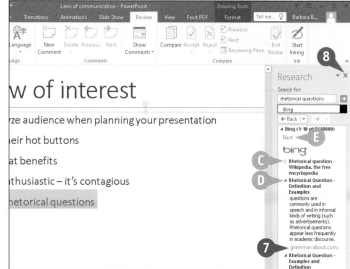

**Can I specify which research sites PowerPoint will
check?**
Yes. With the Research task pane open, click the
Research options link at the bottom. A dialog box
appears with a list of all resources. Click the check box
beside any listed reference, and then click **OK**. The
references you selected now appear in the drop-down list.

**I followed a link but it did not contain the
information I wanted. Is there a way to go
back to the original item that was displayed?**
Yes. Working within PowerPoint, you can click
the **Back** button (← Back ▾) in the Research task
pane. You can also choose another topic in the
Research task pane.

CHAPTER 5

Adding Charts and Tables

Charts and tables give your audience a visual reference when you talk about figures or make comparisons, especially when comparing or reporting on more than two items — for example, regional sales figures for your company's product line. You enter your data and then PowerPoint works its magic to turn your data into colorful, informative graphic representations.

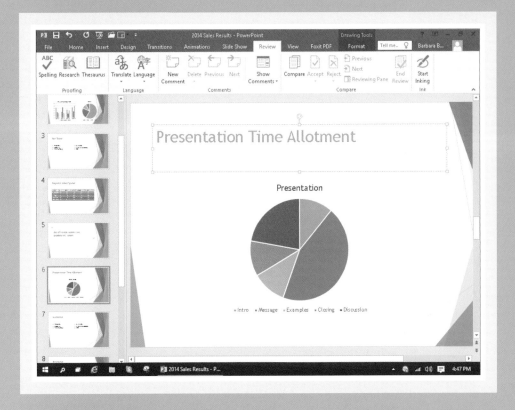

Insert a Table

You can use a table to arrange information in rows and columns for easy data comparison. For example, you might list regions in the far left column of a table, and then compare sales figures for products in two or more other columns. Tables are useful for showing important data to your audience. For example, you might use a table to show the data for a chart and then show the chart on the next slide. You can use a content placeholder to insert a table, and then type data into the table cells.

Insert a Table

Insert a Table

1️⃣ Select a slide with a content placeholder.

2️⃣ Click the **Insert Table** icon (▦).

🅐 The Insert Table dialog box appears.

3️⃣ Click and type the number of columns you want in your table.

4️⃣ Click and type the number of rows you want in your table.

Note: Alternatively, you can click the spinner (⬍) to select the number of columns and rows.

5️⃣ Click **OK**.

The table appears on the slide.

Note: By default, most of the table styles assume that you will enter column headings in the top row of the table. If you need row headings, add an extra column to hold them.

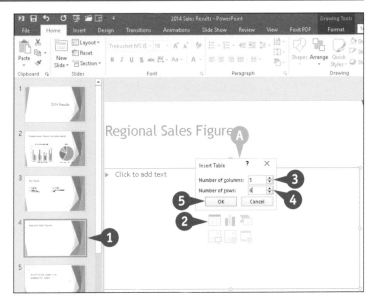

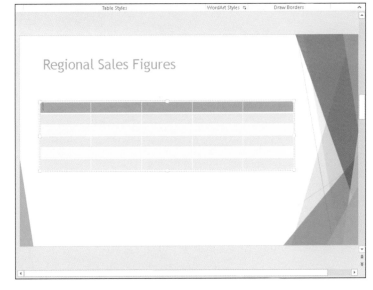

Type Text in a Table

1 Click in the first cell and type a column heading.

This example types Northeast.

2 Press Tab.

B The insertion point moves to the next cell.

Note: You can also click in a cell to type data into it.

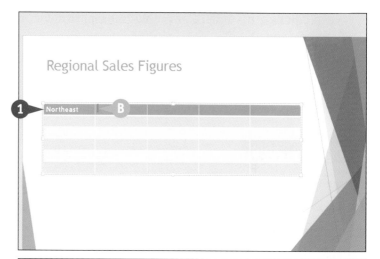

3 Continue adding column headings and cell entries by repeating Steps **1** and **2**.

4 Click outside the table when finished.

C To change table data, click in the cell, edit your entry, and then click outside the table when finished.

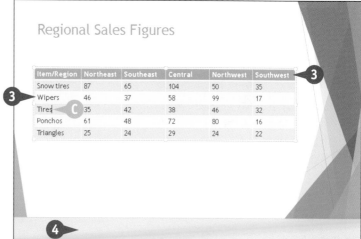

TIP

Can I add and delete rows or columns to and from tables?
Yes. You can insert and delete rows or columns by following these steps:

1 Click a row or column.

2 Click the **Table Tools Layout** tab.

3 To insert, click an **Insert** option.

4 To delete, click **Delete**.

5 Select an option from the menu.

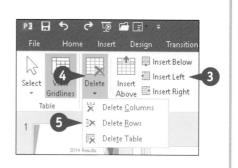

Format a Table

When you insert a table, PowerPoint automatically applies a style to the table based on the theme of the slide. You can add visual impact to your presentation by changing the format of your table. You can add and delete rows and columns, format the text and background, and change the style of the table. Select cells, rows, and columns by clicking and dragging or use the Select button on the Table Tools Layout tab of the Ribbon.

Format a Table

1. Select a slide with a table.
2. Click the table.
3. Click the **Table Tools Design** tab.
4. Click the **Table Styles** down arrow (▼).
5. Click a style from the gallery.

Note: The color scheme is that of the theme but the choices are divided into sections: Best Match, Light, Medium, and Dark.

Ⓐ Click **Clear Table** to remove any previously applied styles.

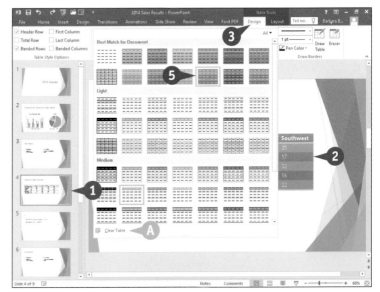

PowerPoint applies the style to the table.

6. Click a row to select it.

You can also click and drag across cells or text.

This example selects the third row.

7. Click the **Quick Styles** down arrow (▼).
8. Select a style from the gallery.

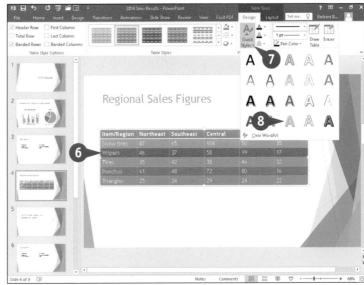

PowerPoint applies the style to the selection.

9 Click and drag across rows to select them.

This example selects all the rows.

10 Click the **Borders** button ▼ (not shown).

11 Click a border from the menu.

PowerPoint applies the style to the selection.

12 Click the **Home** tab.

13 Click the **Bold** button (**B**).

14 Click the **Italic** button (*I*).

15 Click the **Center** button (≡).

PowerPoint applies the formatting changes to the selection.

Note: Click other style buttons such as **Underline** (**U**) or **Right Alignment** (≡) to achieve different effects.

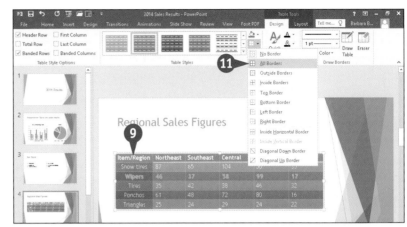

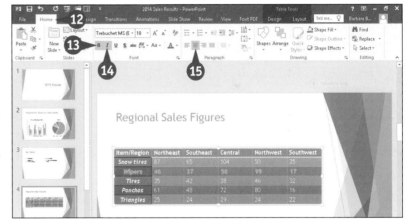

TIP

Can I make size adjustments to the table?

Yes. You can resize your table as follows:

1 Click in the table.

2 Position the mouse pointer over a handle.

3 Click and drag the handle to size the table.

4 Position the mouse pointer over a cell border separating rows or columns.

5 Click and drag the border.

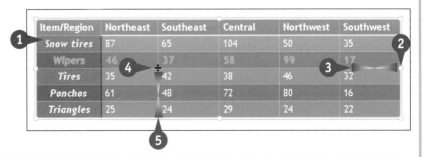

Insert a Chart

Charts present information visually and help the audience understand your point. They give an instant impression of trends, or they compare sets of data, such as sales growth over a several-year span. Charts tell a story with a brief viewing and can convey statistical information quickly. You can add these visual-analysis tools to your presentation to convey summarized information quickly to your audience. To use this feature, you choose the chart type and then type chart data into a spreadsheet.

Insert a Chart

Create a Chart

1. Select a slide with a content placeholder.

Note: To learn how to select a slide, see Chapter 2.

2. Click the **Insert Chart** icon (▥).

   The Insert Chart dialog box appears.

3. Click a chart type category.

4. Click a specific chart type.

5. Click **OK**.

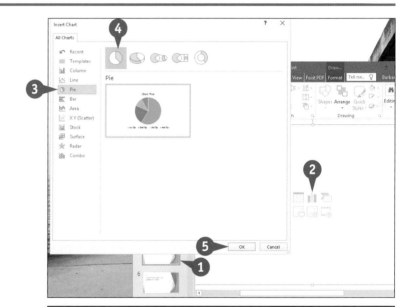

The chart appears, along with sample data in a separate spreadsheet window.

Note: Entering data is similar to entering data into an Excel worksheet.

6. Click in the grid to activate the spreadsheet.

7. Delete any unneeded information in rows or columns.

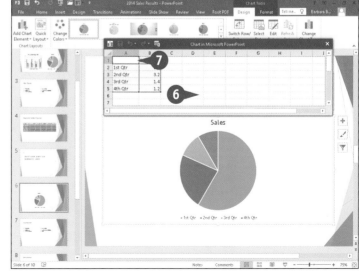

Enter Chart Data

1 Type column headings in row 1.

2 Type row labels in column A.

A You can click the **Edit Data in Microsoft Excel** button (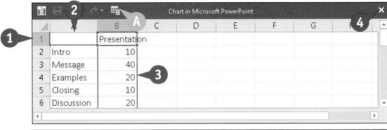) to open an Excel spreadsheet and enter your data.

3 Type your data values in the cells.

Note: You can click a cell and type to enter new data, and double-click a cell to edit existing data.

4 Click the **Close** button (✕) to close the worksheet.

The spreadsheet window closes and the chart appears on the slide.

5 Click outside the chart when finished.

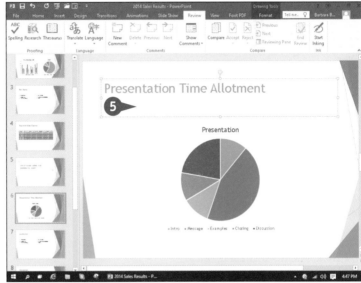

TIP

Can I format the numbers on the axis or data labels?

Yes. To format the text, click the text box or a single element, click the **Home** tab, and then edit as you would other text (see Chapter 4). To format the position and colors of the data series, legend, or labels, double-click the item you want to format and the Format Pane opens. Click the buttons next to the styles you want to use. Options differ for different chart categories.

Format a Chart

When you insert a chart, PowerPoint automatically applies a style to the chart based on the theme of the slide. Charts present information visually, so choice of color is important. You can change the formatting of charts to make specific data stand out. To format any object on a chart, you click it and then use the formatting tools on the Chart Tools Design and Home tabs to change it to your liking. Try to keep the chart relatively simple, though — the less complicated and cluttered it is, the easier it will be for the audience to understand.

Format a Chart

1 Click anywhere on a chart.

2 Click the **Chart Tools Design** tab.

3 Click the **Chart Styles** (not shown).

4 Hover the pointer over the different styles in the gallery.

You see a preview of the style on your slide.

5 Click the chart style from the gallery that you want to use.

The chart reflects the change in chart style.

6 Click the **Plus** icon (+).

The Chart Elements box opens. You can add or remove chart elements using this box. For example, you can include data labels or a legend.

Note: Only elements used in your chosen chart appear in the list, so you may see different options than those shown in the figure.

7 Position the mouse pointer to the right of Data Labels, or the chart element you added, and click the arrow (▶) that appears.

8 Click an item from the selection.

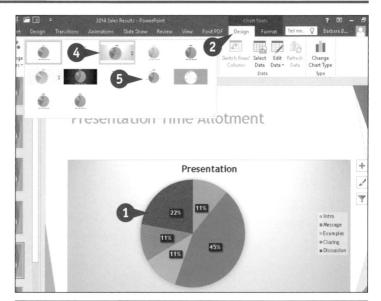

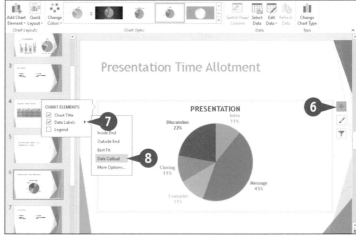

The data labels (or your chosen element) appear.

9 Click the plot area.

10 Click the **Chart Tools Format** tab.

11 Click **Shape Fill**.

Ⓐ You can alternatively make a selection from the Shape Styles gallery.

Ⓑ You can choose from specialized fill options such as a picture, or different gradients and textures.

12 Click a color from the gallery.

The plot area changes color.

13 Click outside the chart and then click the chart.

Note: To format, click a section of the chart, be it a pie slice, bar, or dot. To format a single item in the chart, click it twice (not a double-click). The same applies to the data labels.

14 Click **Shape Effects**.

15 Click one of the effects; the example uses Bevel.

16 Click an item from the gallery.

PowerPoint applies the formatting to the chart.

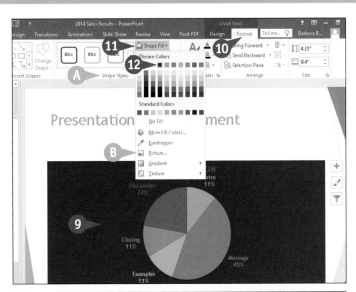

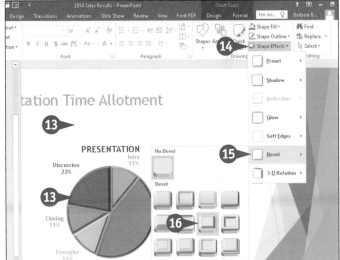

TIP

Can I change the type of a chart?
Yes. Follow these steps:

1 Follow Steps **1** and **2** in this section.

2 Click **Change Chart Type**, which is on the far right of the Ribbon.

3 In the Change Chart Type dialog box, click a chart type category.

4 Click a specific chart type and click **OK**.

PowerPoint changes the chart type to the one you selected.

Edit Chart Data

It is not unusual for chart data to change over time. You can update your chart with the most recent information by opening the data spreadsheet and changing the data. You need not show all the spreadsheet data in the chart. If you decide not to display all the data, you can remove data elements such as data series or categories from the chart without deleting that information from the spreadsheet. You can later bring removed data back by reversing the process. Alternatively, you can delete the data from the spreadsheet.

Edit Chart Data

1. Click anywhere on a chart.

2. Click the **Filter** icon ( ).

   The Chart Filters box opens. You can add (☑) or remove (☐) the data elements with this box.

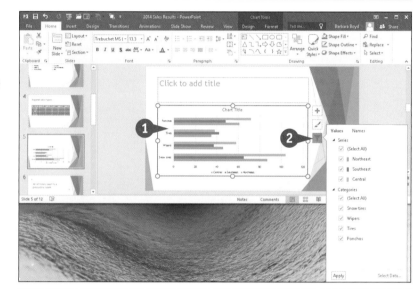

3. Click a series (☐ changes to ☑).

   This example hides the Central series.

4. Click a category (☐ changes to ☑).

   This example hides the Ponchos category.

5. Click **Apply**.

   PowerPoint removes the data elements.

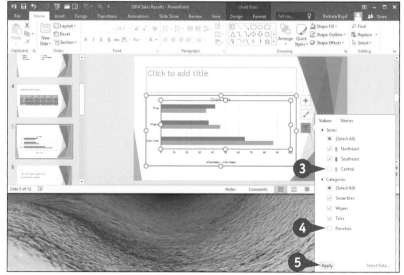

6 Click the **Chart Tools Design** tab.

7 Click **Edit Data**.

The data spreadsheet appears.

8 Double-click a cell to edit the data.

This example is editing cell B4.

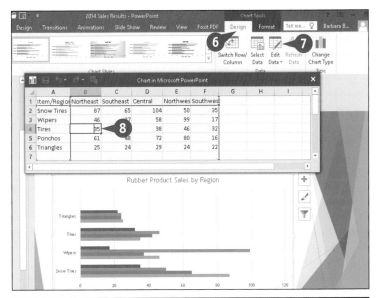

9 Type a new row label in cell A7.

10 Type new data in row 7.

A The chart updates with a new series for the added column.

B The chart updates with a new category for the added row.

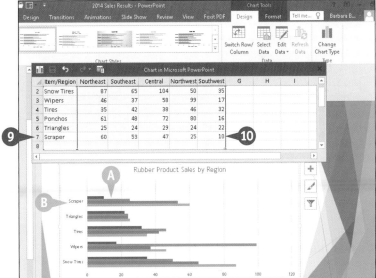

TIP

Can I import data from an Excel spreadsheet?

Yes. It is often easier to work in Excel, or use existing data. Open the Excel file with the desired data, click and drag to select the data you want to use, and then press to copy the data. Next, open the PowerPoint presentation where you want to place the data from Excel. Create a slide per the section "Insert a Chart," and click the **Chart Tools Design** tab, then click **Select Data**. Finally, click in the first cell (A1) and press Ctrl + V. The chart now reflects the data you pasted from Excel.

Insert a SmartArt Graphic

SmartArt graphics are diagrams that illustrate a process, workflow, or structure. You can use SmartArt graphics or SmartArt diagrams to quickly present concepts in an easily understandable way. For example, a diagram can show the workflow of a procedure or the hierarchy in an organization. Some SmartArt layouts are text only, whereas others involve text and pictures. You might use a SmartArt picture layout to show the four seasons, and a SmartArt text graphic to describe the steps for starting a race. PowerPoint offers many SmartArt layouts to help you communicate with your audience graphically.

Insert a SmartArt Graphic

1. Click a slide that has a content placeholder.

2. Click the **Insert a SmartArt Graphic** icon (🖼).

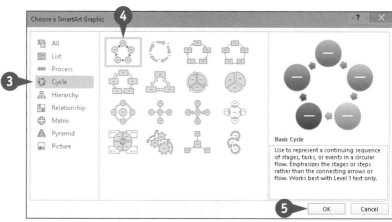

The Choose a SmartArt Graphic dialog box appears.

3. Click a diagram category.

Note: Click **All** and drag the scroll bar to see all the layouts.

4. Click a specific diagram layout.

5. Click **OK**.

The dialog box closes and the SmartArt graphic diagram appears on the slide.

6 Click the **Expand** button (◁) to open the Text pane (◁ changes to ▷).

Ⓐ You can click the **Text Pane** button on the Ribbon to open the Text pane.

7 Click **[Text]** next to a bullet.

[Text] disappears and the insertion point takes its place next to the bullet.

Note: You can also edit text directly in the graphical element.

8 Type the text for the element.

9 Repeat Steps **7** and **8** to type text into other graphical elements.

10 Press Enter.

Ⓑ PowerPoint adds a graphical element.

11 Click outside the SmartArt graphic when you are finished.

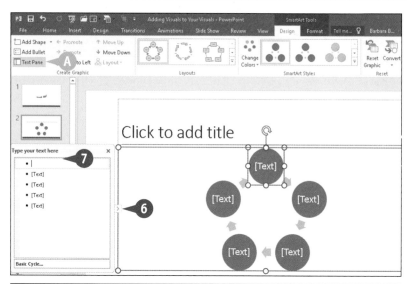

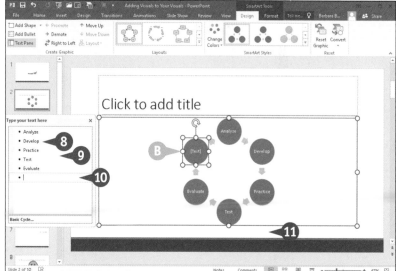

TIPS

Can I add more elements in the SmartArt graphics diagram if I am not using the Text pane?

Yes. Click an element next to where you want the additional element. Click the **Smart Tools Design** tab. Click the **Add Shape** down arrow (▼). The list gives you options about where to place the new element. Click a selection from the list.

Can I have fewer elements than the SmartArt graphic template?

You can remove elements in the Text pane. Click a bullet item and then press Backspace; the SmartArt graphic will have one less element and the bullet on the Text pane will be removed.

Edit SmartArt

After you create a SmartArt graphic, you can change its look and contents at any time. For example, you can change a SmartArt graphic to a different layout, edit the text, change its color, give it a 3-D effect, or even mix different shapes. You can also format text by changing the font color or style, or by making the font bold or italic. This versatility enables you to create the perfect diagram that sends a specific message to your audience.

Edit SmartArt

1. Click anywhere in the SmartArt graphic to select it.

2. Click the **SmartArt Tools Design** tab.

3. Click the **Expand** button (☰) to open the Text pane (☰ changes to ☰).

4. Click any text in the Text pane or on any element to edit the text.

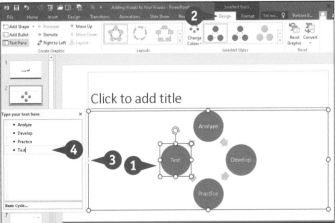

5. Click the **Collapse** button (☰) to close the Text pane (☰ changes to ☰).

6. Click the **SmartArt Styles** down arrow (☰).

   The SmartArt Styles gallery appears.

7. Click a style from the gallery.

Ⓐ The gallery shows diagrams from the same category as the current one. Click **More Layouts** to see all the diagram options.

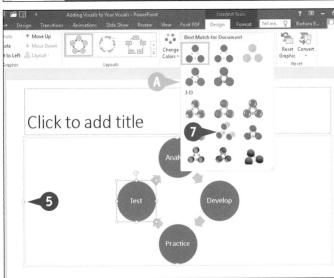

The SmartArt graphic changes style.

8 Click the **SmartArt Layout** down arrow (⏷).

The SmartArt Layout gallery appears.

9 Click a layout from the gallery.

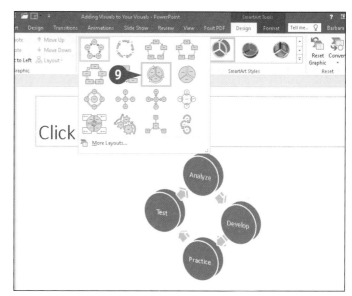

The SmartArt graphic changes layout.

10 Click a single element to select it.

11 Click the **SmartArt Tools Format** tab.

12 Click **Smaller** or **Larger** to change the element's size.

13 Click a Shape Styles command to change the color, border color, or special effect of the shape.

14 Click a WordArt Styles command to change the color, border color, or special effect of the font.

The element reflects the changes you made.

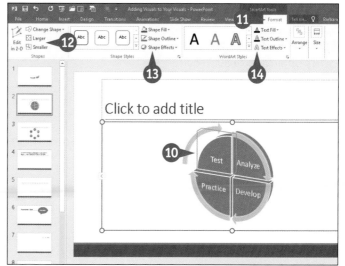

TIP

Are there color themes for the SmartArt graphics?

Yes. Follow these steps to choose from a variety of color themes.

1 Click a SmartArt graphic to select it.

2 Click the **SmartArt Tools Design** tab.

3 Click **Change Colors**.

4 In the Primary Theme Colors gallery, click a color theme.

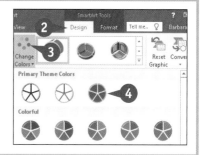

Using SmartArt Layout Effects

You can make pictures stand out by combining them with SmartArt graphics, which can more effectively communicate your message than arranging the pictures on the slide with a list of bullet points. SmartArt graphics enable you to group pictures and then apply text to the individual pictures or the entire group. You can also apply a workflow or hierarchy to pictures using SmartArt graphics. For example, you could build an organization chart with a photo of each team member along with his or her name and position.

Using SmartArt Layout Effects

Apply a Layout

1 Select pictures in Normal view.

Note: To select multiple pictures, click the first picture and then press **Ctrl** while clicking additional pictures.

2 Click the **Picture Tools Format** tab.

3 Click **Picture Layout**.

The gallery of picture layouts appears. Hover the mouse pointer over a picture layout to see a preview.

4 Click a picture layout.

PowerPoint applies the SmartArt graphics picture layout to the pictures.

5 Click the **[Text]** to type labels or information.

Change a Picture

6 Click a picture.

7 Click the **Picture Tools Format** tab.

8 Click the **Change Pictures** icon (🖼).

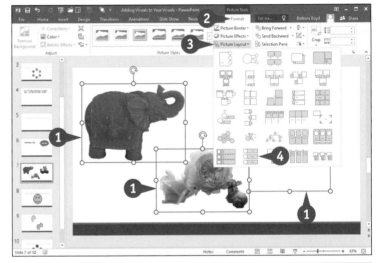

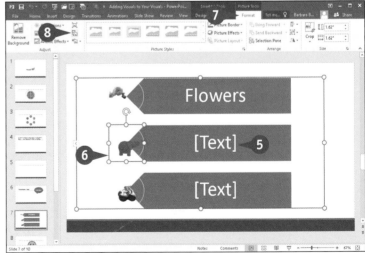

The Insert Pictures dialog box appears.

9 Click **From a file**.

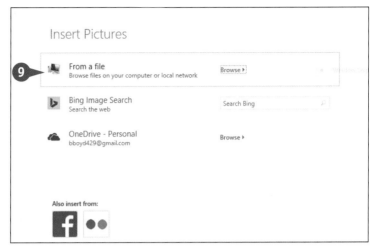

The Insert Picture dialog box appears.

10 Click the folder containing the picture file.

11 Click the picture.

12 Click **Open**.

A PowerPoint changes the picture to the image you selected.

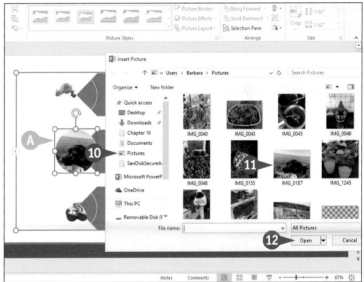

Can I change the order of the pictures?
Yes. Click a picture in the SmartArt layout, and then click the **SmartArt Tools Design** tab. Click either **Move Up** or **Move Down**, and the order of the picture changes accordingly.

Can I add another picture holder?
Yes. Click the SmartArt layout, click the **SmartArt Tools Design** tab, and then click **Add Shape**. You can also move a picture from one side of SmartArt to the other; click the SmartArt, click the **SmartArt Tools Design** tab, and then click **Right to Left**.

CHAPTER 6

Working with Clip Art, Shapes, and Objects

Adding graphic elements such as clip art and shapes to your slides can enhance the words on your slides and improve the effectiveness of your presentation. Although you can use placeholders, you can also place graphic elements anywhere on a slide — you are not bound by placeholders. You can also use color and various formatting options to make your presentation picture-perfect.

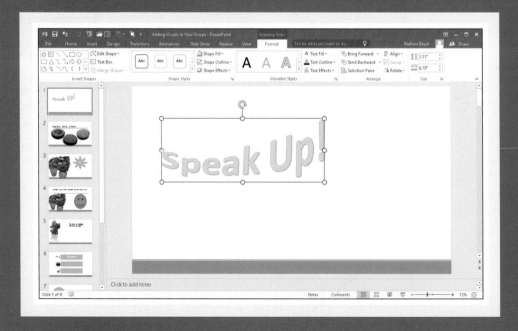

Insert Clip Art

*C*lip art can be interesting drawings, silhouettes, cartoons, caricatures, and other nonphotographic representations. You can add clip art to slides to make them interesting and engaging. Clip art is usually easier for an audience to see because it lacks the detail of a photo. You can search for clip art by keyword with the online feature in PowerPoint, or you can insert your own clip art from your computer. You can insert clip art anywhere on your slide without using a content placeholder, which gives you complete flexibility with how you use it.

Insert Clip Art

1 Select a slide in Normal view.

Note: To learn how to select a slide, see Chapter 2.

2 Click the **Insert** tab.

3 Click **Online Pictures**.

A You can also click the **Online Pictures** button ( ) in a content placeholder.

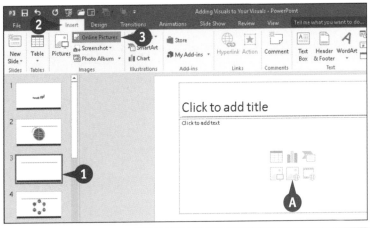

The Insert Pictures dialog box appears.

4 Type a keyword or phrase in the **Bing Image Search** search box.

5 Click the **Search** icon ( ).

6 Click and drag the scroll bar to scroll through and view the images.

7 Click an image from the gallery.

8 Click **Insert**.

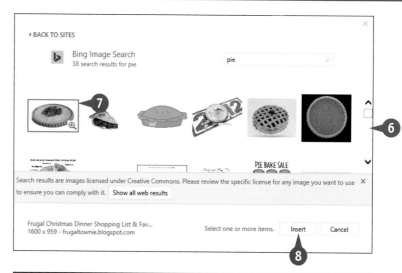

The clip art appears on the slide.

Note: See the sections "Move Objects" and "Resize Objects" to learn how to position and size the clip art.

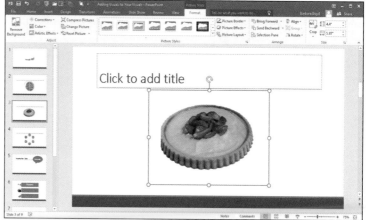

TIPS

Can I search the entire Internet for clip art?
Yes. First, try the Bing Image Search feature. If unsuccessful, search the web with your browser and save an image to your computer. Then click **Pictures** on the Insert tab and use the Insert Picture dialog box to browse to your saved clip art.

Do I need to be concerned about copyright?
Yes. The images in the Bing search results are available under a Creative Commons license; you should credit the source in your presentation. And you may not be able to use the image for commercial purposes. You can search online for stock image providers, some of which offer royalty-free clip art.

Select Objects

You will often need to format or reposition slide objects such as shapes or pictures. To change an object on a slide, you must first select it. When you click the border of an object to select the entire object, the border becomes solid; when you click the text within an object to select the text, the border becomes a dashed outline. You can also select (or hide) objects in the Selection pane.

You must select an entire object to format or reposition it. You can format specific text by selecting only that text.

Select Objects

1 Select a slide in Normal view.

2 Click an object or text box.

If you click a text box, the insertion point appears within the text and the border becomes a dashed outline.

Note: When you click a text box, the first click places an insertion point within the text and the border becomes a dashed outline. Click the border and it becomes a solid line, selecting the entire box as an object.

A The object's contextual tab appears on the Ribbon.

3 Press **Ctrl** while you click additional objects.

Note: You can also select multiple objects by clicking and dragging on the slide around them.

4 Click the **Drawing Tools Format** or **Picture Tools Format** tab.

Which one you see depends on the type of object you click; you may see both if you have mixed object types.

5 Click **Selection Pane**.

The Selection pane appears.

An item appears in the Selection pane for every shape and placeholder on the slide.

An object is selected or highlighted in the Selection pane if you select it on the slide.

6 Click an item in the list.

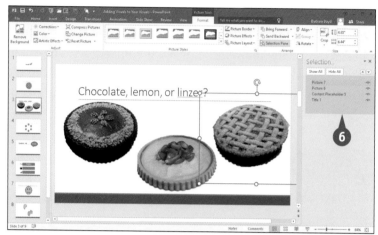

7 Click the **Eye** icon (changes to —) to hide an object.

PowerPoint hides and selects the objects.

You can click the **Dash** icon (—) to expose a hidden object.

Note: You can select multiple objects in the Selection pane by pressing Ctrl while clicking them.

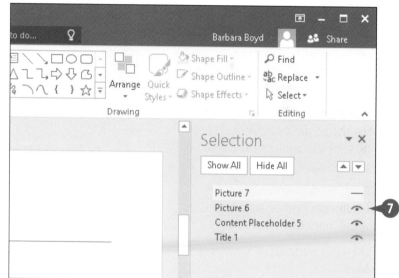

TIPS

Can I change the names that PowerPoint gave my shapes?

Yes, you can change them in the Selection pane. Click the name that you want to change, then double-click it. When the insertion point appears in the text, delete the name that PowerPoint has assigned. Type the name that you want and press Enter.

I unintentionally clicked a shape while selecting multiple shapes. Can I deselect it without starting all over?

Yes. That can also happen when you click and drag around a group of objects on a slide — you may get one that you do not want as part of the selected group. Press Ctrl while clicking a shape that is part of the selected objects to deselect it.

Move Objects

The position of the various objects on a slide can affect the message you want to convey. When you insert an object, such as a picture, text box, placeholder, or shape, it usually does not appear in the location where you want it. When you insert a slide, you may prefer to position the text and content placeholders in a different location than the standard layout. You can reposition objects on a slide, putting them in a more strategic place, by clicking and dragging them.

Move Objects

1. Click the middle of an object to select it.

2. Click and drag the object to a new position.

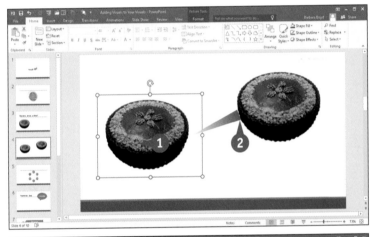

When you release the mouse button, the object appears in its new position.

3. Click anywhere outside the shape when finished.

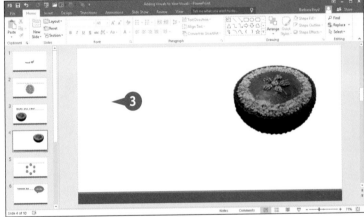

Resize Objects

After placing an object on a slide, you will often want to resize it. For example, when you insert a picture, it may be too small for your audience to see, or it may be bigger than the slide. You can resize objects such as charts, WordArt, pictures, and shapes on your slide to optimize their visual impact.

When you select an object, handles appear on the border; you click and drag a handle to resize the object. Dragging a corner handle while pressing the Shift key retains the object's original proportions.

Resize Objects

1 Click an object to select it.

A Handles (⬦) appear on the border around the object.

2 Position the mouse pointer over a handle on the border of the object.

3 Click and drag outward to enlarge it or inward to shrink it (the double-arrow pointer changes to a crosshair pointer).

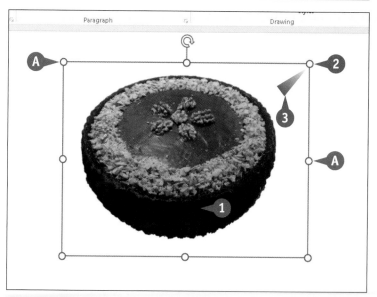

When you release the mouse button, the object appears at its new size.

4 Click anywhere outside the object when finished.

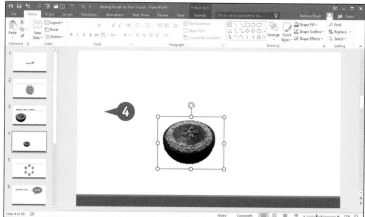

Change Object Order

When you work with multiple objects, you may want to stack them in layers so that they overlap as objects do in real life; or you may want to overlap them to create a special effect or make them appear three dimensional. For example, if you want to create a shadow effect for an object, the shape that you use as the shadow must be behind that object. Controlling which object appears in front of another object is called ordering. PowerPoint includes a feature that makes ordering objects easy and fast.

Change Object Order

1. Click the **Home** tab.
2. Click **Select**.
3. Click **Selection Pane**.

   The Selection pane appears.

4. Select an object behind other objects.

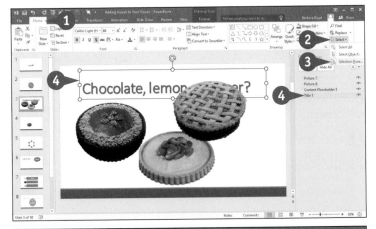

5. Click the **Bring Forward** button (▲).

   The object moves in front of the other objects.

Ⓐ You can click the **Send Backward** button (▼) to send an object behind the other objects.

6. Click outside the object when finished.

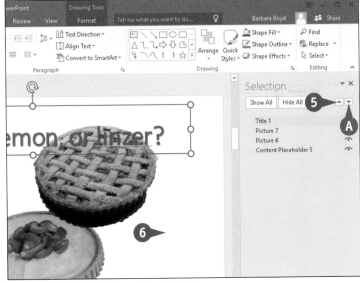

Group and Ungroup Objects

Y ou may create a set of objects that you want to move or format as a unit. For example, you may draw a car using ovals and lines. After assembling the car, not having to move its pieces individually would save you the time and effort of reassembling the pieces in a new location. Grouped objects act as a single object. After grouping objects, changes you make then apply to all the objects in the group, whether you reposition, resize, or format them. Grouping enables you to save time by applying changes to multiple objects.

Group and Ungroup Objects

1 Select multiple objects.

Note: See the section "Select Objects" to learn how to select multiple objects.

2 Click the **Picture Tools Format** tab.

3 Click the **Group** button (⊞).

4 Click **Group**.

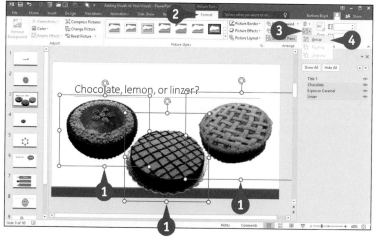

A A single selection box appears around the grouped objects.

B The group appears in the Selection pane.

5 If not already selected, select the grouped objects.

6 Click the **Picture Tools Format** tab.

7 Click the **Group** button (⊞).

8 Click **Ungroup**.

The objects ungroup.

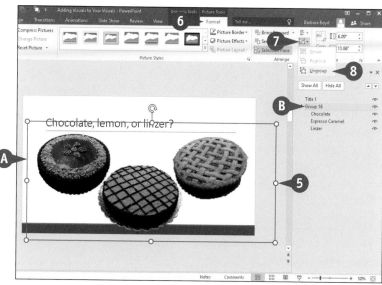

Draw a Shape

There are many predefined shapes that you can easily draw on a slide to add visual interest. For example, you might want to draw an arrow between two charts to indicate before and after results. The available shapes range from simple geometric squares and circles to thought bubbles and arrows. You can choose these shapes from a gallery and draw them by simply clicking and dragging. You can type text into many of the shapes and change the formatting of the shape, the border, and the text. The Shape gallery even includes action buttons that run simple actions.

Draw a Shape

1. Select a slide in Normal view.

2. Click the **Insert** tab.

3. Click **Shapes**.

   The gallery of shapes appears.

4. Click the shape you want to draw.

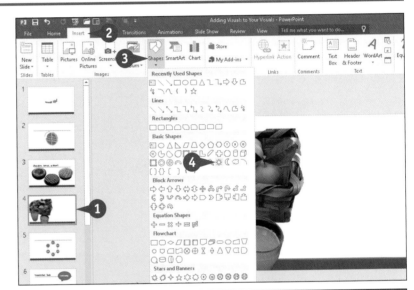

   The gallery closes, and the mouse pointer changes to the crosshair pointer.

5. Click the slide to insert the shape.

   When you release the mouse button, the shape appears.

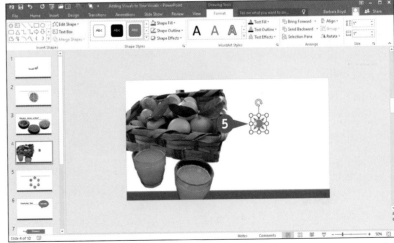

Note: You can also click and drag the crosshair pointer to size the shape while inserting it, or resize it later as explained in the section "Resize Objects."

Note: You can use the Rectangle or Oval shape to draw a square or circle. Press Shift as you drag to keep the shape perfect.

Add Text to a Shape

You can spice up your text boxes by adding a colored or patterned shape behind them, or you can add text directly to a shape. For example, you can use an arrow with text in it to describe something on your slide. The text appears within the shape, and the shape effectively becomes a fancy text box. You lose some versatility using shapes with text because shapes lack some of the automation that text boxes have. For example, they do not automatically enlarge or shrink based upon the amount of text you type.

Add Text to a Shape

1 Right-click the shape in which you want to add text.

2 Click **Edit Text**.

The insertion point appears inside the shape.

3 Type your text.

4 Click anywhere outside the shape when finished.

The text appears in the shape.

Note: If the text you type exceeds the width of the shape, PowerPoint continues the text on the next line automatically. You can force a new line by pressing Enter.

Note: Click and drag across the text to edit it as you would other text in PowerPoint.

Merge Shapes

Powerpoint gives you the flexibility to create and use your own shapes by merging two or more shapes together. For example, you may need a shape that is a circle with a star cut out of the center to frame a person's picture. You can also fragment multiple shapes for a puzzle effect, or merge a variety of slide objects — standard geometric shapes, pictures, and clip art. After merging shapes, the new shape works just like any other distinct shape on a slide. You need one geometric shape plus one or more other objects to merge shapes.

Merge Shapes

① Insert and overlap multiple shapes similar to the example.

Note: To insert a shape, see the section "Draw a Shape."

Note: Some shapes in the example are transparent so you can see each shape completely.

② Click two overlapping shapes while pressing Ctrl.

③ Click the **Drawing Tools Format** tab.

④ Click the **Merge Shapes** button (⊘).

⑤ Click one of the merge options: **Union**, **Combine**, **Fragment**, **Intersect**, or **Subtract**.

Ⓐ When you click **Subtract**, the second shape you click is removed, leaving a portion of the first shape clicked.

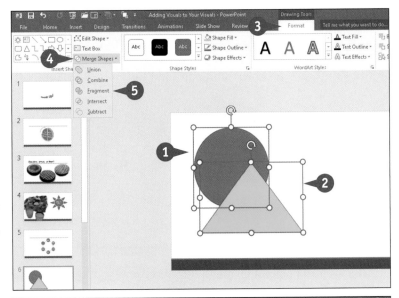

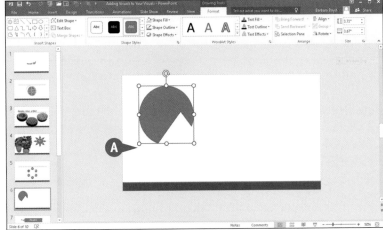

B When you click **Intersect**, the area where the two shapes intersect remains.

C When you click **Fragment**, the two shapes (including the overlapping part) separate so you can move them independently.

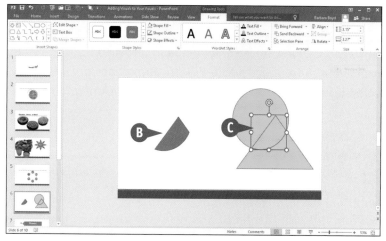

D When you click **Union**, the shapes become a new shape.

The border extends around the entire shape.

E You can click the Undo button to undo your changes.

Note: You can click and drag on the slide around multiple shapes to select them.

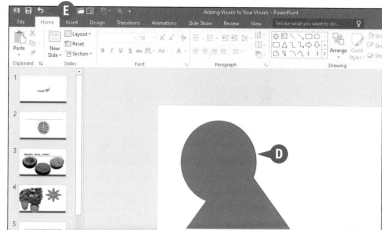

TIPS

I saw a nice effect where characters were made from a picture. Can I create that?

Yes. Insert your picture and type your characters into a placeholder or WordArt. Place the characters over the picture. Format the characters the way you want them — you cannot format after the merge because the characters become a shape. Click the picture first and then click the words while pressing Ctrl. Click the **Merge Shapes** button (⊘) and then click **Intersect**.

I want everything except where my two shapes overlap. Can I do that?

Yes. You can combine the shapes. Click the **Merge Shapes** button (⊘) and then click **Combine**. Combine is the opposite of Intersect — it removes the intersection from the overlapping shapes.

Format Objects

You can adjust the formatting of an object to make it more visually appealing or easier to see against a slide background. For example, you can add a fill color, modify the font, change the thickness or color of lines, and modify arrow styles. Details and fine-tuning such as object formatting make your presentation pop — you can produce objects very specific to your needs and adjust the colors of objects to look good against the background of the slide and other objects on the slide.

Format Objects

1 Click the object to format.

Note: You can learn how to select and format text in Chapter 4.

2 Click the **Drawing Tools Format** tab.

3 Click the **Shape Styles** down arrow (▽).

As you hover the mouse pointer over a color, you see a preview of the color on your object.

4 Click a color scheme from the gallery.

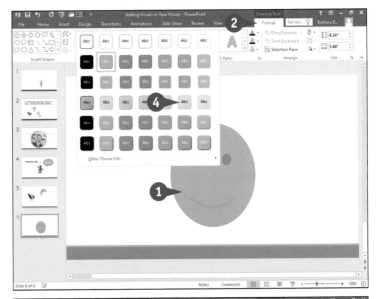

The color scheme changes.

5 To choose a color that is not part of the theme, click **Shape Fill**.

As you hover the mouse pointer over a color, you see a preview of the color on your object.

6 Click a color from the color palette.

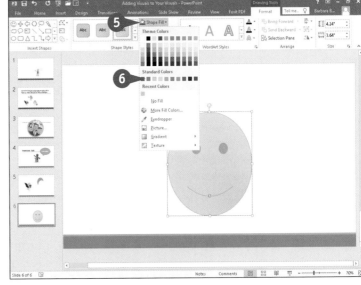

The shape changes color.

7 Click **Shape Outline**.

8 Click **Weight**.

A You can change the border color.

B You can change the border style.

9 Click a weight from the menu.

This example changes the weight of the shape's border.

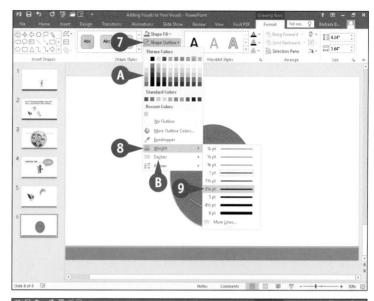

PowerPoint applies your changes.

10 Right-click the object.

The shortcut menu appears.

C You can also use the Mini Toolbar to apply formatting.

11 Click **Format Shape**.

The Format Shape task pane appears; you can use the task pane to perform any formatting.

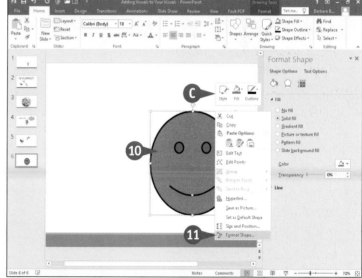

TIPS

I want every shape that I draw to appear with a blue fill color. Is there a quick way to do that?
Yes. Draw any shape and then click **Shape Fill** on the Drawing Tools Format tab. Click the blue fill color you want, then right-click your shape and click **Set as Default Shape**. Shapes you insert will now appear in blue.

Can I make an object transparent?
Yes. Open the Format Shape task pane, and then click the **Fill** icon (⬧). Click **Fill** if that section is not expanded. If not selected, click **Solid Fill** (○ changes to ◉). Type a percentage into the **Transparency** text box or use the Transparency slider or spinner (⬧) to adjust the transparency.

Color with the Eyedropper

You can match colors by sampling a color from anything on your slide and then applying it to anything on the slide that you select. Matching colors is important because color is essential to the look and feel of your presentation. The Eyedropper enables you to match colors with a couple of clicks, saving you time. You can sample from anything on your slide such as the background, text, objects, and even pictures!

Color with the Eyedropper

1 Select the object whose color you want to change.

2 Click the **Drawing Tools Format** tab.

3 Click **Shape Fill**.

4 Click **Eyedropper**.

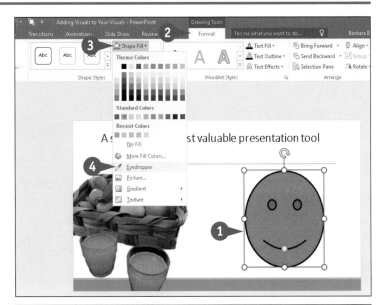

The Eyedropper pointer appears.

5 Position the Eyedropper pointer over the color you want to sample.

6 Click the object.

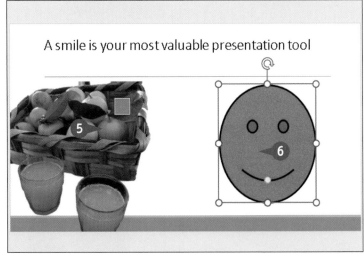

The object now matches the color of the sampled color.

7 Click the border of an object that contains text.

Note: Optionally, you can change the color of specific text by selecting only that text within the object.

8 Click the **Home** tab.

9 Click the **Font Color** button (🅰).

10 Click **Eyedropper**.

The Eyedropper pointer appears.

11 Position the Eyedropper pointer over the color you want to sample.

12 Click the object that contains text.

The text now matches the color of the sampled color.

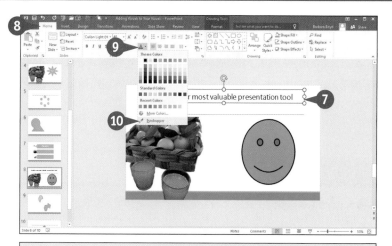

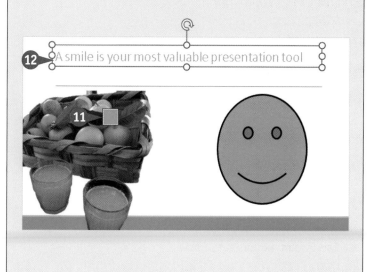

TIPS

Can I sample a color from a different slide than the slide that holds the object whose color I want to match?
No. As soon as you click a slide in the Slide Thumbnails pane, you lose the Eyedropper pointer. You can copy and paste the object onto the slide with the sample color, match the color, and then delete the object from the slide where you pasted it.

Why does the Eyedropper feature not seem to work when I click a placeholder containing text?
The insertion point is between characters. You must either click the placeholder border to select the entire placeholder or click and drag across text to select specific text.

Apply a New Effect

You may want to give an object a special effect to make it stand out or link it to an important point in your presentation. You can use shape effects to add dimension and realism to the object's appearance. For example, you can apply a reflection effect that gives the appearance of the object reflecting in a lake. You can also give an object a soft, blurred border, or give it a shadow or glow. When you select an object, the contextual Format tab that appears on the Ribbon provides you with many tools to apply effects and formatting to the object.

Apply a New Effect

1 Click an object to select it.

2 Click the **Picture Tools Format** tab.

3 Click **Picture Effects**.

Note: For a shape, you would click **Shape Effects**.

4 Click a picture effect.

This example selects the Reflection effect.

5 Click a variation of the effect.

You see a preview of the effect as you hover the mouse pointer over the various choices.

A PowerPoint applies the special effect to the object.

B You can right-click the picture to open the Format pane, which offers options to make more precise changes.

6 Click anywhere outside the object when finished.

Note: When you move or resize a picture with an effect, the effect is moved or resized, too.

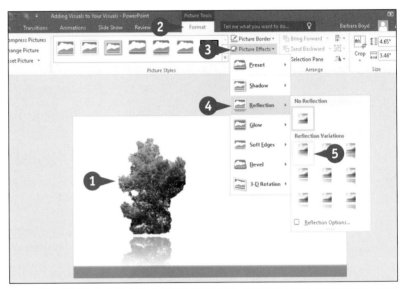

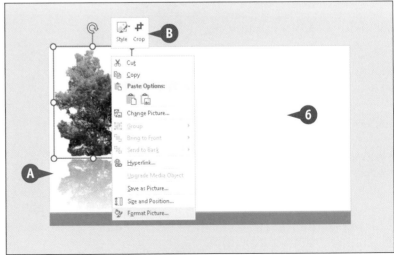

Add a Text Box

Y ou can add a text box anywhere on a slide, which enables you to have almost unlimited versatility with text. Unlike a placeholder, a text box does not automatically produce a bulleted list. A text box is great for freeform text and automatically enlarges, shrinks, and wraps text, depending on the amount of text you type. Keep in mind that text box contents do not appear in Outline view.

Add a Text Box

1 Select a slide in Normal view.

Note: To learn how to select a slide, see Chapter 2.

2 Click the **Insert** tab.

3 Click **Text Box**.

The mouse pointer changes to the Text box insertion pointer.

4 Click where you want to place the upper left corner of the text.

The text box appears with an insertion point inside.

5 Type your text.

6 Click anywhere outside the text box when finished.

Note: You can adjust the text box width; the height adjusts automatically based on the amount of text you type. You can also move the text box anywhere. For more information, see the sections "Resize Objects" and "Move Objects."

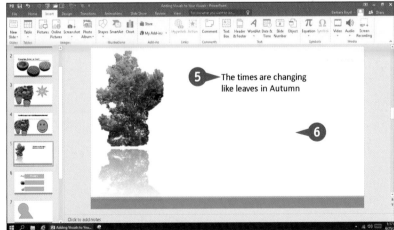

Add WordArt

The WordArt feature enables you to create special effects with text. You can distort WordArt text and apply interesting color styles. For example, if you have a picture of a product, you can use the WordArt feature to bend a phrase over and around the picture. Or, you can emphasize an important word or phrase anywhere on your slide. You can even create a simple logo! WordArt is an object that you can move, resize, or format using techniques discussed earlier in this chapter.

Add WordArt

1 Select a slide in Normal view.

Note: To learn how to select a slide, see Chapter 2.

2 Click the **Insert** tab.

3 Click **WordArt**.

The WordArt gallery appears.

4 Click a WordArt style.

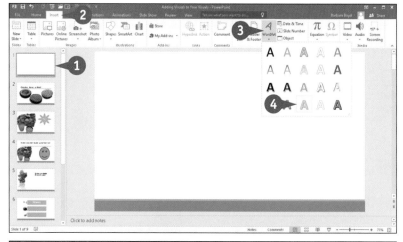

The WordArt appears on the slide ready for you to type a word or phrase.

5 Type your text.

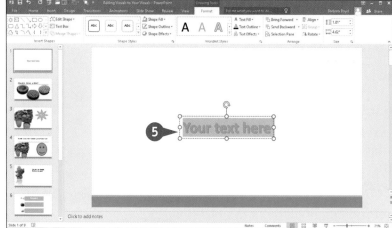

This example creates the text, "Speak Up!"

As you type, the WordArt automatically sizes itself.

6 Click the **Drawing Tools Format** tab.

7 Click the **Text Effects** button (A).

8 Click **Transform**.

The Transform gallery appears.

As you hover the mouse pointer over different effects, you see a preview of them on your text.

9 Click a variation from the gallery.

PowerPoint applies the special effect to the WordArt.

10 Resize the WordArt as needed to distort the effect.

11 Drag the handles on or inside the WordArt border to change the distortion of the effect.

Note: There may be multiple handles.

You can use other tools on the Drawing Tools Format tab to format the WordArt.

12 Click outside the object when finished.

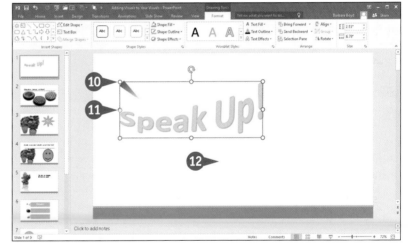

TIPS

I created a WordArt object, but then realized it contains a typo. Is there any way to change it?
Yes. Click the object just like any text box or placeholder. The insertion point appears within the text of the WordArt so that you can make the necessary changes.

How do I change the style and color of the WordArt?
Click the WordArt object, and then click the **Drawing Tools Format** tab when it appears. Click the **WordArt Styles** down arrow (▼). When the WordArt gallery appears, choose a WordArt style.

Arrange Objects with Smart Guides

Symmetry helps your audience concentrate on your message rather than be confused by a jarring display. For example, you may want similar objects on a slide to be proportionate to and equidistant from each other. In PowerPoint, instead of manually moving objects to align them by sight, you use Smart Guides. Smart Guides enable you to align objects, center objects, resize multiple objects to the same proportions, and arrange objects equidistant from each other — all in real time. Using Smart Guides lends precision to your presentation.

Arrange Objects with Smart Guides

1 Insert three similar objects, such as clip art or pictures, onto a slide that contains a placeholder.

Note: See the section "Insert Clip Art" for more information.

2 Resize an object so it is a different size from the others.

Note: See the sections "Move Objects" and "Resize Objects" for more information.

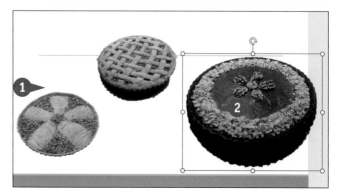

3 Click and drag an object until the left edge aligns with a placeholder.

A red, dashed line appears, indicating that the object is aligned with the placeholder.

4 Release the mouse button.

5 Click and drag an object until the top edge is aligned with another object.

Red, dashed lines and arrows appear, indicating that the object is aligned with the other objects.

6 Release the mouse button.

7 Click and drag the resized object so the top is aligned with and equidistant from the others.

Red, dashed lines and arrows appear, indicating that the object is aligned with the other objects.

8 Release the mouse button.

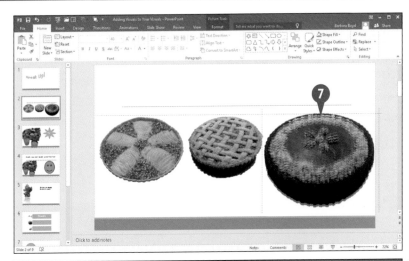

9 Resize the object to be the same size as the others.

Red, dashed lines and arrows appear, indicating that the object is aligned with the other objects.

10 Release the mouse button.

PowerPoint aligns the objects.

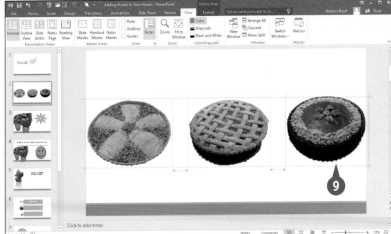

How are Smart Guides different from gridlines and guidelines?
Smart Guides change as you move and resize objects. They are particularly helpful in making objects equidistant from each other. Smart Guides appear and disappear as you move objects around. You need to be very close to an aligned position for them to appear, and so they can be challenging to use. Gridlines and guidelines are continuously visible while they are enabled. Gridlines can help you plot objects on a slide, whereas guidelines are movable and particularly useful for lining up objects with background features. All these tools have similar uses, but some are more helpful than others with certain tasks.

Using the Grid and Guides

Lining up objects by sight can be frustrating; the grid and guides help you position and align objects with precision. The grid looks like graph paper lines on your slide; guides run across the entire slide and can help you line up objects with details on the slide background. If you need to make small, fine adjustments to positioning, you can make the distance between gridline points small, or make the distance large for easier alignment. You can also have objects snap to the gridline for easy and fast alignment.

Using the Grid and Guides

1 In Normal view, click the **View** tab.

2 Click the check box to enable **Gridlines** (□ changes to ✔).

3 Click the check box to enable **Guides** (□ changes to ✔).

4 Position the mouse pointer over the guide until it changes to the mouse splitter.

5 Click and drag the guide to move it in a position to align two objects.

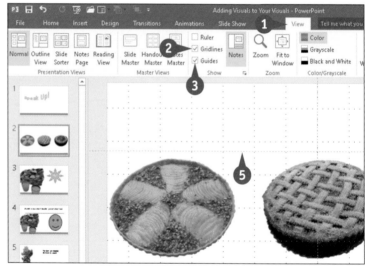

6 Click the dialog box launcher (⌐a).

The Grid and Guides dialog box appears.

7 Select the **Snap objects to grid** check box (□ changes to ✔).

Ⓐ You can change the spacing of the gridlines.

Ⓑ You can deselect the **Smart Guides** check box to disable Smart Guides (✔ changes to □).

8 Click **OK**.

Objects will now snap to the gridlines as you move them.

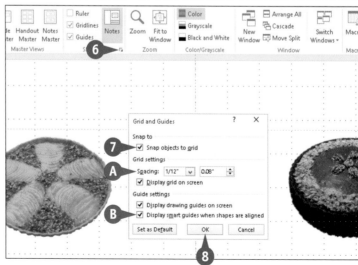

Nudge Objects

Sometimes, you may want to move an object by very small increments. For example, you may want two objects to touch, but not overlap. Using the mouse to perform delicate and precise movements can be tricky, yet these small details can be important to a presentation. Nudging is a feature that moves objects by small increments using keystrokes. The nudge feature enables you to move a selected object incrementally to the right, left, up, or down on the slide. You can use nudging together with the grid and guidelines to align objects perfectly.

Nudge Objects

1 In Normal view, select an object.

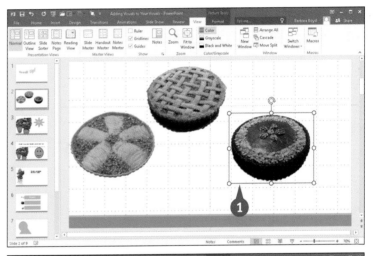

2 Press ⬆, ➡, ⬅, or ⬇ as many times as needed to nudge the object in the desired direction.

This example presses ➡ 15 times to move the object over one gridline.

3 Click outside the object to deselect it.

Note: If an object has a background, the background may cover parts of another object when you nudge it closer. See Chapter 7 to learn how to remove the background from clip art or a picture.

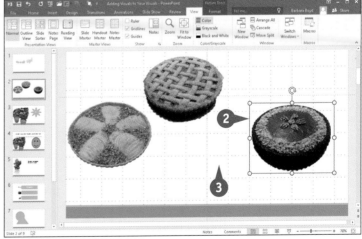

Align Objects

Instead of using Smart Guides, you can align objects relative to each other quickly and easily with menus you find on the Ribbon. For example, you can align several objects at the same position as the leftmost object, or you can distribute objects evenly relative to one another. This enables you to align many objects perfectly with a couple of clicks, as opposed to the Smart Guides feature, which performs alignment in a very convenient way, but with only one object at a time.

Align Objects

1 Select multiple objects.

Note: See the section "Select Objects" to learn how to select multiple objects.

2 Click the **Picture Tools Format** tab.

3 Click the **Align** button (⬚).

4 Click the **Align Middle** option in the menu.

The middle of all the selected objects aligns with the middlemost object.

5 Click **Distribute Horizontally**.

A You can click **Align to Slide** to make the objects align with the edges and center of the slide as a reference.

B You can click **Align Selected Objects** to make the objects align with each other.

The objects distribute evenly horizontally.

Note: Align Middle refers to the horizontal axis, whereas Align Center refers to the vertical axis. If you choose the inappropriate one, your objects will stack rather than align.

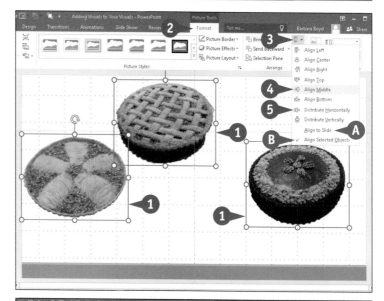

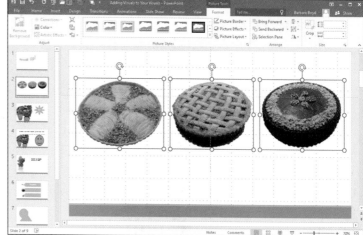

Flip and Rotate Objects

Sometimes when you combine several shapes to create a more complex graphic or you want a picture to appear more dramatic, you can rotate it. For example, you may have a triangle shape as a hill with a clip art car going up the hill. PowerPoint enables you to rotate an object or quickly flip it horizontally or vertically to accomplish that dramatic effect. The Picture Tools Format tab offers all the flip and rotation tools, but you can also click and drag to rotate the object.

Flip and Rotate Objects

Flip Objects

1 Click an object to select it.

2 Click the **Picture Tools Format** tab.

3 Click **Arrange**.

4 Click **Rotate**.

Note: For SmartArt, you must first click **Arrange** after clicking the SmartArt graphic and before clicking **Rotate**.

5 Click **Flip Horizontal**.

A The object flips horizontally.

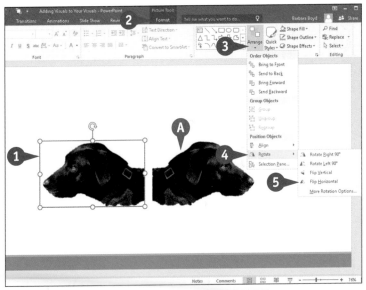

Rotate Objects

1 Click an object to select it.

2 Position the mouse pointer over the rotation handle.

3 Click the rotate handle (⟳).

The rotation pointer changes to the rotation movement arrows.

4 Drag clockwise or counterclockwise.

When you release the mouse, the object stays at the new angle.

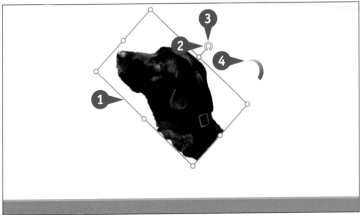

CHAPTER 7

Incorporating Media

PowerPoint enables you to add visual and sound effects that enhance your presentations. You can place photographs, videos, and audio clips anywhere on your slides. You can add dramatic artistic effects to your photographs or remove the background from them. PowerPoint lets you edit photos and videos directly. Finally, you can insert or link to media from the Internet.

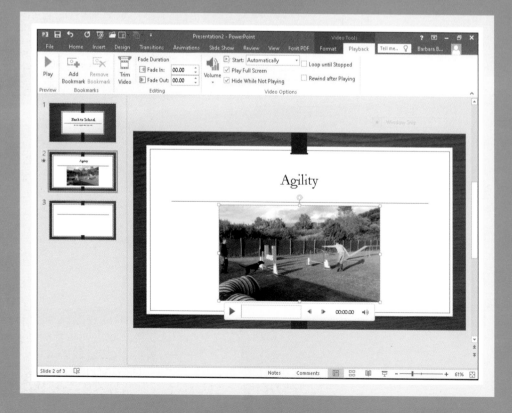

Insert a Picture

Images illustrate your points and enhance your presentation. You can insert various types of images into placeholders or as independent objects, which gives you more versatility when you work with them. Pictures include digital photos, scanned images, clip art, and bitmaps. These can come from your own collection on your computer, such as your company logo or a picture of your product, or a Bing search of the Internet. After you insert an image file, it becomes an object on your slide. To learn how to move, resize, and format objects, see Chapter 6.

Insert a Picture

From Your Computer

1. Select a slide in Normal view.

2. Click the **Insert** tab.

3. Click **Pictures**.

Note: If you use a layout with a placeholder, click the **Pictures** (⬚) icon.

The Insert Picture dialog box appears.

4. Select the folder containing the file you want to insert.

5. Click the file.

6. Click **Insert**.

Ⓐ The image appears on your slide. Resize and position the image as needed, as explained in Chapter 6.

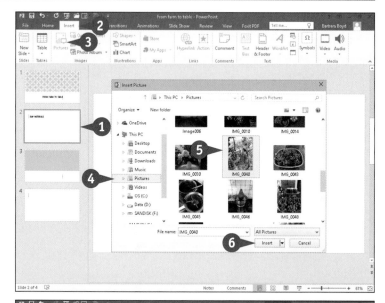

From an Online Source

1 Select a slide in Normal view that contains a placeholder.

Note: If you want the picture to occupy most of the slide, choose a slide layout such as **Picture with Caption**.

2 Click the **Insert Online Picture** icon ( ).

The Insert Online Pictures dialog box appears.

3 Type a keyword in the Bing Image **Search** text box.

4 Click the **Search** icon ( ).

5 Click a picture from the gallery.

6 Click **Show all web results** for even more results.

7 Click **Insert**.

PowerPoint inserts the selected picture into the placeholder.

B Note the picture description, picture size, and the hyperlink to the website where the picture originates.

C Some of these pictures are not royalty-free.

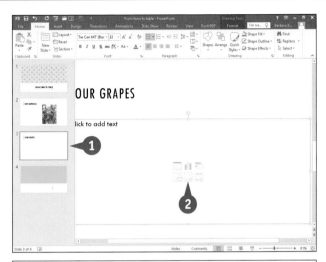

TIP

Will large image files slow the performance of my presentation and can I do anything to fix it?
Yes, to both questions. You can compress the image to improve performance without a noticeable compromise to your image quality. However, compressing pictures permanently changes the images — you cannot reverse those changes. After selecting a picture, follow these steps:

1 On the **Picture Tools Format** tab, click the **Compress Pictures** icon ( ).

2 In the Compress Pictures dialog box, click to disable ( ) **Apply only to this picture** so all pictures in your presentation are compressed.

3 Click **Screen** (changes to) for a resolution you can show to an audience with a projector.

4 Click **OK** to compress the pictures.

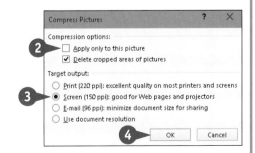

Add a Border

Some clip art images have transparent backgrounds, but sometimes the background of the picture or clip art does not blend with the background of the slide. After you insert a picture, you may want to set it apart from the rest of the slide by adding a border to it. A border helps the image stand out from other items on the slide and makes a clear break from the background of the slide. You can format the border by changing the thickness, making it something other than solid, or converting it to a different color.

Add a Border

1 Click a picture.

2 Click the **Picture Tools Format** tab.

3 Click **Picture Border**.

4 In the gallery that appears, click a border color.

A The border appears around your picture.

B Click **Eyedropper** to match the border color to a color on your photo, as explained in Chapter 6.

5 Click **Picture Border**.

6 Click **Weight**.

7 Click **More Lines**.

The Format Picture pane opens.

8 Click the **Compound** button (≡⁻) to choose a multiline border, which gives your picture a nice matted look.

C Click **Dash type** (⁝⁻) to choose between dashes or dots.

D Click **Join type** to choose square, round, or mitered corners.

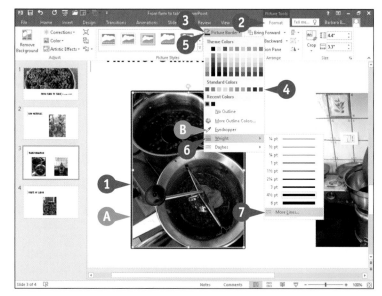

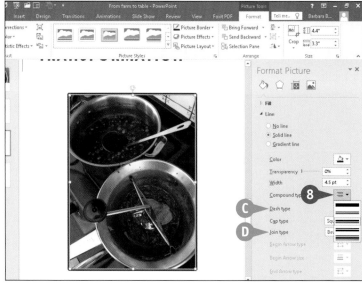

Adjust Brightness and Contrast

Many times, a picture is not perfect when you take it, or it does not show well on a screen. You can adjust the brightness and contrast of a picture in PowerPoint to improve the quality and maximize its visual impact. Brightness indicates how bright or dark the entire picture is. Contrast indicates how well you can see shades and colors against each other in the picture. Typically you want the picture to be as bright and as high contrast as possible for it to be easy for the audience to see.

Adjust Brightness and Contrast

1 Click a picture.

2 Click the **Picture Tools Format** tab.

3 Click **Corrections**.

The gallery of corrections appears.

4 Click a **Brightness/Contrast** option from the gallery.

A You can also apply a **Sharpen/ Soften** effect.

B You can click **Picture Corrections Options** for more detailed options.

PowerPoint adjusts the brightness and contrast.

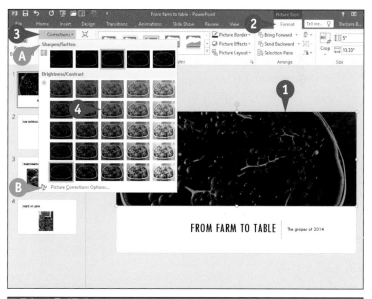

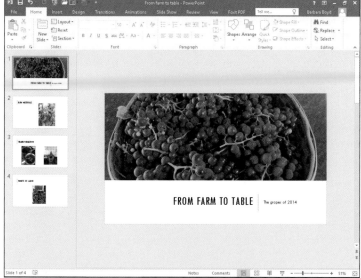

Adjust Color

You can adjust the color of your pictures to make them pleasing to the eye, or recolor them for interesting effects. For example, you may want to apply a monochrome effect in a color that matches the color scheme of your presentation, or fade the colors to give the photo a vintage or retro mood. Standard color variations are determined by the theme of the presentation, but many other variations are also available. Best of all, you can make the changes right in PowerPoint!

Adjust Color

1. Click a picture.

2. Click the **Picture Tools Format** tab.

3. Click **Color**.

   The gallery of colors appears.

4. Click your choice of **Color Saturation**, **Color Tone**, or **Recolor** options.

   This example selects a saturation option.

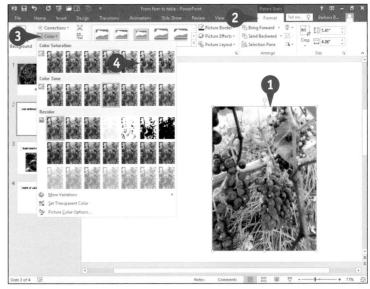

PowerPoint adjusts the color.

Note: Color Saturation determines how much color is in the picture and varies anywhere from black and white to a lot of color.

Note: Color tone affects the actual color — for example, a change in color tone may give the white items in your picture a slightly yellow hue.

Using Artistic Effects

You may want to apply an effect to a photo so it matches the look of your presentation or to give a stock photo a custom design. For example, you can make a picture look as if an artist sketched it. Several artistic effects are available in PowerPoint, so there is no need to use a separate program to give your picture a special effect. You can apply effects such as pixelation, blurring, and pencil sketch without leaving PowerPoint.

Using Artistic Effects

1 Select a picture.

2 Click the **Picture Tools Format** tab.

3 Click **Artistic Effects**.

The gallery of artistic effects appears.

4 Click an artistic effect.

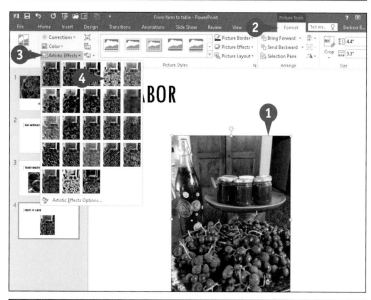

PowerPoint applies the artistic effect. This example selects Pencil Sketch.

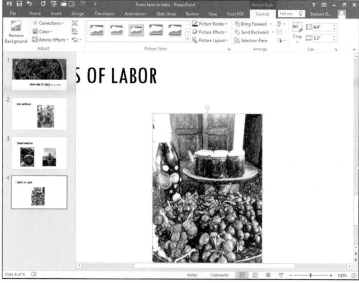

Crop a Picture

A picture often contains things that you would rather not have in the image. For example, you may have a picture of top management at a sporting event, but want to cut out the rest of the crowd in the bleachers. Cropping trims the edges from a picture in the same way as cutting them with a pair of scissors. You can crop a picture to show only the main subject. You can then resize the cropped picture to best fit the slide layout, and the objects in the picture change size accordingly and proportionately.

Crop a Picture

1 Select a picture.

2 Click the **Picture Tools Format** tab.

3 Click **Crop**.

Black crop marks (◣) appear around the picture.

4 Position the mouse pointer over a crop mark.

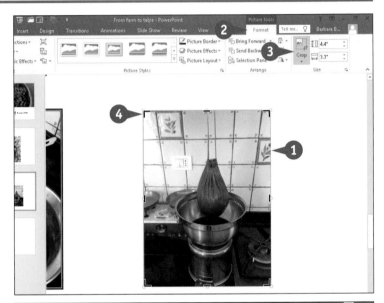

5 Click the crop mark.

6 Drag the crop mark inward to remove part of the picture.

Ⓐ Press and hold the Ctrl key while dragging the crop mark to crop equally from opposite sides of the image.

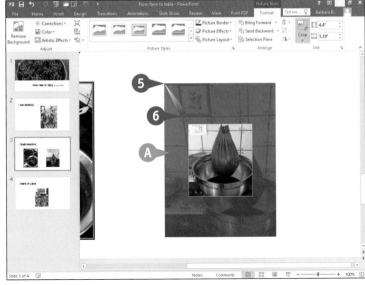

When you release the mouse button, you can see both the original picture and the cropped picture.

7 Click **Crop**.

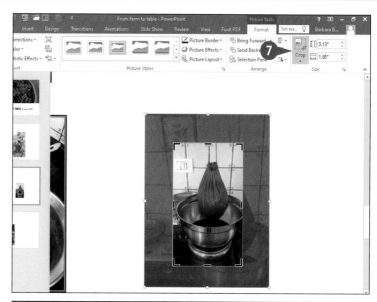

PowerPoint crops the picture.

8 Move and resize the picture if needed.

Note: See Chapter 6 to learn how to move and resize objects.

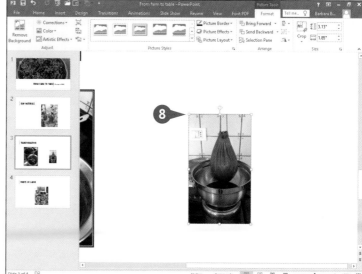

TIP

Can I crop a picture to an interesting shape?
Yes. There are two ways to crop to a shape. The first way is to click a picture and then click the **Picture Tools Format** tab. Click the **Picture Styles** down arrow (▼), and then click an option from the gallery. This method also includes a picture effect such as a picture frame. The second way is to crop to a shape without a picture effect, click the **Picture Tools Format** tab, and then click the **Crop** down arrow (▼). Click **Crop to Shape** and then click one of the myriad options from the Shapes gallery; the picture crops to that shape.

Remove the Background from a Picture

You may want to remove the background of a picture so you can work with just the main subject of the picture. Using the Remove Background feature in PowerPoint, you can remove the background from a picture easily and simply, and superimpose the remaining image onto a slide background or possibly another picture. This automated feature helps you avoid the inconvenience of importing the picture into PowerPoint after using a separate program to remove the background.

Remove the Background from a Picture

1 Select a picture.

2 Click the **Picture Tools Format** tab.

3 Click **Remove Background**.

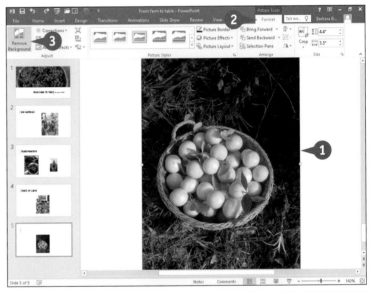

The background becomes magenta and PowerPoint automatically attempts to detect the object in the foreground. A marquee with handles appears.

4 Click and drag a handle to resize the marquee.

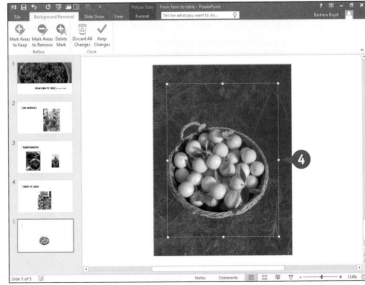

126

5 Repeat Step 4 with the various handles until PowerPoint detects the foreground object that you want.

Note: Very small adjustments to the marquee help PowerPoint determine the object that you want in the foreground.

6 Click **Keep Changes**.

A To revert without saving changes, you can click **Discard All Changes**.

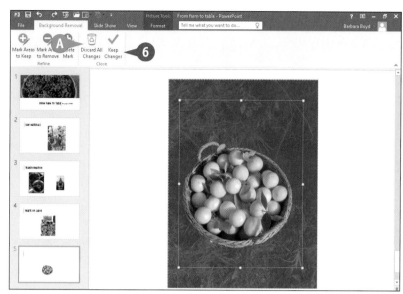

PowerPoint removes the background and only the foreground subject remains.

TIP

How can I include or exclude an image detail?
You can fine-tune the detected object. To add an area for inclusion:

1 Click **Mark Areas to Keep** in the Refine group.

2 Click and drag across the magenta area that includes your detail.

A PowerPoint includes the detail and marks it with a plus sign.

B To erase the mark so that the detail is excluded, click **Delete Mark** and then click the mark.

Insert a Screenshot

You may create a document on your computer that you want to incorporate as an image in your slide show. For example, you may want to show how your software works to a potential client or a map that shows your store locations. You can take a screenshot of an open window or a section of the computer display and insert it onto a slide without leaving PowerPoint. The Screenshot feature is a fast and convenient way to take a snapshot of something on your computer and put it into a presentation.

Insert a Screenshot

Choose an Open Window

1. Select a slide in Normal view.

2. Click the **Insert** tab.

3. Click **Screenshot**.

   The Available Windows gallery appears. Windows that are open, but not minimized, appear in this gallery.

4. Click a window in the gallery.

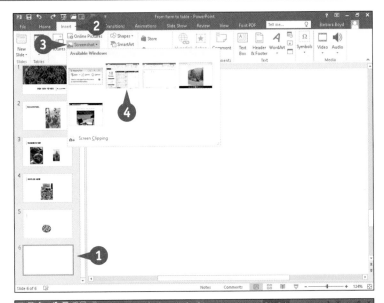

PowerPoint inserts the window screenshot onto the slide.

Note: Only windows that are not minimized appear in the Available Windows gallery. If you want to take a screenshot of a window, it must be restored or maximized.

Choose a Section of the Screen

① Repeat Steps **1** to **3** in the previous subsection.

The Available Windows gallery appears.

② Click **Screen Clipping** (not shown).

The PowerPoint window disappears, showing whatever is under it. The mouse pointer changes to the crosshairs pointer.

③ Click and drag across the section of screen that you want in your screenshot.

The PowerPoint window reappears and the screenshot appears on the slide. You can size and position the screenshot as needed.

Note: To capture a screen on a Windows tablet, press and hold 🪟 and then press the volume down button. Screenshots are saved in the Screenshots folder inside the Pictures folder. Crop and edit the image as explained previously.

Note: To learn how to position and resize objects, see Chapter 6.

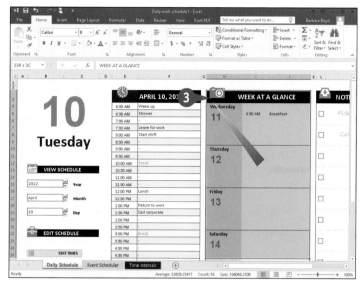

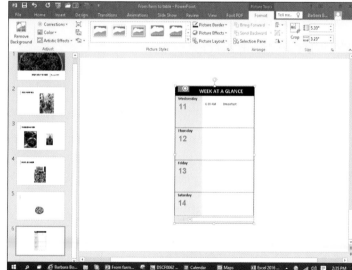

TIPS

When I use the Screen Clipping option, how do I get the correct screen?

When you minimize the PowerPoint window, you see what is directly under it. Minimize all active windows on your computer and then use the Windows taskbar to restore the window of interest — if you want your Desktop, restore nothing. Now restore PowerPoint and perform the Screen Clipping process.

How do I take a screenshot of two or more windows?

Minimize all windows. Restore and arrange the windows you want in the screenshot. Restore the PowerPoint window and click the **Insert** tab. Click **Screenshot**, and then click **Screen Clipping**. Click and drag across the windows with the crosshairs pointer.

Create a Photo Album

You can set up slides so that they advance automatically, and you can also play an audio clip across slides and have it loop indefinitely. This is a perfect scenario to show a photo album. You can then create a professional-quality photo album and show it like any other slide show or set it up to flip through the pictures automatically, complete with background music! The procedure described here creates a new presentation.

Create a Photo Album

1 Open a new or existing PowerPoint file.

2 Click **Insert**.

3 Click the **Photo Album** down arrow (▼).

4 Click **New Photo Album**.

The Photo Album dialog box appears.

5 Click **File/Disk**.

The Insert New Pictures dialog box appears.

6 Click the folder that holds your picture files.

7 Click pictures that you want in your photo album while pressing Ctrl to select multiple files. All selected pictures appear in the photo album.

8 Click **Insert**.

The Insert New Pictures dialog box closes.

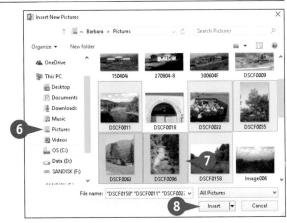

The Photo Album dialog box reappears.

9 Click a picture to view it.

10 Click the **Picture layout** drop-down arrow (∨) and select a layout.

A You can see a preview of the layout when you click it.

B You can use these picture correction features if you select only one picture.

C You can click to select one or more pictures to move or remove them.

D This option is available only when the layout has multiple pictures.

11 Click **Create**.

PowerPoint creates the photo album.

Note: You can design a photo album like any other presentation.

Note: Click **Edit Photo Album** from the Photo Album drop-down menu on the Insert tab to change the pictures in the slide show.

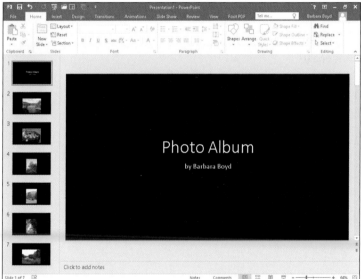

TIP

What is the New Text Box button in the Photo Album dialog box?
You may want to include an explanation or comments about your photographs on a slide. You can click the **New Text Box** button and PowerPoint inserts a text box in the Pictures in Album list. You can move the text box or a photograph within the list by clicking it and then clicking the **Move Up** (↑) or **Move Down** (↓) buttons. After you create the photo album, you can click the text box on the slide and type your text. You can insert multiple text boxes into your photo album or even into a slide.

Insert Video and Audio Clips

You can enhance your slide show by inserting video or audio on a slide. An instructional video can explain a complex task, whereas a funny video can liven up your presentation. PowerPoint recognizes videos in a variety of formats, such as Windows Media Video (WMV) files and Motion Pictures Experts Group (MPEG) files. Use an audio clip to play interesting sounds, such as applause, during a slide, or play an audio clip as background audio during several slides or an entire slide show.

Both audio and video clips use the steps in this section — except when you insert audio, a megaphone icon appears on the slide rather than a video.

Insert Video and Audio Clips

1 Select a slide in Normal view.

2 Click the **Insert** tab.

3 Click **Video** or **Audio**.

4 Click an option in the drop-down menu.

This example chooses **Video on My PC**.

Ⓐ If you use a layout with a content placeholder, click the **Insert Video** icon (⬚) and then click the **Browse** button next to From a File.

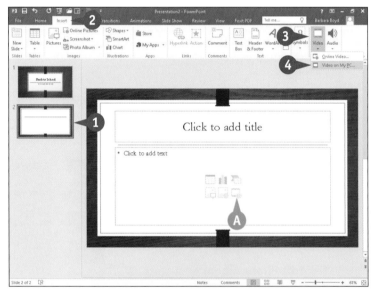

The Insert Video or Insert Audio dialog box appears.

5 Select the folder or external drive containing the file.

6 Click the file.

7 Click **Insert**.

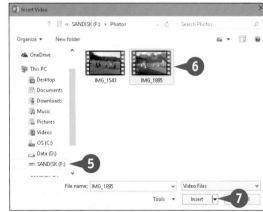

The video or audio appears on your slide.

Note: You can size and position a video as needed. To learn how to position and resize objects, see Chapter 6.

Ⓑ The Control bar appears when you position the mouse pointer over the clip.

8 Click **Play** (▶ changes to ❚❚).

Ⓒ You can click anywhere on the scrubber bar to jump to any part of the clip.

Ⓓ You can click the **Move Forward** (❙▶) and **Move Back** (◀❙) buttons to jump forward or backward 0.25 seconds.

Ⓔ You can click the **Volume** button (◀») to adjust the sound.

9 Click **Pause** (❚❚ changes to ▶).

The video or audio stops playing.

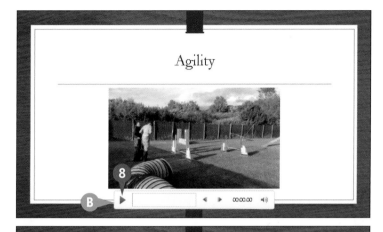

TIP

Can I play the video in full screen during the slide show?
Yes. To make the video play full screen, click the video, click the **Video Tools Playback** tab, and then click the **Play Full Screen** check box (☐ changes to ☑) in the **Video Options** group.

Record an Audio Clip

You can draw your audience into your slide show by playing audio — such as interesting sound effects, background music, and voiceovers — at just the right time during the show. For example, you may want applause when a slide with sales figures appears. You may also want to display your presentation when you cannot be present to speak in person. For example, you may have a looping presentation on display at a kiosk or on your website. PowerPoint lets you record audio clips that link directly to slides. You can record an audio clip in PowerPoint and insert it directly into a slide without using different software to record it first.

Record an Audio Clip

1 Select a slide in Normal view.

2 Click the **Insert** tab.

3 Click **Audio**.

4 Click **Record Audio**.

Note: You need a microphone built in or attached to your computer to perform this task.

The Record Sound dialog box appears.

A Click **Cancel** to abort the recording and discontinue insertion of the audio.

5 Click in the **Name** text box.

6 Type a name for your recording.

7 Click the **Record** button (●).

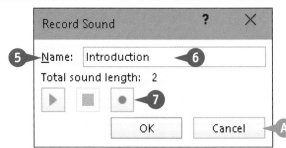

⑧ Record your audio into the microphone.

⑨ When you are finished, click the **Stop** button (■).

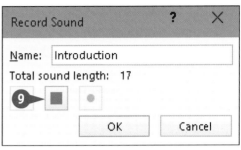

⑩ Click the **Play** button (▶) to listen to your recording.

Ⓑ You can click the **Record** button (●) to continue recording additional audio.

⑪ Click **OK** when you complete your recording.

⑫ Click the **Audio Tools Playback** tab.

⑬ Click **Play** on the Ribbon or on the playback controls on the slide.

The audio plays.

Ⓒ You can click **Volume** to adjust the sound.

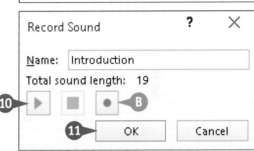

TIPS

What is the Play in Background button?
The **Play in Background** button enables the audio clip to start automatically when the slide appears. The audio does not stop — it plays across multiple slides, looping until you stop it or the show ends. These settings appear as check boxes on the **Audio Tools Playback** tab.

Can I have sound play for a few minutes before I begin and then fade it out?
Yes. Click your audio and then click the **Audio Tools Playback** tab. Click the arrows on the spinner next to **Fade In** and **Fade Out** to set the duration of the fade.

Trim Audio Clips

You may have an interesting part of a song to play for your audience, or a clip from an interview to share with them, but you do not want to play an entire audio clip. You might have an audio clip that you recorded and inserted directly onto a PowerPoint slide, but it needs to be shorter. In any of these cases, you can trim the audio clip directly in PowerPoint to make it the perfect length for your purpose. This handy feature saves you the inconvenience of trimming the audio clip in a different program and then importing it into PowerPoint.

Trim Audio Clips

1 Click an audio clip.

2 Click the **Audio Tools Playback** tab.

3 Click **Trim Audio**.

The Trim Audio dialog box appears.

4 Click the slider where you want to listen to the audio.

Note: Do not click the slider if you want to start listening from the beginning.

5 Click the **Play** button (▶ changes to ❚❚).

6 Listen and find where you want to trim the beginning and end of your audio.

7 Click the **Pause** button (❙❙ changes to ▶) to stop the audio.

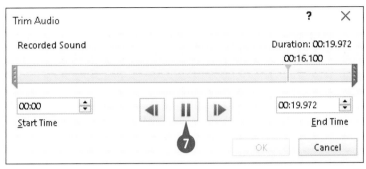

8 Click and drag the green marker where you want to trim the beginning of the audio.

9 Click and drag the red marker where you want to trim the end of the audio.

10 Click **OK**.

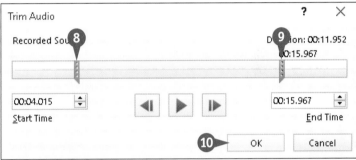

The dialog box closes and PowerPoint trims the audio to the length that you specified.

11 Click **Play** (▶ changes to ❙❙) to listen to the trimmed audio.

Note: Trimming an audio clip is reversible. Repeat this process to reverse it.

FROM FARM TO TABLE   The grapes of 2014

TIPS

What happens when I set the Start setting to Automatically?
You can start both audio and video clips in two ways. You can start them when you click them, or they can start automatically when the slide appears when you set Start to Automatically.

How does the Play across Slides option work?
When you enable (☑) **Play across Slides**, an audio clip plays until it ends, even if you advance to other slides. If you do not want the audio to end, enable (☑) **Loop until Stopped**.

Trim Video Clips

Videos are usually not the length you want for your presentation, and so you will probably want to trim them. You may want to play only a snippet of a video during a presentation to show a little information about something, or you may have a leader or trailer in the video that you do not need your audience to see. PowerPoint gives you the convenience to trim the video right on the slide so you do not have to leave PowerPoint and use other software to do it.

Trim Video Clips

1 Click a video clip.

2 Click the **Video Tools Playback** tab.

3 Click **Trim Video**.

The Trim Video dialog box appears.

4 Click and drag the green marker where you want the video to begin.

The video frame that plays at that time appears in the window.

5 Click and drag the red marker where you want the video to end.

The video frame that plays at that time appears in the window.

6 Click **OK**.

The dialog box closes and PowerPoint trims the video to your specifications.

7 Click the **Video Tools Playback** tab.

8 Click **Play** (▶ changes to ⏸) to view the trimmed video.

TIPS

What is the Fade Duration?

The Fade Duration fades the beginning or end of the video. The length of time the fade effect lasts is determined by the time you set in the Fade In and Fade Out text boxes. The effect gives your video a soft feel.

What is the Hide While Not Playing feature?

The Hide While Not Playing feature hides the video if it is not playing. You need to start the video automatically, because you cannot manually start the video when it is hidden. This feature is convenient because the video clip hides after it finishes playing so that you can show the rest of the slide.

Insert Video from the Internet

The Internet has an unlimited amount of clip art and pictures, which you learn how to access earlier in this chapter. The Internet is also a great source of video clips. Some media is royalty-free and some is licensed under Creative Commons. Make sure you have permission to use the media you want to use in the way you want to use it and give credit where credit is due.

Although searching the Internet for video can be cumbersome, PowerPoint has a search feature that saves you time and effort. You can insert the perfect video directly into your presentation using keywords.

Insert Video from the Internet

1 Select a slide in Normal view.

2 Click the **Insert** tab.

3 Click **Video**.

The Insert Video dialog box appears.

4 Click **Online Video**.

A If you are using a layout with a placeholder, click the **Insert Video** icon (▢).

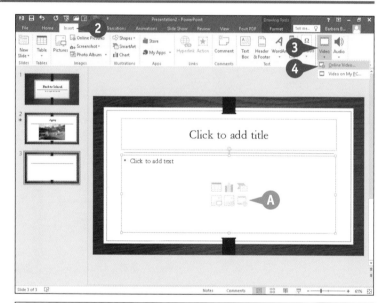

5 Click in the YouTube Search text box and type a keyword.

6 Click the **Search** icon (🔎).

B If you have a specific YouTube video you want to use, copy the embed code from it on the YouTube website and paste it in the field on the Insert Video dialog box.

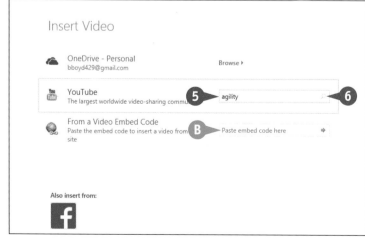

The YouTube results appear.

C Note the video description.

7 Click **Insert**.

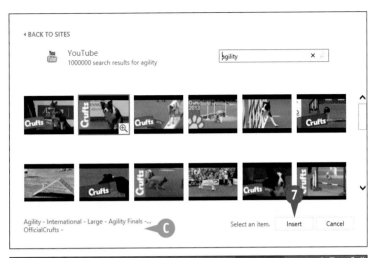

The video you selected appears on the slide.

D Resize and move the video as you would an object.

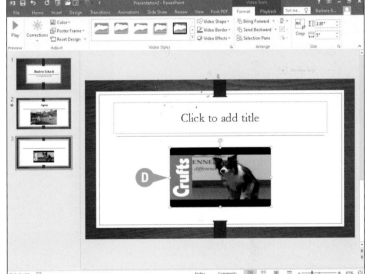

TIPS

What is the SkyDrive search option in the Insert Pictures and Video dialog box?

Microsoft has a convenient, free service called OneDrive where you can store and share files in your own space. For example, you can load pictures to OneDrive and give your friends access to it so they can download your pictures to their computer. PowerPoint accesses your OneDrive directly to search and download pictures into your presentation.

Can I also download sound clips from the Internet?

Yes, but you have to find them with your search engine and download them to your PC; then click the **Insert** tab, click **Audio**, and choose **Audio on My PC**.

Insert a Hyperlink

Hyperlinks change your PowerPoint presentation from a traditional slide show to an interactive extravaganza. A hyperlink can perform a variety of actions during a PowerPoint slide show. It gives you an easy way to go to a different, non-sequential slide in your slide show. It can open another PowerPoint presentation or open a document from another Office application. A hyperlink also provides a way to open and create an email message — helpful for presentations that people watch on your website — and gives you the convenience of opening a web page from your slide show. Using hyperlinks enables you to run a smooth presentation and impress your audience.

Insert a Hyperlink

Go to a Slide in the Current Presentation

1 Click inside a placeholder where you want to insert the hyperlink.

Note: To use an object as the button to the hyperlink, select it in the slide before clicking Insert.

2 Click the **Insert** tab.

3 Click **Hyperlink**.

The Insert Hyperlink dialog box appears.

4 Click in the **Text to display** text box.

Note: If you select an object as the hyperlink button, this box reads <Selection in Document> and you cannot edit it.

5 Type a name for your hyperlink.

6 Click **Place in This Document**.

7 Click the slide you want to link to.

8 Click **OK**.

PowerPoint inserts the link to the slide.

Note: You can have more than one hyperlink on the same slide. Repeat the steps to add others.

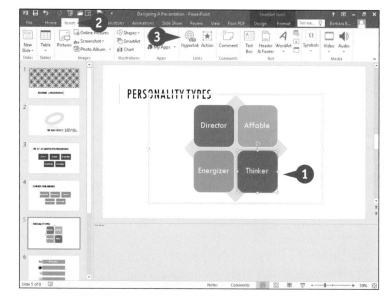

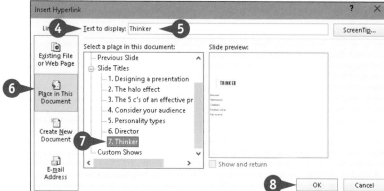

Open a File

1 Repeat Steps 1 to 4 in the subsection "Go to a Slide in the Current Presentation."

2 Click **Existing File or Web Page**.

3 Click **Current Folder**.

4 Click the **Look in** drop-down arrow (⌄).

5 Navigate to and click the folder that contains the file you want to open.

6 Click the file to open.

7 Click **OK**.

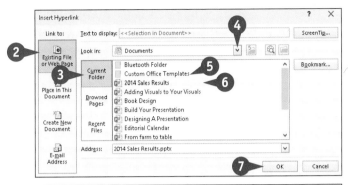

Open a Web Page

1 Repeat Steps 1 to 4 in the subsection "Go to a Slide in the Current Presentation."

2 Click **Existing File or Web Page**.

3 Click **Browsed Pages**.

4 Scroll through the list of web pages you have visited and click the one you want to link to.

A Click the **Browse the Web** button (🔍) to open the page you want to link to, then return to PowerPoint; you find the page in the Browsed Pages list.

5 Click **OK**.

B PowerPoint places the link on your slide.

During the slide show, click the text to follow the link.

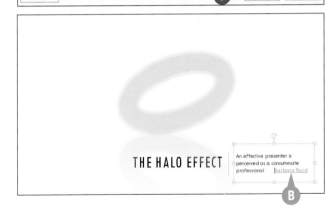

TIPS

How do I remove a link to a file but leave the link text?

Right-click the hyperlink and click **Edit Link** on the shortcut menu. When the Edit Hyperlink dialog box opens, click **Remove Link**. The link text remains, but PowerPoint removes the link.

Can I give the hyperlink a longer description?

Yes. You can do this by creating a ScreenTip. Right-click the hyperlink, and click **Edit Link** on the menu. In the Edit Hyperlink dialog box, click the **ScreenTip** button. In the ScreenTip dialog box, type the description and click **OK**. If your ScreenTip feature is enabled, the ScreenTip appears in a little box when you position the mouse pointer over the link during the slide show.

CHAPTER 8

Enhancing Slides with Action

Animations and transitions create action in your slide show presentations. Animations give movement to text and objects so a slide show does more than display static bullet points or still images. Transitions add an interesting effect when the slide show advances from one slide to another.

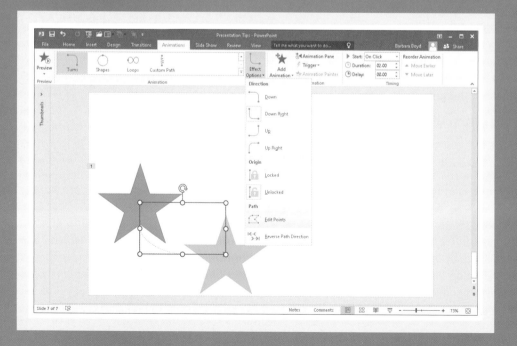

Understanding Animations and Action Buttons

You can engage your audience with animations, which emphasize text and objects on a slide so that they appear at different times and with special motions. A classic example is animating bullet points to move onto the screen one at a time. Action buttons trigger various functions during a slide show, such as moving to a particular slide or opening a different application or file. You should use animations sparingly because too many can distract your audience from your content.

What Is Animation?

In PowerPoint, *animation* refers to object motion on slides. You can apply one or more animation types to one object: An entrance animation brings an object onto the slide; an exit animation takes an object off the slide; and an emphasis animation does something to an object while it is on the slide, such as rotate or spin it. For example, you can have a ball bounce onto the slide and then have it spin. And, you can find predesigned animations online.

How Animations Work

Let your imagination come alive with animation! Using the Animation pane, you can apply animations to objects one at a time and one after another. You can run them automatically when the slide advances, trigger them through the previous animation, or trigger them manually by clicking the slide. You can also run the animation for a particular object by clicking it. You can set an animation to run after a delay, which you can configure and adjust. You can also arrange the sequence order of animations.

How Action Buttons Work

Action buttons and their sibling hyperlinks (see Chapter 7) turn static presentations into dynamic ones. For example, for a client presentation, you can jump to the slide related to a question instead of wading through your entire show. You can draw an action button on a slide and set the action that occurs when you click the button. For example, clicking the action button might open an external document such as a proposal, take you to a different slide, or update the data on a chart. You can assign various standard actions to an action button or trigger macros with them.

Preview Animations and Action Buttons

To create a professional presentation, choose appropriate effects and always make sure they run properly. Both the Animation pane and the Animations tab on the Ribbon offer a Play button to easily review the animation. Previewing the behavior of an action button or hyperlink is not as easy; you must run the slide show and click the button to verify its behavior. Animations and action buttons add complexity to your slide show, so use them sparingly and thoroughly review them before showing your slide show to an audience.

Explore the Animation Pane

Designing and running animations can be a complicated business, and it is nice to have a central place from which to do it. PowerPoint provides you with a handy tool called the Animation pane to help you manage animations. The Animation pane enables you to reorder the animations, see what objects they move, view and set the duration of the animations, and set the trigger for each animation. You can also perform these tasks on the Animations tab of the Ribbon. Click the Animation Pane button on the Animations tab to show the Animation pane.

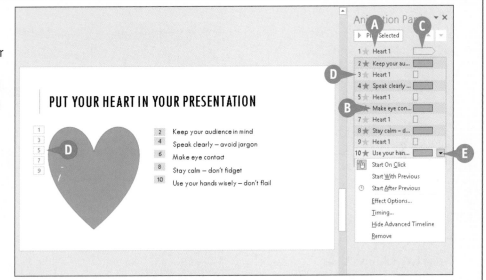

Ⓐ Animation List

PowerPoint lists each animation in the order that it runs; each animation is attached to an object, which is also listed. Green items are entrance animations, yellow items are emphasis animations, and red items are exit animations.

Ⓑ Animation Description

Position the mouse pointer over the animation to view its trigger and name.

Ⓒ Duration Bars

These bars show the timing and duration of each animation. Position the mouse pointer over the bar to view the duration time.

Ⓓ Sequence Numbers

These numbers correlate with the sequence numbers attached to the objects and appear both in the Animation pane and on the actual slide. Click either number to select the animation.

Ⓔ Animation Settings

Click the down arrow (▼) on any animation to change its settings.

Apply an Animation

Add some excitement and creativity to your presentation by designing it with some animation! You can have your bullet points fly onto the slide point by point to keep your audience focused on one point at a time. You may decide to have SmartArt appear one piece at a time, or have a picture zoom into the slide and then do a turn! You can use the Animations tab on the Ribbon to apply an animation to any slide object.

Apply an Animation

Apply to Clip Art or a Picture

1 Select an object to animate.

You can apply the same animation to multiple objects by selecting them all at the same time.

Note: See Chapter 6 to learn how to select objects.

2 Click the **Animations** tab.

3 Click the down arrow ($\overline{\overline{\vee}}$) in the Animation group.

The gallery of animations appears.

4 Click an animation.

Note: When applying an entrance animation, place your object where you want it to end.

A PowerPoint applies the animation to the object and assigns it a sequence number.

B PowerPoint places an animation icon (★) next to the slide thumbnail.

Note: You can apply multiple animations to one object.

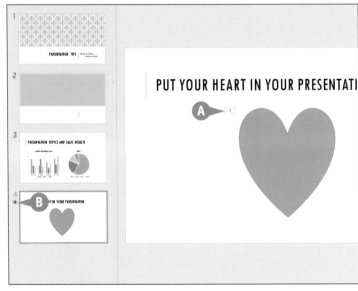

Apply to Bullets

1 Select a placeholder with bullet points, or click the border to select the entire placeholder.

2 Click the **Animations** tab.

3 Click the down arrow (⩔) in the **Animation** group.

4 Click a transition.

C You can click these menu items to see more animations.

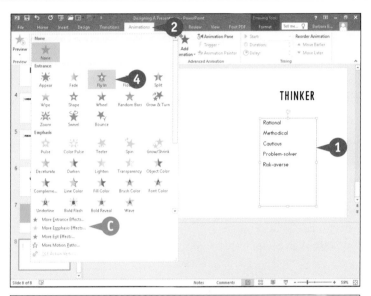

D PowerPoint applies a sequence number to each bullet on the placeholder.

During the slide show, one bullet point will fly onto the slide every time you click the mouse button.

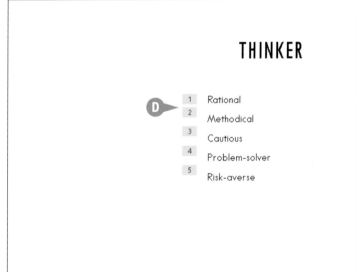

TIPS

Does PowerPoint offer animation templates?
Yes, you find them online. Click the **File** tab and then click **New**. Type **animation** in the Search field to see results. You can download animated books, 3-D cubes, tipping scales, and more, and then simply type or paste your text or images. See Chapter 3 for online template specifics.

How do I use the different types of animations?
Combine an entrance or exit animation with one or more emphasis animations. For example, to compare a new car to an old car, use an entrance animation to "drive" each car on to the slide, then you use emphasis animations to make the new car glow and the old car teeter. An exit animation can make the old car fade off the slide.

Preview an Animation

You can see each and every animation in your presentation simply by running the slide show, but if you are working on the animation for a slide, previewing animations in Slide Show view is not very convenient. To be efficient and effective, you need a way to look at the animation while on the slide you are designing. You can see the animation on individual slides in Normal or Slide Sorter view. Previewing the animation of a slide enables you to verify that the animation works as expected and is appropriate for the slide's content.

Preview an Animation

1 Select a slide with animation in Normal view.

Note: You can also preview animations in Slide Sorter view.

2 Click the **Animations** tab.

All the animation sequence numbers appear.

3 Click **Preview**.

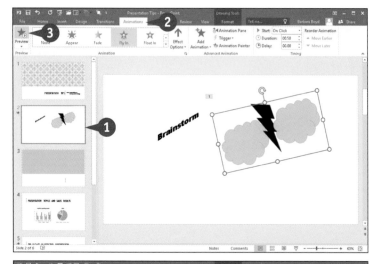

PowerPoint runs all animations on the slide.

Ⓐ In this example, the word brainstorm flies in from the bottom left and ends at the top right.

Note: You can also preview animations by running the entire slide show. See Chapter 13 to learn how to run a slide show.

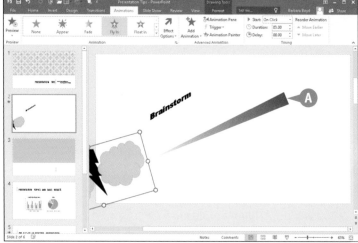

Add an Animation

You can apply different animations to different objects on a slide, and you can also apply multiple animations to one object. This enables you to make an object perform a variety of movements, creating a complex special effect. For example, you can have a ball bounce onto the slide, grow larger, do a spin, and then glow or pulse. Simple is usually best, so try not to create too much complexity. The animation should always relate to your words at that point in the presentation.

Add an Animation

1 Select an object that already has an animation.

2 Click the **Animations** tab.

3 Click **Add Animation**.

The gallery of animations appears.

Ⓐ Use the scroll bar to see more animations.

4 Click an animation.

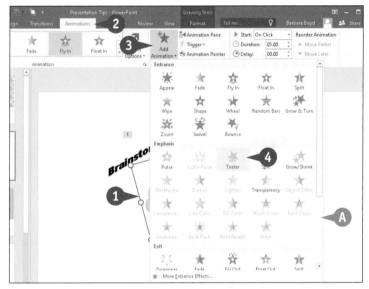

Ⓑ An additional sequence number appears.

In this example, the object has two animations that will run sequentially. The Teeter animation will run second because its sequence number is 2.

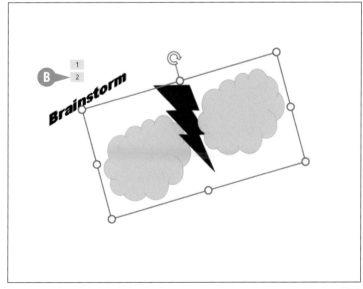

Change Animation Effects

PowerPoint gives you the flexibility to choose the motion of an animation. For example, the Fly In animation can bring the object onto the screen from any direction. For complex objects made from multiple parts, such as SmartArt, the animation can appear on the screen as one piece, in pieces simultaneously, or in pieces at separate times. You can move a shape and its text separately. You have complete control over the animations, which can emphasize even simple objects.

Change Animation Effects

1 Select a slide with animation in Normal view.

2 Click the sequence number of the animation you want to change.

3 Click the **Animations** tab.

4 Click **Effect Options**.

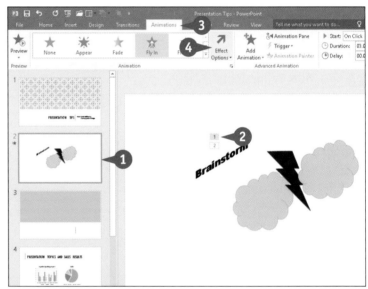

The gallery of effects appears.

5 Click an effect from the gallery.

Note: For objects with multiple pieces, there are two additional options: All at Once and By Paragraph. Click **All at Once** to have multiple pieces move independently but at the same time. Click **By Paragraph** to have multiple pieces appear separately.

PowerPoint changes the effects for the animation.

Ⓐ To change the actual animation, select a different animation from the Animation gallery.

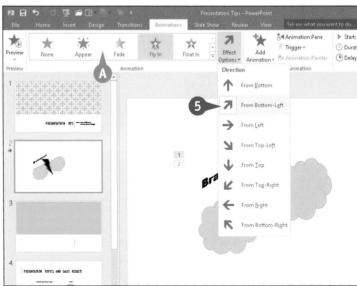

Change the Animation Trigger

Something must trigger an animation to run, and you can determine what that trigger is. The trigger can be the appearance of the slide on the screen, it can be you clicking anywhere on the slide, or it can be you clicking a particular object on the slide. You can also trigger the animation to run with or after another animation. The default trigger is clicking the slide, but you can change it to any of the other triggers. Clicking the slide or an object on the slide gives you complete control over when the animation runs.

Change the Animation Trigger

Create a Standard Trigger

1. Click the **Animations** tab.

2. Click an animation.

3. Click the **Start** down arrow (▼).

4. Click a start option.

   This example chooses With Previous, which runs the animation simultaneously with the previous animation.

Note: If the other object has more than one animation, the previous animation refers to the last of the multiple animations.

Ⓐ On Click runs the animation when you click the slide.

Ⓑ After Previous means that the animation will automatically run after the previous animation ends.

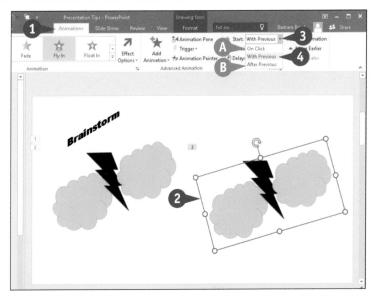

Create a Trigger with Click of Object

Ⓒ The sequence number becomes a lightning bolt, which indicates it has a trigger.

1. Click **Trigger**.

2. Click **On Click of**.

3. Click an object name.

   The animation will now run when you click that object during your slide show.

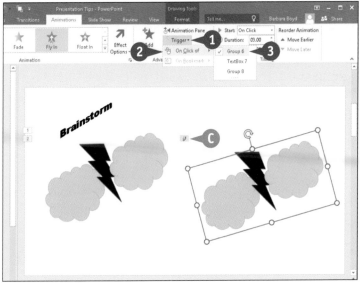

Modify Animation Timing

Timing is everything, even with animation. You can modify the duration of your animation — *duration* is the amount of time the animation runs from beginning to end. You can also change the delay time between the animation's trigger and its start. For example, if you set an animation's trigger to Previous Animation and the Delay to one second, the animation will start one second after the previous animation ends. This flexibility enables you to be very exact while creating an effect that will have maximum impact on your audience.

Modify Animation Timing

1 Click the **Animations** tab.

2 Click **Animation Pane** to open the Animation pane if it is not open.

3 Click an animation.

The trigger of the selected animation is After Previous.

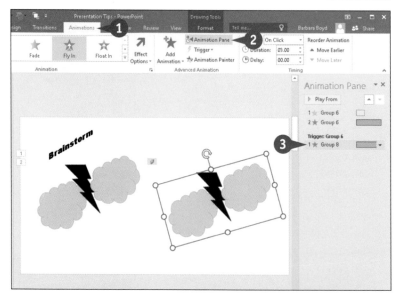

4 Click the **Duration** spinner (⬍) or type a number into the text box to adjust the length of time that the animation runs.

5 Click the **Delay** spinner (⬍) or type a number into the text box to adjust the delay between the trigger and when the animation starts.

6 Click **Preview**.

This example sets the duration to 4.00 and the delay to 1.00. The third animation will now start after a 1-second delay and last for 4 seconds.

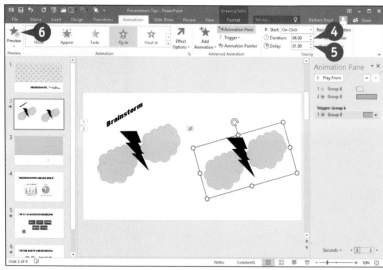

Reorder Animations

After applying multiple animations on a slide, you can change the order in which the animations play on the slide during your presentation. You can arrange the order of the animations in many ways. You can even run an animation of one object, then an animation of another object, and then more animations of the first object. Each bullet on a placeholder can be animated, and you can treat bullets as a group or individually when reordering animations.

Reorder Animations

1 Select a slide that contains multiple animations.

2 Click the **Animations** tab.

3 Click **Animation Pane** if it is not open.

4 Click an animation.

5 Click an order option for the animation.

This example selects Move Later.

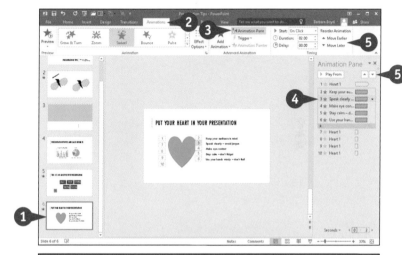

Ⓐ The animation changes position in the list.

This example arranges the animations in the list so the heart pulses before each bullet.

Ⓑ You can click **Preview** to view the animation.

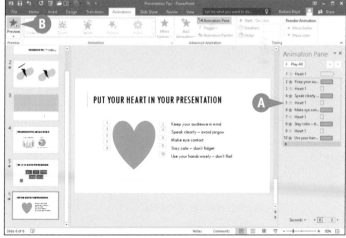

Add a Motion Path

The shape and length of an object's trajectory as it bounces or flies onto the slide are determined by the animation you choose. PowerPoint enables you to design your own trajectory when you use a motion path, which is another kind of animation. With a motion path, you determine the object's location on the slide, the starting point of the animated movement, and the ending point of the movement. The object's location on the slide and the starting location of the motion path do not need to be the same.

Add a Motion Path

1 Click an object.

2 Click the **Animations** tab.

3 Click the **Animation** down arrow (⏷).

4 Click and drag the scroll bar to the bottom to see the motion paths.

A Click **More Motion Paths** to see an additional 63 motion paths.

B Click **Custom Path** to design a freestyle trajectory.

5 Click a motion path.

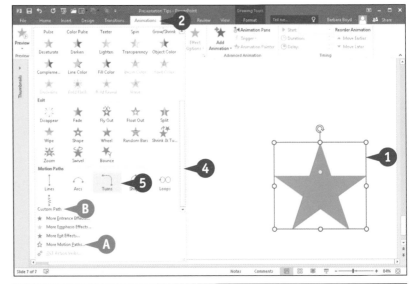

The motion path appears.

The green and red markers indicate the beginning and end of the motion.

6 Click the motion path if it is not selected.

7 Click **Effect Options**.

8 Click one of the directions to change the trajectory of the motion.

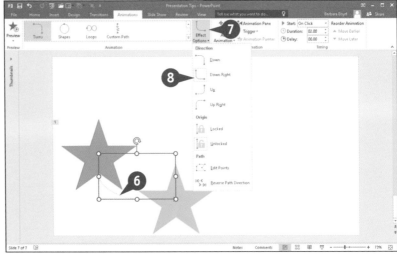

9 Click **Edit Points**.

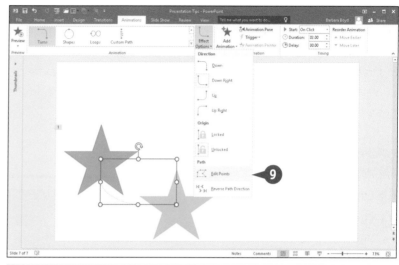

The motion path enters edit mode.

10 Click and drag anywhere on the line to change the shape of the motion path.

11 Click and drag the handle on the blue line to distort the motion path.

C You can click **Preview** to see the movement of the motion path.

Note: To see more motion effects settings such as adding a smooth start or end, open the Animation pane and click the down arrow (▼) next to the animation you are working on, and then click **Effect Options**.

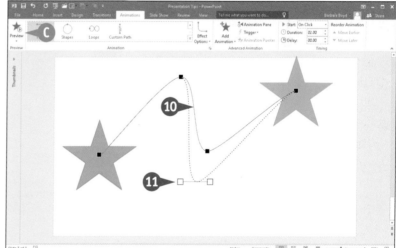

TIP

Is there a way to change the size of the motion path without changing the shape of the line?
Yes. Click and drag a handle on the border to change the size of the motion path without changing its shape.

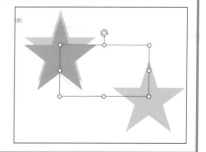

Remove an Animation

As you experiment with various animations, it is useful to know how to add them, as well as how to remove them. If your enthusiasm for animations gets the better of you, PowerPoint makes it quick and easy for you to remove some of them. The most convenient way to remove an animation is in the Animation pane.

Remove an Animation

1. Click the **Animations** tab.

2. Click **Animation Pane** if it is not open.

3. Click an animation.

4. Click the down arrow (▼) next to the animation.

5. Click **Remove**.

Note: You can also click an animation and then press Delete.

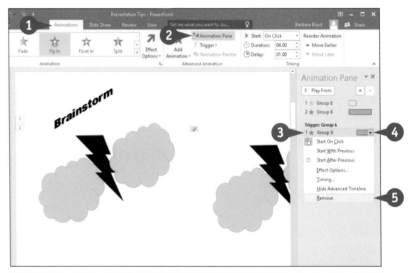

Ⓐ PowerPoint removes the animation from the object.

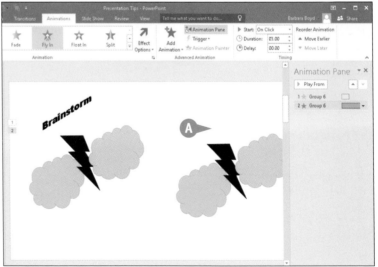

Apply a Transition

Moving from one slide to the next is called a *transition*, and it offers yet another opportunity to add variety to your presentation. With transitions, you can vary the way a slide appears, such as fading from one slide to the next. You can apply a transition in Normal or Slide Sorter view to a single slide, multiple slides, or all slides. You may want to use the same transition throughout your presentation, or mix it up and use various transitions on different slides — as with animation, however, try not to overwhelm your audience with too many transitions.

Apply a Transition

1 In Normal view, select the slides to which you want to apply a transition.

2 Click the **Transitions** tab.

3 Click the **Transitions** down arrow (⩯).

The gallery of transitions appears.

4 Click a transition.

A Apply the **Random** transition to randomly apply a different transition to each slide in your presentation.

PowerPoint applies the transition to the selected slides.

B The transition icon (★) appears beside the slide's thumbnail.

C You can click **Effect Options** to change the direction of the transition movement.

D You can click **Apply To All** to apply the transition to all slides.

E You can click **Preview** to see the transition.

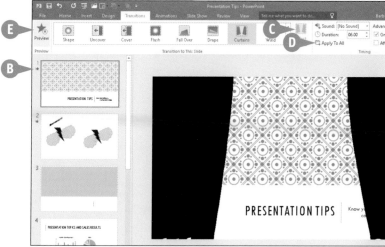

Remove a Transition

Sometimes while designing a presentation, you may apply a transition and then decide that it just does not work. As you experiment with various transitions, you need to know how to apply them as well as how to remove them. Using too many transitions in a presentation can be distracting for your audience, so if you decide your presentation is too complex, you may want to remove some of the transitions. PowerPoint enables you to quickly remove a single transition or all of them from your presentation.

Remove a Transition

1 Select a slide with a transition in Normal or Slide Sorter view.

2 Click the **Transitions** tab.

3 Click the **Transitions** down arrow ().

The gallery of transitions appears.

4 Click **None**.

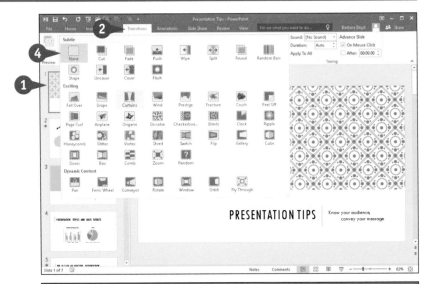

PowerPoint removes the transition and the transition icon disappears from the slide.

Ⓐ You can click **Apply To All** to remove transitions from all slides in the presentation.

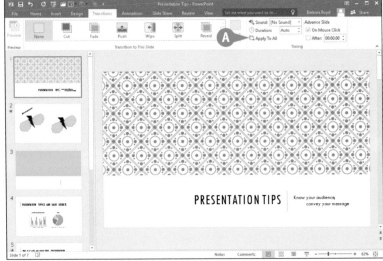

Advance a Slide after a Set Time Interval

When you run a slide show, you can use one of two methods to advance from slide to slide. You can advance slides manually by clicking the slide, or you can set a timer that automatically advances to the next slide after a set amount of time. For example, if you are showing a presentation with pictures of a house, you may want to advance the slides automatically every ten seconds while you talk about the house. You can change these settings in Normal view, but Slide Sorter view is preferable.

Advance a Slide after a Set Time Interval

1 Select a slide with a transition in Slide Sorter view.

2 Click the **Transitions** tab.

3 Click the **After** check box (☐ changes to ☑); this makes the slide automatically advance.

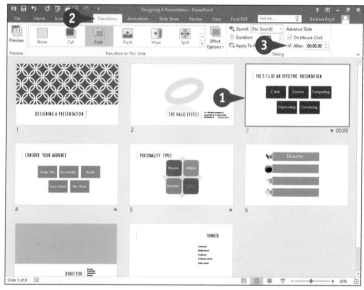

4 Click and hold the spinner (⬍) to set a time interval.

Ⓐ The time interval appears under the slide.

Ⓑ If you leave the **On Mouse Click** check box selected (☑), you can also advance the slide by clicking your mouse.

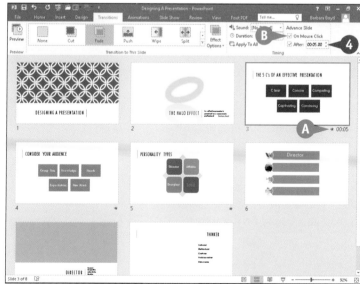

Add a Transition Sound

You can apply a sound to one or more slides in a presentation to accent important transitions. PowerPoint offers 19 sounds or you can use your own. When used appropriately, transition sounds draw the audience's attention to important information that appears on the subsequent slide. You can apply a sound without using a visual transition.

Transition sounds are different from inserting an audio file that plays when a specific slide is shown or in the background during your presentation, which is explained in Chapter 7.

Add a Transition Sound

1 Select a slide to which you want to add a transition sound in Normal or Slide Sorter view.

2 Click the **Transitions** tab.

3 Click the **Sound** down arrow (▼).

4 Click a sound.

Ⓐ Click **Other Sound** to open the Add Audio dialog box and choose an audio file stored on your computer.

Ⓑ Click **Loop Until Next Sound** to play the sound continuously until another sound is played.

PowerPoint applies the sound to the transition.

5 Click **Preview** to hear the sound.

Note: Preview is available only if you apply a visual transition to the slide, not just a sound. To hear a transition sound without a visual transition, you must play the slide show.

Note: Repeat Steps **1** to **3** and then select **[No Sound]** from the menu to remove a sound from a transition.

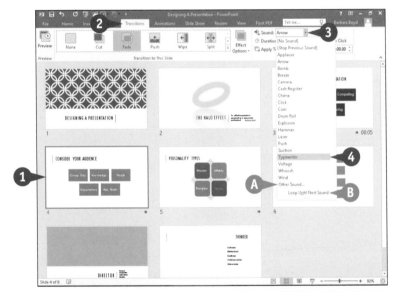

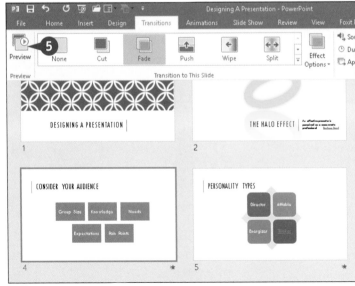

Set a Transition Speed

You can further customize a visual transition or a transition sound by changing the transition speed. The transition speed controls the rate at which the transition effect plays. Transitions are set with a default run speed that seems to be the right speed for each particular transition, but you may need a faster or slower transition speed. For fade-and-dissolve transitions, you might prefer a slow transition speed so the audience gets the full effect. For transitions such as wipes, you might prefer a faster speed that keeps the slide show moving.

Set a Transition Speed

1. Select a slide with a transition in Normal or Slide Sorter view.

2. Click the **Transitions** tab.

3. Click the **Duration** spinner (⊜) to change the transition speed.

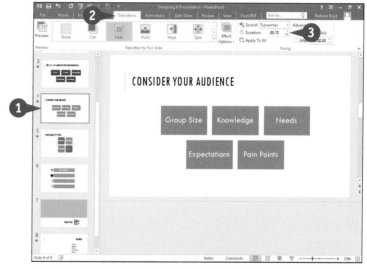

4. Click **Preview** to view the transition at the speed you specified.

   The transition plays.

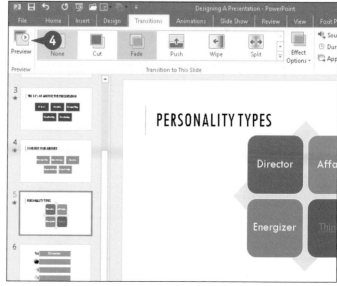

Insert an Action Button

Action buttons enable you to jump quickly and easily to a slide during a slide show. You can also use them to activate a hyperlink that opens a web page, another presentation, or a document from another application such as Excel. There are various standard actions that you can assign to an action button, and if you are advanced enough to use macros, action buttons can also trigger them.

Jumping to a web page requires an Internet connection. Any document that opens via an action button must be available on your computer.

Insert an Action Button

① Select a slide in Normal view.

② Click the **Insert** tab.

③ Click **Shapes**.

Hover the mouse pointer over the action buttons at the bottom of the gallery to see a preview of their functions.

④ Click an action button style.

The mouse pointer turns into cross hairs.

⑤ Click where you want the button.

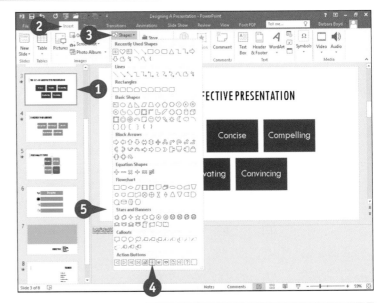

Ⓐ The action button appears and the Action Settings dialog box opens.

⑥ Click **Hyperlink to** (○ changes to ◉).

⑦ Click the **Hyperlink to** down arrow (▼).

⑧ You can click one of the hyperlink choices and click **OK**. This example uses **URL**.

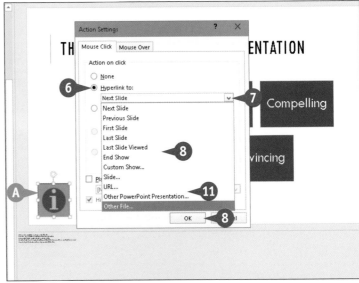

The Hyperlink to URL dialog
box appears.

9 Type the URL.

10 Click **OK**.

11 On the Action Settings
dialog box, choose **Other
File** or **Other PowerPoint
Presentation** and the dialog
box shows the directory of
your computer.

12 Click the desired folder and
file.

13 Click **Open**.

Note: If you choose a
PowerPoint presentation, you
are further prompted to choose
which slide to link to.

14 Click the button during the
slide show.

The assigned action takes
place. This example opens
a URL.

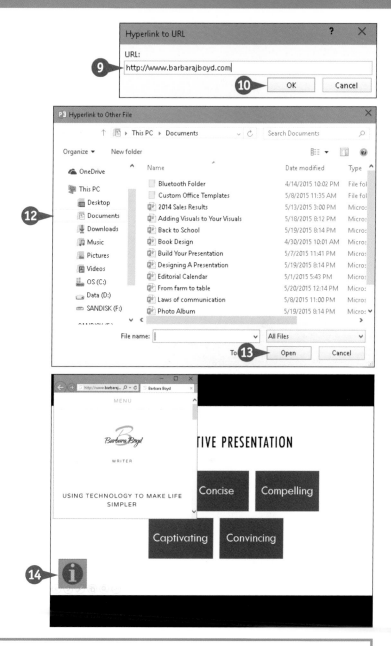

**My web page address is long. Is there a better way to enter it
in the text box besides typing it?**
Yes. Open your web browser and browse to the web page that
you want to open during the slide show. Select the URL and press
Ctrl+C to copy the address. Edit the action button and then
press Ctrl+V to paste the URL into the text box.

**What if I want to change what an
action button does?**
Right-click the action button and then
click **Edit Hyperlink**. This displays the
Action Settings dialog box, where you
can make your changes.

CHAPTER 9

Organizing Slides

After you have created a number of slides, you should check to ensure that the overall flow of your presentation makes sense. A great place to organize your slides is in Slide Sorter view. This view displays a thumbnail (little picture) of each slide. You can use the thumbnails to move, copy, and hide slides with ease.

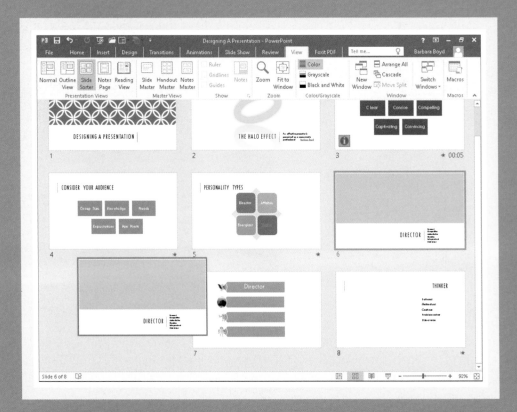

Go to an Individual Slide

When you are working in Slide Sorter view, it is sometimes useful to go to Normal view, where you can view a slide in detail. Sometimes you will see a slide in Slide Sorter view and want to revise it. While in Slide Sorter view, you can quickly and easily change to Normal view while keeping the slide selected to see it in detail. Although you can select a slide and then click the Normal View icon, these steps show a faster way to display an individual slide.

Go to an Individual Slide

1 Click the **View** tab.

2 Click **Slide Sorter**.

3 Double-click the slide that you want to see in detail.

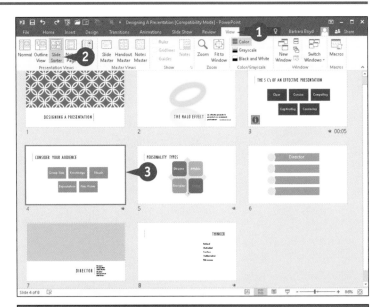

A The slide appears in Normal view.

B You can click the **Slide Sorter View** icon (⊞) to switch back to that view.

C Scroll through the thumbnail pane and click another slide to jump to it.

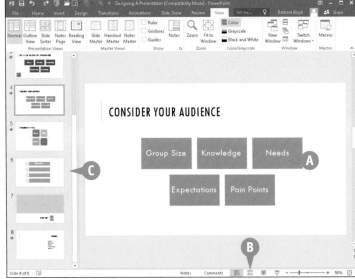

Move a Slide

A good presentation conveys a sequence of ideas in a logical progression. When creating a presentation, you often must reorganize slides to get that sequence right. For example, a presentation on how to create a presentation would begin with audience analysis, message development, slide creation, revision, and rehearsal — all in that order. PowerPoint has the ability to easily move slides so you can quickly order them as necessary.

Move a Slide

1 Click the **Slide Sorter View** icon (⬛).

Slide Sorter view appears.

2 Click and drag a slide thumbnail to the desired location.

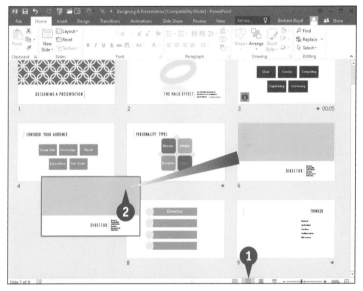

A When you release the mouse button, the slide appears in its new position.

Note: Press and hold Ctrl as you drag to create a duplicate slide in the new position.

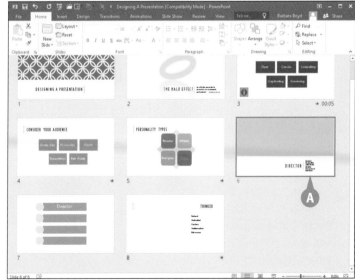

Copy and Paste a Slide

If you create presentations about similar subjects, you may want to copy a slide from one presentation to another to save time. The ability to copy the slide from one presentation to another means you do not need to re-create the slide; you can simply copy and paste it. You can also click and drag a slide from one presentation to another to copy it. If you want to copy many slides from one presentation to a new one, save the original file with a different name and delete the files you do not need.

Copy and Paste a Slide

1 Select the slide(s) you want to copy in Slide Sorter view.

Note: See Chapter 2 for a way to insert slides from another file using the Reuse feature.

Note: To select multiple slides, click the first slide, and then press Ctrl while clicking additional slides.

2 Click the **Home** tab.

3 Click the **Copy** button (📋).

4 Switch to a presentation that is open.

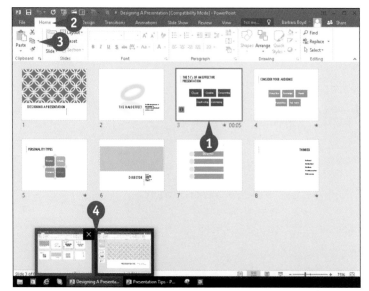

5 In Slide Sorter view, click in between the slides where you want the copied slide to appear.

The insertion point appears.

6 Click the **Home** tab.

7 Click **Paste**.

Ⓐ The copied slide(s) appears in the presentation.

Ⓑ You can maintain the slide's original formatting by clicking the **Paste Options** down arrow (▼) and then clicking the **Keep Source Formatting** button (📋).

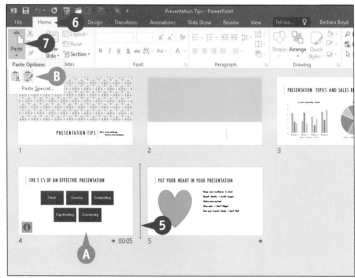

Hide a Slide

Hiding a slide prevents it from appearing during the slide show. By hiding slides, you can create an abbreviated slide show without deleting any slides. For example, you may need to give a short presentation to executives, but a detailed presentation of the same slide show to managers. You can hide slides, give the presentation, and then unhide them. Hiding slides saves you time by enabling you to prepare only one slide show for two audiences. Hiding slides is also a good way to temporarily remove them to see how your presentation flows without them.

Hide a Slide

1 Select the slide(s) you want to hide in Slide Sorter view.

Note: To select multiple slides, click the first slide, and then press **Ctrl** while clicking additional slides.

2 Click the **Slide Show** tab.

3 Click **Hide Slide**.

Note: Hyperlinks to hidden slides still work even though the slide is hidden. If during the course of your presentation you find you need to show the hyperlinked hidden slide, click the hyperlink to open it.

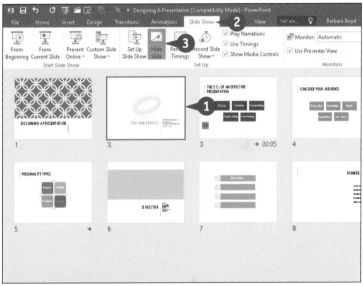

A A diagonal line appears through the slide number, indicating that the slide will not appear during the slide show.

Note: To redisplay hidden slide(s), repeat Steps **1** to **3**.

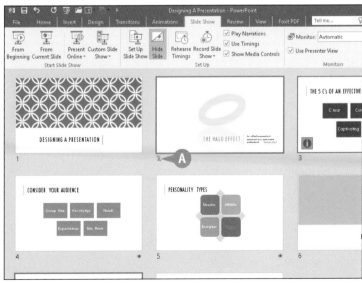

Zoom In the View

You can view a slide in greater or lesser detail by changing the zoom level. In Slide Sorter view, if you want to view many slides at once, you can select a smaller zoom percentage so that the slides are smaller and more fit in the available space. That approach can help you find a slide more quickly. You can also apply a larger zoom percentage so that you can see fewer slides but in more detail. In Normal view, zooming in can help you move objects with more precision, whereas zooming out helps you see the overall effect of your slide.

Zoom In the View

1 In Slide Sorter view, click the **View** tab.

2 Click **Zoom**.

The Zoom dialog box appears.

3 Double-click the **Percent** text box and enter a number.

Ⓐ You can also click a zoom percentage option.

4 Click **OK**.

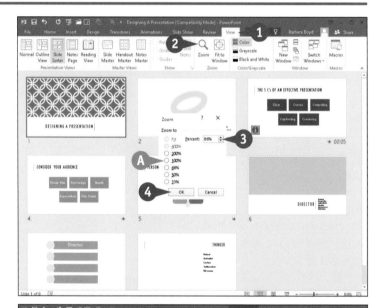

Ⓑ In Normal view, repeat Steps **2** to **4**.

Ⓒ You can also click and drag the **Zoom** slider to zoom, or click the **Zoom In** button (➕) or the **Zoom Out** button (➖) at each end of the slider.

PowerPoint displays the slides at the specified zoom level.

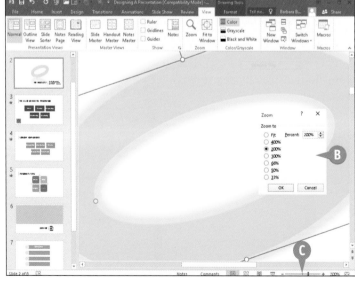

172

Change Aspect Ratio

You may find yourself presenting the same slide show on different screens, such as a widescreen or standard monitor, a notebook monitor, or a projector. Most of these devices' screens have one of two aspect ratios: 4:3 (standard) or 16:9 (widescreen). You can change the aspect ratio and use any template to design a presentation, but the fonts and objects on your slides may become distorted. Try to design your presentation in the proper aspect ratio from the beginning — if you must change the aspect ratio of a template, do it before any design work to avoid potential distortion.

Change Aspect Ratio

1 In Normal view, click the **Design** tab.

This presentation is in a 16:9 format.

2 Click the **Slide Size** down arrow (⌄).

3 In the Slide Size menu, click an aspect ratio from the list.

A sizing dialog box may appear.

4 Click **Maximize** or **Ensure Fit** in the dialog box.

Note: Ensure Fit resizes objects to ensure that they fit on the slide. Maximize does not resize objects, but objects may fall off the edge of the slide as a result.

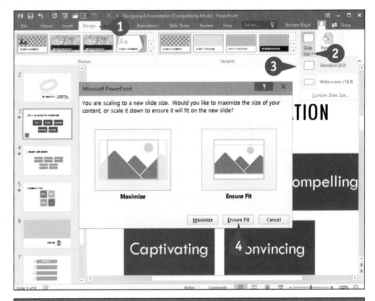

PowerPoint changes the aspect ratio of the presentation.

Note: When you change aspect ratio, AutoFormat may adjust fonts and lines. Changing the aspect ratio in a presentation may skew the slide background and may resize and distort objects. Always inspect your presentation after changing the aspect ratio to see if anything changed.

Change Slide Orientation

Typically, slide shows are presented horizontally in the landscape orientation; portrait orientation is vertical, like a business letter. The landscape orientation is made to fit a monitor, widescreen monitor, or projector screen. There are times when you may want your presentation in the portrait orientation — possibly while you print the slide show or to show two slide shows side by side on a screen. You can change the orientation of your presentation, though changing orientation distorts objects on the slides; if you want a show in portrait orientation to retain its quality, you should change orientation first, then design it.

Change Slide Orientation

1 In Slide Sorter view, click the **Design** tab.

2 Click the **Slide Size** down arrow (▼).

3 Click **Custom Slide Size**.

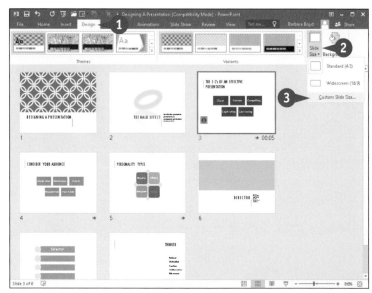

The Slide Size dialog box appears.

4 Click **Portrait**.

Ⓐ You can also click the **Slides sized for** down arrow (▼) to choose a specific size, such as A4 or 35mm slides.

5 Click **OK**.

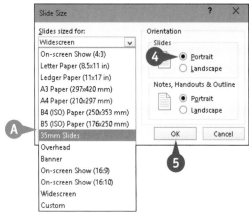

174

The scaling dialog box appears.

6 Click **Ensure Fit**.

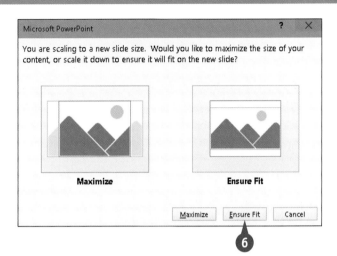

B The slides change to the chosen orientation.

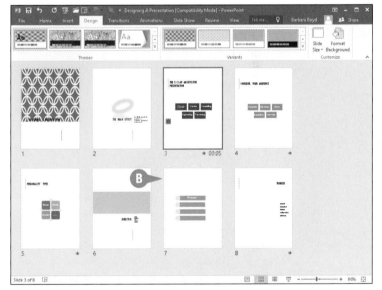

TIP

What happens if I don't choose Ensure Fit?

When you choose **Ensure Fit**, PowerPoint makes automatic adjustments so everything on your slide appears in the new format or orientation, which may distort objects or layouts and cause your slides to look awkward. If you don't choose **Ensure Fit**, some items such as long text boxes may not fit on the slide and will run off the page. If this happens, you must manually resize the text box to fix the new orientation.

View Slides in Grayscale

There are times when you may want to view your design work in black and white or grayscale — sometimes for dramatic effect, sometimes for practical reasons. For example, in a presentation with a colorful background, it can be easier to view slide content in grayscale. You can view grayscale slides in Normal, Slide Sorter, or Notes Page view.

Grayscale presents slides in shades of gray. Black and white is extreme because it uses no shading.

View Slides in Grayscale

1 In Normal view, click the **View** tab.

2 Click **Grayscale**.

The presentation appears in grayscale and an additional tab called Grayscale appears.

3 Click the **Grayscale** tab.

4 Click an object in the presentation.

5 Click **Light Grayscale**.

Ⓐ The object changes appearance.

⑥ Click **Back to Color View**.

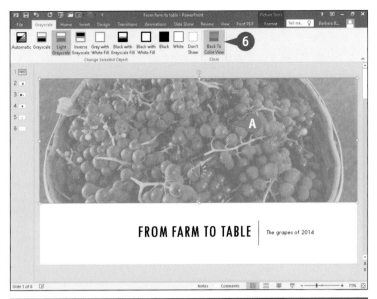

The presentation returns to color view.

Note: If you plan to print the slides in grayscale, you may want to switch to grayscale periodically during the design to see how it looks. See Chapter 15 to learn about printing your presentation.

TIP

I want only one image in grayscale. Do I change it with these tools?
No. The grayscale tools on the View tab affect the entire presentation. To change a single image, click the image and then click the **Picture Tools Format** tab. Click **Color** and choose a grayscale tone. See Chapter 7 to learn about adjusting color.

Group Slides into Sections

You may need to present multiple topics in your slide show, calling for a logical separation between topics. For example, you may want to have different themes for morning and afternoon. A presentation on Microsoft Office may need three distinct sections for three different applications: Word, Excel, and PowerPoint. Instead of creating separate presentations, you can easily separate one presentation into sections to avoid finding yourself at the podium fumbling with your computer searching for the correct presentation. The sections exist independently, enabling you to easily apply different formats to each section while keeping the sections together in one presentation.

Group Slides into Sections

1 In Slide Sorter view, click the slide that you want to begin your new section.

2 Click the **Home** tab.

3 Click the **Section** down arrow (⬇).

4 Click **Add Section**.

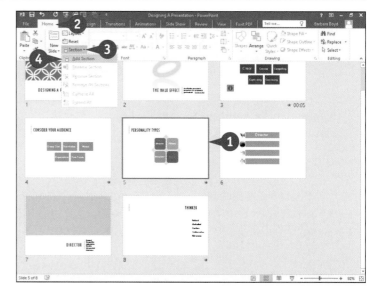

A PowerPoint inserts a section before the slide that you selected.

Note that the beginning part of the presentation becomes a section, too.

5 Click a section you want to rename.

6 Click the **Section** down arrow (⬇).

7 Click **Rename Section**.

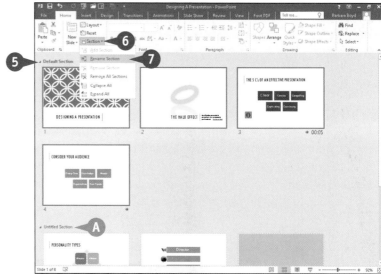

The Rename Section dialog box appears.

8 Type a new name.

9 Click **Rename**.

B PowerPoint renames the section.

10 Click a section.

11 Click the **Design** tab.

12 Click a variation from the Variants group.

C PowerPoint changes the theme for the section.

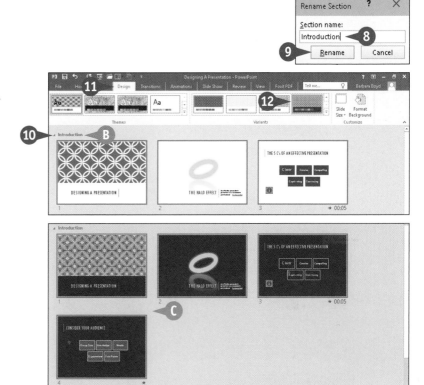

TIP

Can I get rid of a section of my presentation?
Yes. You can remove a section, which deletes the slides contained within, or simply collapse it, depending on your needs. Use the commands on the section menu or do the following:

1 Click the section.

2 Press Delete.

A To collapse or expand a section, you can click the collapse (▟) or expand (▷) icon next to the section name.

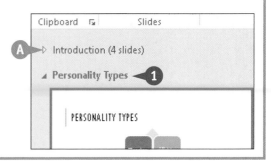

CHAPTER 10

Working with Outlines

If you have a text-heavy presentation, Outline view provides an easy, convenient way to enter text into your presentation. It helps you organize your thoughts into a simple hierarchy so that you can focus on the flow of ideas in the presentation. As a bonus, the outline is an excellent resource to write a report to accompany your presentation.

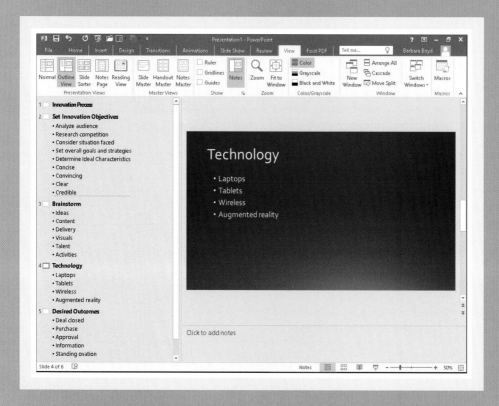

Display Outline View

Outline view is the same as Normal view except the Outline pane replaces the Slide Thumbnails pane. Typing text into a slide in Normal view can be cumbersome — you need to move and manage text and bullets. In Outline view, you simply type text into an outline and PowerPoint adds slides, inserts text into them, and manages bullets. When you finish working with the text, you can switch to Normal view to work on the slide design. You can easily move between Outline view and other views so that you can alternate between typing text and designing the slides.

Display Outline View

1 Click the **View** tab.

2 Click **Outline View**.

PowerPoint displays Outline view.

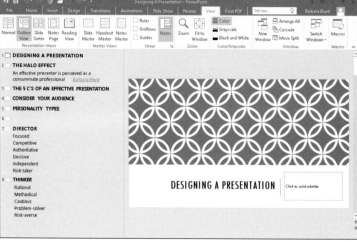

Understanding How Outline and Slide Content Relate

You can enter presentation text in Outline view or directly on a slide in Normal view. Typing text into a slide in Normal view can be cumbersome and time consuming — you need to move and manage text and bullets, possibly from slide to slide. In Outline view, you type text in a familiar outline form. To take advantage of Outline view, you must first become familiar with it. You can work more effectively when you understand how the contents of the outline and slides relate to each other.

One Heading, One Slide

Every top-level heading (a heading at level one in the outline) is the title of a slide. When you type text in a title placeholder on a slide, it appears as a level-one heading in the outline. When you type a level-one heading in the outline, PowerPoint adds a slide and the level-one heading appears in the title placeholder on the slide.

DIRECTOR
Focused
Competitive
Authoritative
Decisive
Independent

Bullet to Bullet

The second level of headings in an outline becomes the bullets in the content placeholder on the corresponding slide. If you have more than one level of bullets in the outline, there will be multiple levels of bullets on the slide, and vice versa. As you type, PowerPoint manages the bullets, but you can change the way they look.

THINKER
Rational
•Reserved
•Subtle
Methodical
•Questioning|

Images

Images never appear in the outline. You place images on slides and you see them in the Slide pane. You can insert graphics or pictures in a content placeholder, in a header or footer, or in any available location on the slide. An advantage of Outline view is that graphics do not appear in the outline, so you can concentrate on text.

Special Text

Special text elements include headers, footers, text boxes, tables, charts, and WordArt. Many graphics have text elements. Text elements such as these appear on a slide, but they do not appear as part of the outline.

Enter Presentation Content in an Outline

Outline view provides the easiest way to enter text into your presentation. You can build the text for a presentation very quickly with Outline view. You build your outline by typing text and using the Enter and Tab keys, just like any other outline. PowerPoint automatically adds slides for each first-level item in the outline. You can watch the slide develop as you type the text. The first slide in your outline automatically becomes the presentation's Title slide. Additional slides use a Title and Content slide layout automatically, although you can change the layout later.

Enter Presentation Content in an Outline

1 Start a new presentation.

Note: See Chapter 1 to learn how to start a new presentation.

2 Click **View**.

3 Click **Outline View**.

Outline view appears.

4 Click in the Outline pane next to the Slide icon (▢).

5 Type a line of text; the text appears on the slide as you type.

6 Press Enter.

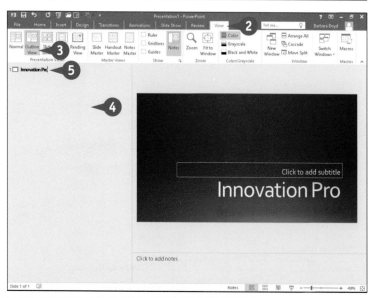

A The insertion point advances to the next line and PowerPoint adds a second slide, a Title and Content slide.

7 Click the **Home** tab.

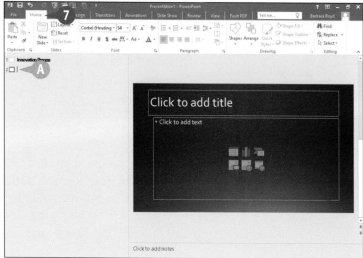

184

8 Type a second line of text and press **Enter**; the text appears on the slide as you type.

The insertion point moves to the next line.

B Press **Tab** to move the insertion point one tab to the right, becoming the first bullet on the second slide.

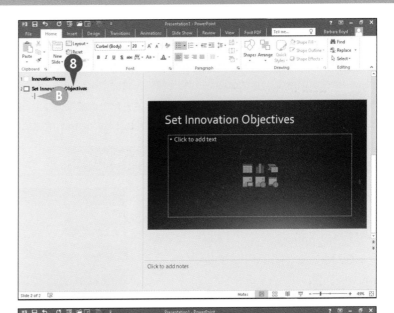

9 Type text for the bullet item and then press **Enter**.

The insertion point moves to the next line.

10 Repeat Steps **8** and **9** to add bullet items as needed.

C Press **Shift** + **Tab** to move the insertion point left; a Slide icon appears, and PowerPoint adds a third slide, a Title and Content slide.

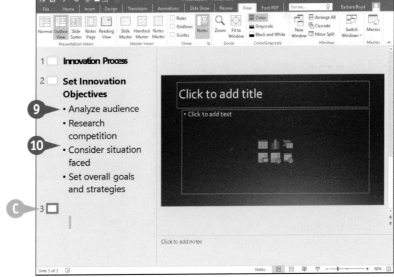

TIP

Is there a way to enlarge the Outline pane and make the font bigger to view my outline text?
Yes. Position the mouse pointer over the border between the Outline pane and the Slides pane until it changes to the mouse splitter. Click and drag the border to the right to enlarge the pane, and click and drag to the left to make it smaller. To increase the font size of the outline, click anywhere in the Outline pane and then click **Zoom** on the View tab. When the Zoom dialog box appears, select a bigger zoom percentage and then click **OK**.

Move Slides and Bullet Points in an Outline

Even with the best intentions of planning and research, presentation content evolves. For example, you may review your presentation and decide on a more logical flow for the information, or new sales figures may arrive at the last minute and you want to add them. A great advantage of Outline view is the ability to move bullet points and text around — even from slide to slide. You can also easily promote and demote bullet points from one level to another. You can even rearrange slides, bullet points, and text in your presentation by dragging and dropping them in the Outline pane.

Move Slides and Bullet Points in an Outline

1 Click the **View** tab.

2 Click **Outline View**.

3 In the Outline pane, click the **Slide** icon (□) for the slide you want to move.

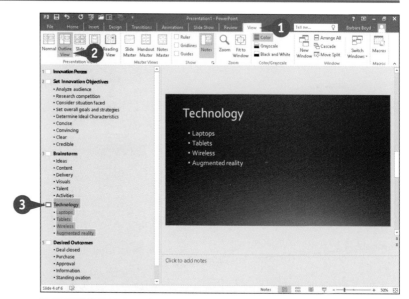

4 Click and drag the **Slide** icon (□) to the desired position using the horizontal line as a guide.

Note: You can click the **Undo** button (↺) on the Quick Access Toolbar if you make a mistake.

Note: You can also select text and then cut, copy, and paste it in the Outline pane.

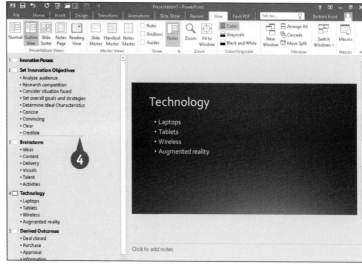

Ⓐ When you release the mouse button, the slide content moves to where you dragged it.

⑤ Click the sub-bullet of a bullet point.

⑥ Click and drag the bullet item to a new location in the bulleted list.

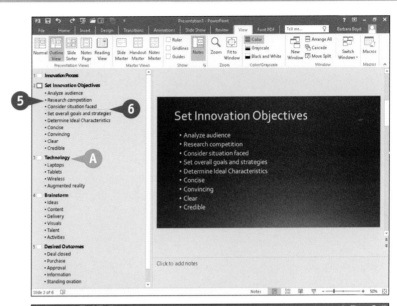

Ⓑ When you release the mouse button, the bullet item moves to where you dragged it.

Note: You can use this method to move a bullet item from one slide to another.

Note: You can click and drag text to select it and then drag it to another location.

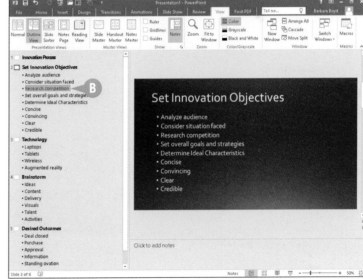

TIPS

I dragged my slide to another location and now I have more bullet points on the slide. What happened?

You probably dragged the slide to a spot inside another slide. Dragging a slide into a group of bullet points on a second slide breaks the second slide apart and places the bottom bullet points of the second slide on the moved slide.

Are there any other actions I can execute by dragging bullets?

Yes. You can promote and demote bullet points in the outline. Click and drag a bullet left or right until the vertical line representing its outline position reaches the desired outline level. Release the mouse and the bullet point moves.

Promote and Demote Items

As you build and reorganize presentation content, you may need to move bullet points in the outline so that they become sub-bullet points, a method called *demoting*. Conversely, you can move sub-bullet points to become higher-level bullet points or even slides, which is called *promoting*. Changing the levels of bullet points and slides is cumbersome if you are working on the actual slide in Normal view. You can save a lot of time and effort using the Outline pane, where you can promote and demote items with keystrokes and command button clicks on the Ribbon.

Promote and Demote Items

1 In Outline view, click the **Home** tab.

2 Click anywhere in a bullet point.

3 Click the **Demote** button (≡).

Note: Alternatively, you can press Tab .

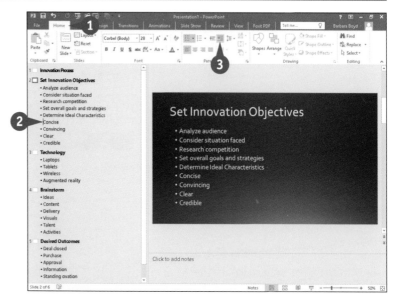

A The bullet point moves to the right, down one level in the outline hierarchy.

4 Click and drag across sub-bullet points to select them.

Note: You can also click and drag across bullet points at different hierarchy levels to perform this task.

5 Click the **Promote** button (≡).

Note: Alternatively, you can press Shift + Tab .

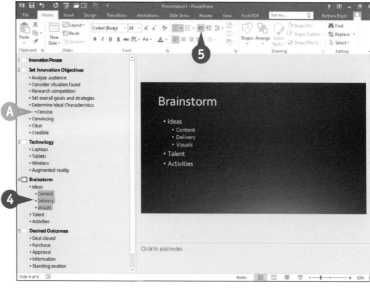

Ⓑ The bullet points move left, up one level in the outline hierarchy.

⑥ Click the sub-bullet of a bullet point.

⑦ Click the **Promote** button (⇤).

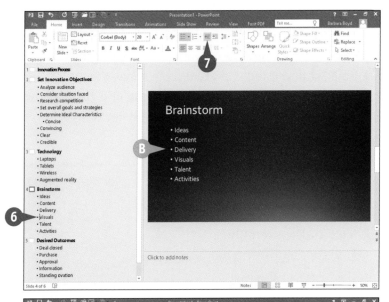

Ⓒ PowerPoint promotes the bullet point to a slide and adds a slide.

Ⓓ The bullet point becomes the title of the new slide. Subsequent bullets move up a level.

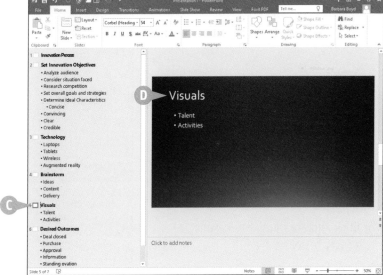

TIP

Can I promote and demote headings directly on a slide?
Yes. However, you cannot promote or demote a slide title. This is a true advantage of using Outline view. In Normal view, you must add a slide and then cut and paste bullet points to promote a bullet point to a slide. To change the level of a bullet point on a slide, click the bullet and then click either **Promote** (⇤) or **Demote** (⇥) in the Paragraph group on the Home tab. The change occurs both on the slide and in the outline. If you click the bullet point text, it does not work — you must click the bullet.

Collapse and Expand an Outline

To see a top-level overview of your presentation, it can be helpful to collapse the outline so you see only slide titles and expand only certain slides to look at the details on them. Collapsing parts of the outline can make your work easier. For example, you may want to collapse the slides that you are finished designing and expand the slides that still need work. You can collapse and expand any part or all of the outline. You can collapse or expand multiple slides. Simply select multiple slides before performing these steps.

Collapse and Expand an Outline

1 Click the **View** tab.

2 Click **Outline View**.

3 Right-click any text within a slide.

The submenu appears.

4 Click **Collapse**.

A Click **Collapse All** to collapse all slides in the presentation.

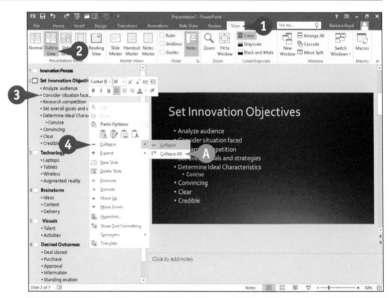

PowerPoint collapses all details and displays a wavy line under the slide title.

5 Right-click a collapsed slide title.

6 Click **Expand**.

B Click **Expand All** to expand all slides in the presentation.

The slide details reappear.

Note: You can also double-click the **Slide** icon (⬜) to collapse or expand slide details.

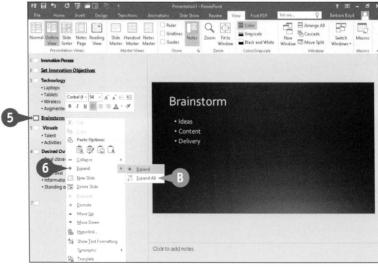

Edit Outline Content

With tools like PowerPoint, a presentation can be a work-in-progress right up to the minute before you step up to the podium. Not only do you want to check for, and correct, typos or factual errors, but you also may think of additional information or a better way to visually emphasize what you want to say as you review and rehearse. Editing an outline is much like editing text anywhere else in PowerPoint, or in any other application for that matter.

Edit Outline Content

1 Click the **View** tab.

2 Click **Outline View**.

3 Click where you want to add or delete text and type to add text, or press **Del** or **Backspace** to delete the text.

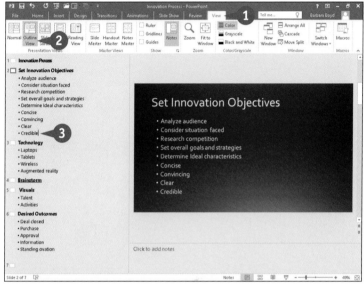

A The outline and the slide reflect the changes you made. In the example, "credible" is changed to "believable" and three lines are deleted.

4 Click the bullet for any bullet point to select the entire bullet point.

Note: You can also click a **Slide** icon (□) to select an entire slide.

5 Press **Del**.

PowerPoint deletes the entire bullet point or slide.

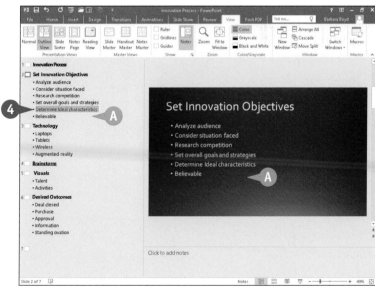

Insert Slides from an Outline

If you already have an outline in another application, such as Microsoft Word, you can use that as the basis for your presentation without retyping it in PowerPoint. For example, you may already have an outline that you used to give a speech or to write a paper. To save time, you can import an outline into a new PowerPoint presentation, and then edit and format that content like any other presentation.

PowerPoint imports outlines that are created in Outline view in Microsoft Word. It also imports text file outlines written in text editors such as Notepad.

Insert Slides from an Outline

1 Click the **File** tab to show Backstage view.

2 Click **Open**.

3 Click **Browse**.

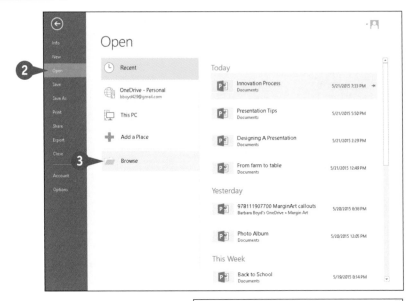

The Open dialog box appears.

4 Click the drop-down arrow (∨).

5 Click **All Outlines**.

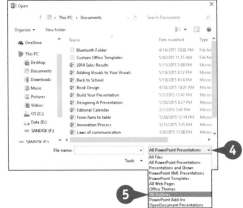

PowerPoint shows all file types that can hold an outline, such as Word files (.docx), text files (.txt), and rich text files (.rtf).

6 Click the folder that holds the outline file you want to import.

7 Click the outline file.

8 Click **Open**.

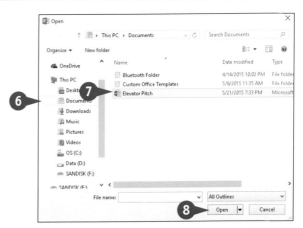

PowerPoint creates a new presentation using your existing outline as the content.

9 Click the **View** tab.

10 Click **Outline View**.

Note: Click the **File** tab to save your presentation, as explained in Chapter 1.

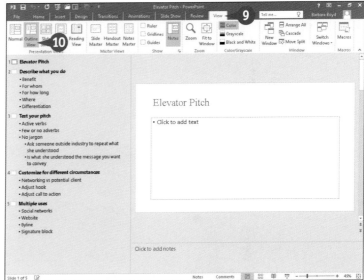

TIPS

All the content in my Microsoft Word outline became slides. What went wrong?

The outline is not in the proper format. The outline needs to be created with the Outline view in Word, which is very similar to typing an outline in PowerPoint. If you need an outline in both Word and PowerPoint, you can create it in either application and export it to the other application.

How does PowerPoint know where to start each slide?

Each top-level heading in the imported outline becomes the title for a new slide — just like a PowerPoint outline. Although you can edit it in PowerPoint, review the outline before importing it. Make sure each slide title is at the top level in the outline.

CHAPTER 11

Using Masters

Masters enable you to make global settings for your slides, such as inserting your company logo or a page number on every slide. Using masters gives your presentation a consistent, cohesive, professional look, which helps your audience remember your message. When you change a master, all slides based on that master also change.

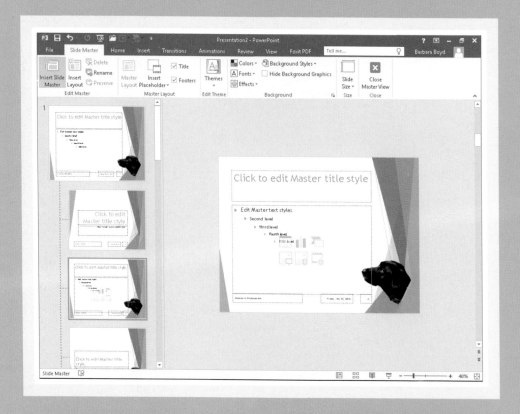

Understanding Masters

Masters are the behind-the-scenes workhorses of PowerPoint templates and layouts. When you create a presentation using a PowerPoint or inline theme or template, it has *masters* that provide the basic structure for each slide template, saving you the time of designing each presentation slide from scratch. For example, the Title and Content slide layout is designed once in the Slide Master view, but you can use it over and over again.

Work with Three Kinds of Masters

The *master slides* consist of a set of slides called the *layout masters*. The top-level layout master, the *slide master,* controls the theme and formatting for all layout masters in the template; there is one layout master for each type of slide layout that you use to build your presentation. PowerPoint offers three master views: *Slide Master* determines how presentation slides look; the *Handout Master* controls how a printed version of your presentation looks; and the *Notes Master* dictates how a printout of your notes looks.

Using Masters to Make Global Changes

If you change the formatting of an element on the slide master, PowerPoint changes that element on all layout masters and all presentation slides. For example, if you add a slide number to the slide master, you see it on all layouts. If you move the title from the top to the bottom of the page of the layout master that controls the Title and Content layout, only slides using the Title and Content layout reflect that change. This saves you time and gives your presentation a consistent look and feel.

How Masters Relate to the Theme

Masters are based on themes. When you apply a theme to your presentation, PowerPoint automatically creates a set of master slides with that theme. You can alter the theme of your master slides and then save it as a new theme. If you apply more than one theme to your presentation, you will have multiple sets of master slides — one for each theme. You can change the design of the layout master of the Title and Content slide in one theme without affecting the Title and Content slides in the other two themes.

Overriding Master Settings

When you make changes to individual presentation slides, those changes take precedence over settings on the corresponding layout master or the slide master. For example, changing the font color of the title placeholder of a Title and Content presentation slide in Normal view does not affect the title placeholder font color of the Title and Content layout master. If you place a graphic on a layout master, you can omit it from the background of an individual presentation slide in Normal view.

Understanding Slide Master Elements

You can use the master slides to create global design settings for your slides. The slide master and layout masters contain placeholders where you can format text. They also contain various placeholders for footer information, slide numbers, and a date. Any change to a layout master is applied to any presentation slide that has its corresponding layout. When you make a formatting change to a placeholder on the slide master, PowerPoint applies that change to any corresponding placeholder anywhere in the presentation. One change can affect many slides, but only for the theme associated with the master slide you are changing.

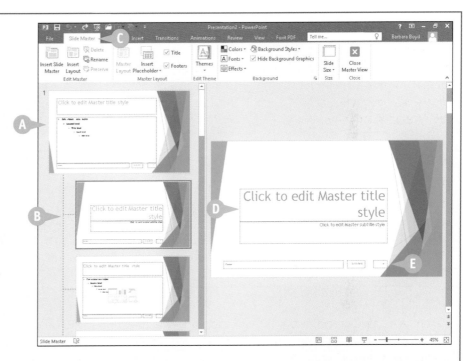

A Slide Master

The slide master is connected to its related layout masters with a dotted line. The Slide Thumbnails pane shows one set of master slides for each theme.

B Layout Masters

Layout masters represent the various slide layouts that you can insert into a presentation, such as the Title and Content layouts. Changes on a layout master affect only those presentation slides with the layout of that particular master.

C Slide Master Tab

Use the Slide Master tab to change master slides — you can design the background of masters, change or insert placeholders, and change theme colors and font schemes.

D Placeholders

You can format an entire placeholder, some of its text, or each bullet point individually by selecting a particular bullet point before formatting.

E Footer, Date, and Slide Numbers

The Date placeholder positions the date on slides; the Page (#) placeholder provides page numbers on slides; the Footer placeholder provides a footer on the slides.

Open and Close Slide Master View

You work with the slide master and layout masters in Slide Master view. Opening Slide Master view automatically displays the Slide Master tab for working with the set of master slides. This tab was created to help you design the master slides, but you can also use the other tabs on the Ribbon. After you make changes to the master slides and close Slide Master view, PowerPoint redisplays whatever view you had open previously — Normal view, Slide Sorter view, or Notes Page view. Global changes to presentation slides due to changes in master slides are reflected there.

Open and Close Slide Master View

1 Click the **View** tab.

2 Click **Slide Master**.

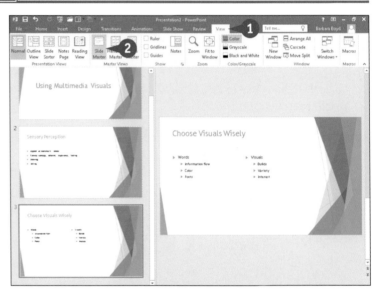

Slide Master view and the Slide Master tab appear.

3 Click the **Slide Master** tab.

4 Click **Close Master View**.

Slide Master view closes and PowerPoint restores the previous presentation design view.

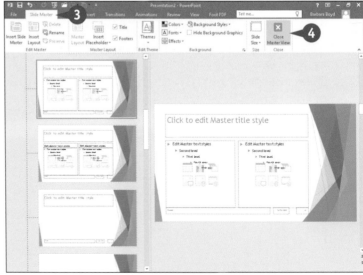

Remove a Placeholder

The layout masters contain placeholders for the slide title, text or graphic content, date, footer, and slide numbers. If you are not using a particular placeholder, you can remove it from the layout masters.

Although formatting changes made to the slide master affect the formatting of associated layout masters, deleting a placeholder from the slide master at the top of the Slide Thumbnails pane does not delete it from the layout masters.

Remove a Placeholder

1 Display Slide Master view.

Note: To display Slide Master view, see the section "Open and Close Slide Master View."

2 Click the layout master that contains the placeholder you want to remove.

3 Click the border of the placeholder to select it. The border becomes solid.

This example selects the subtitle placeholder.

Note: Do not click inside the placeholder, which selects only the text.

4 Press Delete.

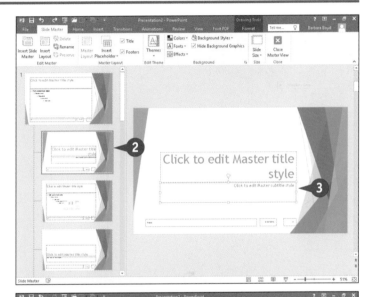

A PowerPoint deletes the placeholder.

Note: If you delete a placeholder from a layout master, PowerPoint does not delete the placeholder from existing presentation slides. Slides inserted in the presentation after you make this deletion from the layout master will not contain the placeholder.

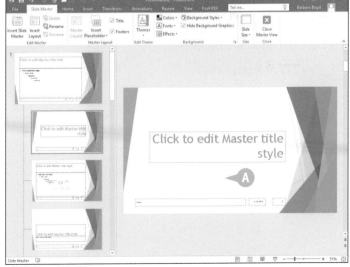

Insert a Placeholder

Sometimes the slide layouts that are available do not meet the requirements of your presentation. You may need to add a placeholder to a layout master to create a slide layout that suits your needs. You can insert a new placeholder in any layout master in Slide Master view. This saves time because you do not have to add the placeholder to every presentation slide that needs one. You can insert placeholders for text or content, plus other types of placeholders like picture or chart placeholders. You can also resize, reposition, or reformat any placeholder at any time.

Insert a Placeholder

1. Display Slide Master view.

Note: To display Slide Master view, see the section "Open and Close Slide Master View."

2. Click a layout master.

   Choose **Blank** or **Title Only** so you do not have to remove existing placeholders.

3. Click the **Insert Placeholder** down arrow (▾).

4. Click a placeholder type.

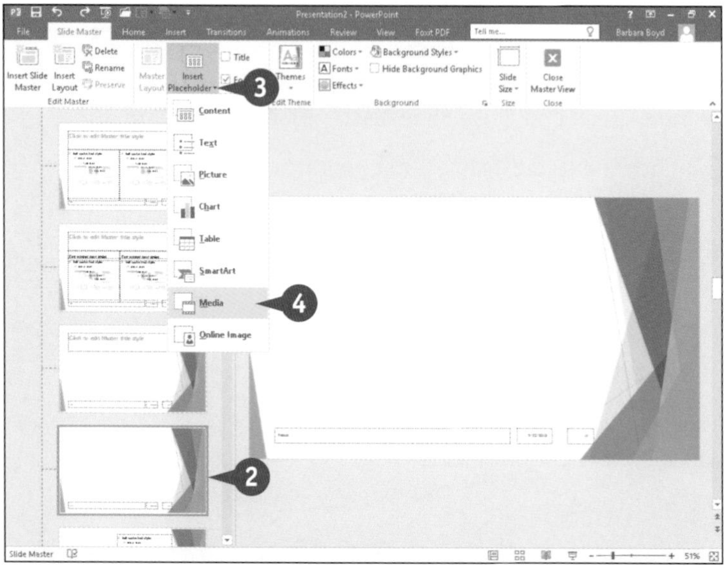

The cross-hairs pointer appears.

5. Click where you want the upper left corner of the placeholder and drag across the slide to where you want the lower right corner of the placeholder.

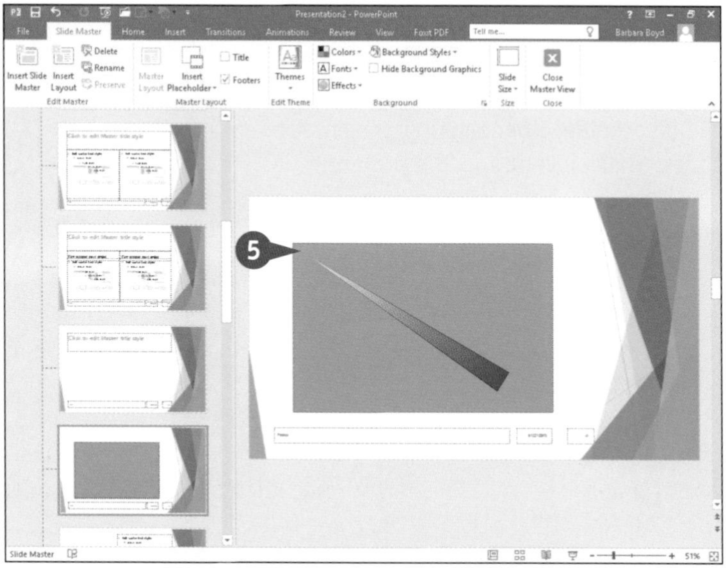

Ⓐ When you release the mouse button, the placeholder appears.

6 With the new placeholder still selected, click the **Home** tab.

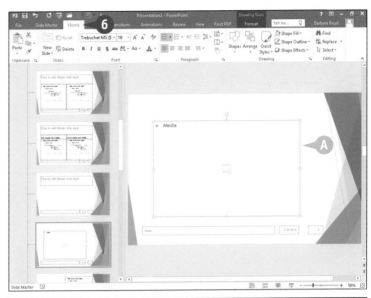

7 Use the tools on the Home tab to format the placeholder.

The example uses the Shape Outline tools to put a frame around a media placeholder.

8 Click outside the placeholder when finished.

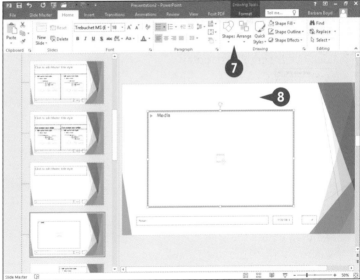

TIP

Is there an easy way to reinstate a placeholder that I deleted from the slide master?
Yes. In Slide Master view, click the **Slide Master** tab and then click the **Slide Master** thumbnail. The slide master is the first slide in the set of master slides, usually the top slide in the Slide Thumbnails pane, unless you have more than one theme in your presentation. Click the **Master Layout** button of the Master Layout group. In the Master Layout dialog box, click the check box for the deleted placeholder (☐ changes to ☑) and then click **OK**. PowerPoint reinstates the placeholder.

Add a Footer

The slide masters have placeholders for footers that you can use to show information such as your company name on slides. You can move the footer anywhere on the master slide. To save time, you can add a footer to a single master slide rather than individual presentation slides.

If you add a footer to the slide master, it appears on all slides. If you add a footer to a layout master, it appears only on presentation slides with that layout. You can also use different footers in the handout master and notes master.

Add a Footer

1. Display Slide Master view.

2. Click the slide master or one of the layout masters.

3. Click the **Insert** tab.

4. Click **Header & Footer**.

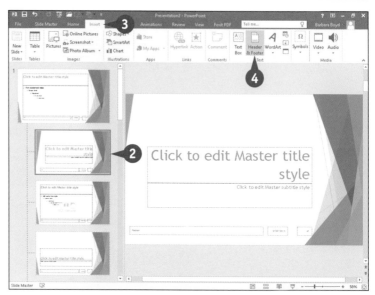

The Header and Footer dialog box appears.

5. Click **Footer** (☐ changes to ✔).

6. Type your information in the text box.

7. Click **Apply**.

Ⓐ You can click **Apply to All** to add the footer to the entire set of master slides.

Note: Adding the footer to the entire set of master slides also applies the footer to all presentation slides.

Ⓑ Click **Don't show on title slide** (☐ changes to ✔) and the footer appears on all slides except the first slide of your presentation.

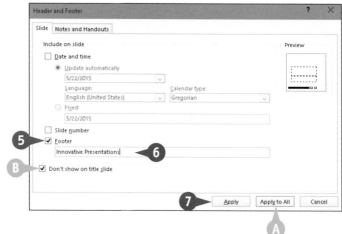

Add a Date

The set of slide masters includes a placeholder for a date. You can add a particular fixed date or one that updates automatically and shows the computer's system date. You can move the date anywhere on the master slide and resize the placeholder if you choose a format larger than the placeholder — for example, the day and month spelled out. To save time, you can add the date to a single master slide rather than individual presentation slides. You can also use dates in the handout master and notes master.

Add a Date

1 Display Slide Master view.

Note: To display Slide Master view, see the section "Open and Close Slide Master View."

2 Click the slide master or one of the layout masters.

3 Click the **Insert** tab.

4 Click **Header & Footer**.

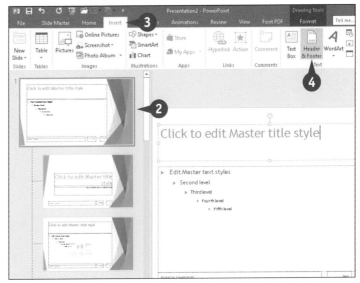

The Header and Footer dialog box appears.

5 Click **Date and time** (☐ changes to ☑).

6 Click the **Update automatically** option (○ changes to ◉).

Ⓐ You can change the format of the date by clicking the down arrow (▼) and selecting a format from the list.

7 Click **Apply**.

Ⓑ You can click **Apply to All** to add the date to all presentation slides.

Ⓒ The date appears on the selected slides.

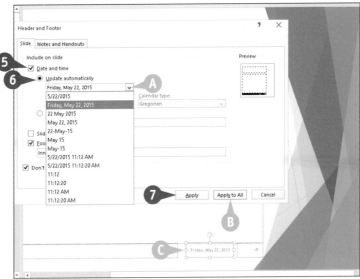

Set Up Slide Numbers

You can have PowerPoint automatically number the presentation slides with the option to not include a slide number on the title slide. You can reposition the slide number placeholder anywhere on the slide master or layout masters. To save time, you can add the slide number to a single master slide instead of numbering presentation slides individually.

You can set up slide numbers on the slide master, which affects all slides; layout masters, which affect only slides with corresponding layouts; or particular presentation slides in Normal view.

Set Up Slide Numbers

1. Display Slide Master view.

Note: To display Slide Master view, see the section "Open and Close Slide Master View."

2. Click the slide master or one of the layout masters.

3. Click the **Insert** tab.

4. Click **Header & Footer**.

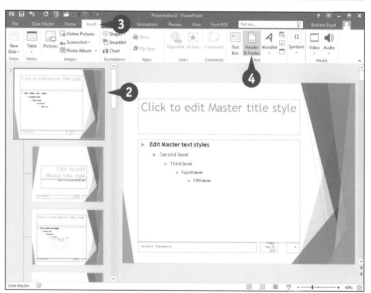

The Header and Footer dialog box appears.

5. Click the **Slide Number** option (☐ changes to ☑).

6. Click the **Don't show on title slide** option (☐ changes to ☑).

7. Click **Apply to All**.

Ⓐ You can click **Apply** to apply slide numbers only to selected slides.

Slide numbers appear on all presentation slides except the title slide.

Insert a Graphic in Slide Master View

You can use Slide Master view to insert a graphic or picture that appears on every slide. For example, your organization or company might want its logo on all slides for professionalism and consistency. You can place a graphic or picture on every slide of your presentation by inserting a single graphic in the slide master.

If you insert a graphic on the slide master, it appears on all slides. If you insert a graphic on a layout master, it appears only on presentation slides with that layout.

Insert a Graphic in Slide Master View

1 Display Slide Master view.

Note: To display Slide Master view, see the section "Open and Close Slide Master View."

2 Click the slide master.

3 Click the **Insert** tab.

4 Click **Pictures**.

The Insert Picture dialog box appears.

5 Click the folder that contains the image file you want to insert.

6 Click the image file.

7 Click **Insert**.

A The dialog box closes and the image appears on the slide master, where you can move, edit, and resize it as needed. (See Chapter 6.) It also appears on all slides.

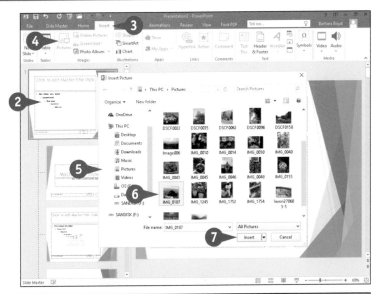

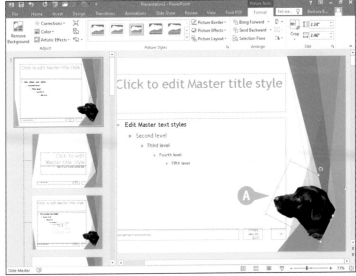

Omit Master Graphics on a Slide

Inserting a graphic on the slide master applies that graphic to all presentation slides; inserting a graphic on a layout master causes that graphic to appear on corresponding presentation slides. You can prevent a slide master graphic from appearing on individual presentation slides. For example, you may need to remove a graphic from a specific presentation slide because the graphic overlaps with other objects, making the information hard to understand. You may also need to remove a graphic from certain slides because it simply does not apply to those slides.

Omit Master Graphics on a Slide

1 Select the slide(s) you want to change in Normal or Slide Sorter view.

Note: To select multiple slides, click the first slide, and then press `Ctrl` while clicking additional slides.

2 Click the **Design** tab.

3 Click **Format Background**.

The Format Background task pane appears.

4 Click **Hide background graphics** (□ changes to ☑).

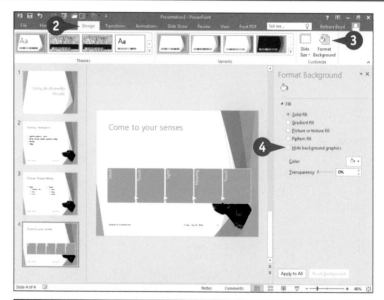

The master graphics disappear from the slide.

5 Click the **Close** button (✕) to close the Format Background task pane.

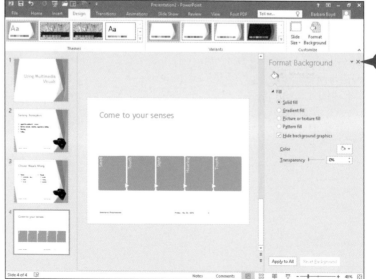

Work with Multiple Masters

You may want to use a few different looks in your presentation. For example, you may use one theme for a morning session and another for an afternoon session of an all-day presentation. You may use different themes to differentiate between sections. Or each member of a presentation team may have a different style.

Occurrence of Multiple Masters

Each theme used within a single presentation has its own set of master slides. Each set of master slides has a slide master, plus one layout master for each slide layout that you see in the Slide Layout gallery, which you see when you insert a slide. Although you can change the theme of your presentation, you cannot change the theme of a set of master slides. You can create a blank set of master slides and design the theme from scratch. Saving your own theme with master slides enables you to create future presentations with that theme.

Masters Are Independent

Changing the slide or layout master of one theme's master slides does not affect the same layout on another theme's master slides. Changes to your slide or layout masters are automatically applied to the presentation slides with that particular slide layout and theme combination. To make a universal change for a specific slide layout — for example, placing the title in the upper right corner of every title slide — you must change each layout master for that slide layout in each set of master slides.

Make Themes in Multiple Masters Consistent

If you use multiple themes (and therefore multiple masters), make sure the themes are complementary. You do this by selecting slide designs with similar color themes, fonts, graphics, and backgrounds that work well together. Avoid mixing and matching themes throughout your presentation.

Multiple Masters and Slides

If your presentation has multiple masters, you choose which layout and theme to use when you insert a new slide or change the layout of an existing slide. You find each theme in the Slide Layout gallery. The various slide layouts are grouped within each theme. For example, if you use three themes in your presentation, you have three Title and Content layout masters, one for each theme, independent from one another. If you change the Title and Content layout master of one theme, it does not affect the Title and Content layout masters of the other themes.

Insert a New Blank Master

If you cannot find a presentation template that you like, or you need a very specific and unique look, you can create your own set of master slides with its own theme. You can insert a blank set of master slides and customize it in Slide Master view. You can then format the text in placeholders, change the background, add graphics, and so on. Chapter 4 tells you how to format text, and Chapters 6 and 7 provide information on working with graphics and media. By changing various elements, you can create a unique master design.

Insert a New Blank Master

1 Display Slide Master view.

Note: To display Slide Master view, see the section "Open and Close Slide Master View."

2 Click **Insert Slide Master**.

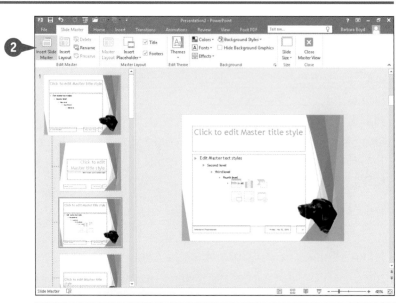

A new set of master slides appears.

A PowerPoint numbers each master.

B You can apply an existing theme to the new set of master slides by clicking the **Themes** button and selecting a theme from the gallery.

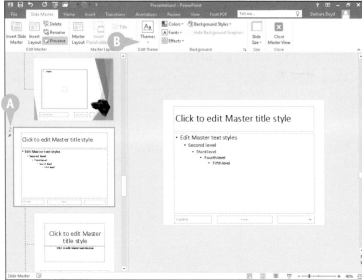

Preserve Master Slides

B y default, PowerPoint removes a set of master slides if you delete all the presentation slides that use it. You can preserve it to avoid its automatic removal. That way, you can use it for future presentation slides. You can also unpreserve a set of master slides. You can manually delete a set of master slides in Slide Master view even if it is preserved.

Preserve Master Slides

1 Display Slide Master view.

Note: To display Slide Master view, see the section "Open and Close Slide Master View."

2 Click the slide master you want to preserve.

Note: You must click a slide master, not a layout master.

3 Click **Preserve**.

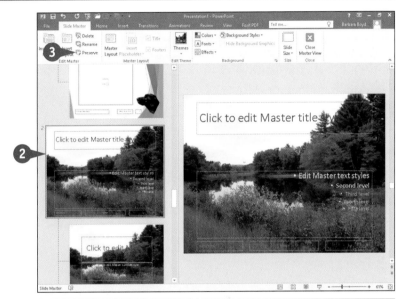

Ⓐ PowerPoint preserves the master and a Preserve icon (✹) appears on the slide master thumbnail.

Ⓑ The Preserve toggle button becomes highlighted.

Note: To reverse the process, perform Steps **1** to **3** again so the Preserve button is no longer highlighted.

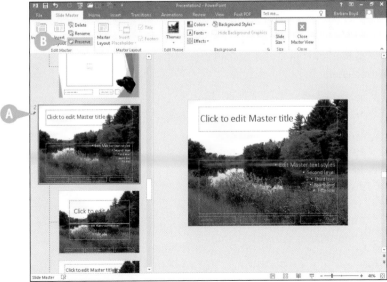

Rename Master Slides

If you insert a blank set of master slides, PowerPoint automatically names it "Custom Design," but you can apply a more descriptive name. For example, if you designed a set of master slides with a landscape photo in the background, you might rename it Garden. You can also rename masters that you use from PowerPoint or another online source. Giving the master slides your own descriptive name makes it easier to select the correct master slides when you apply a layout to a slide in a presentation that uses multiple masters.

Rename Master Slides

1 Display Slide Master view.

Note: To display Slide Master view, see the section "Open and Close Slide Master View."

2 Click the slide master you want to rename.

Note: You must click a slide master, not a layout master.

3 Click **Rename**.

The Rename Layout dialog box appears.

4 Type a name.

5 Click **Rename**.

The dialog box closes, and PowerPoint renames the master slides.

Note: Renaming only changes the names of the sets of master slides within the presentation.

Ⓐ If you add specific backgrounds, font styles, and colors to a set of master slides, you can save it as a theme so you can use it in another presentation. Click the **Theme** down arrow (⬇) and choose **Save Current Theme**. See Chapter 3 to learn more.

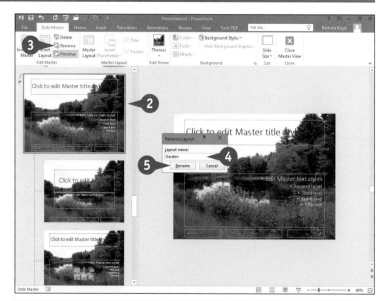

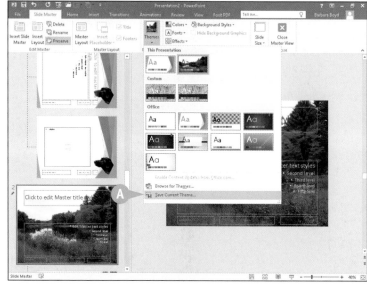

Work with the Handout Master

Although most presenters make notes and/or slides available online so the audience can access them after the presentation, you may still want to give your audience a printed handout of your slides. Handout Master view determines what is printed on the handouts. You can move, resize, and format the font of the handout placeholders — for example, the page number or number of slides per page — to control the appearance of your printed handouts. Any formatting you do on the handout master appears in the handout printout. See Chapter 15 for more about printing.

Work with the Handout Master

1 Click the **View** tab.

2 Click **Handout Master**.

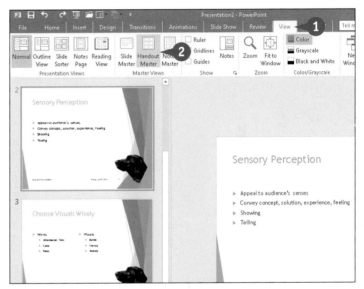

Handout Master view and the Handout Master tab appear.

Ⓐ You can click options to add (☑) or remove (☐) placeholders.

Ⓑ You can click **Fonts** to change the font style of all text placeholders on the page.

Note: You can click commands on the Home tab to format individual placeholders.

Ⓒ Click the **Slides Per Page** down arrow (▼) to choose the number of slides you want displayed on each page.

3 Click **Close Master View**.

Handout Master view closes.

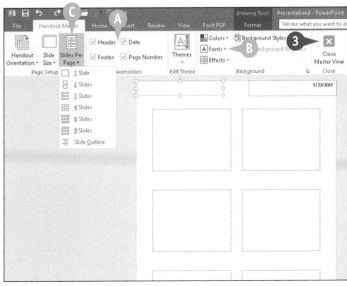

Work with the Notes Master

You can distribute your notes to your audience or only print them for your reference. Either way, the notes master gives you many options for formatting your notes. Changes in the notes master affect the Notes Page view and how the notes pages print. Notes Page view shows what you will see when you print notes pages in Backstage view. The notes master has a placeholder for the slide and for the notes area, as well as placeholders for the header, footer, date, and slide number.

You can modify the format of notes text, move or delete placeholders, and enter headers and footers. See Chapter 15 for information about printing notes.

Work with the Notes Master

1 Click the **View** tab.

2 Click **Notes Master**.

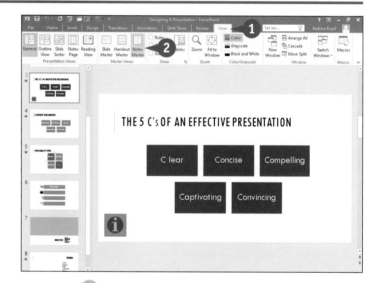

The Notes Master view appears and the Notes Master tab appears on the Ribbon.

3 Click any placeholder border and then drag the placeholder to another location.

4 Click any placeholder border and resize it by clicking and dragging one of the handles.

Ⓐ You can click options to add (☑) or remove (☐) placeholders.

Ⓑ Click the **Notes Page Orientation** down arrow (▼) to change from portrait to landscape.

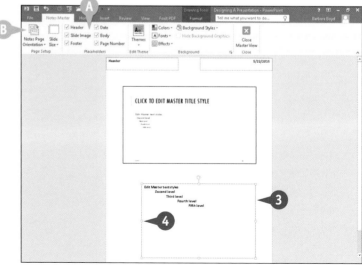

This example resizes and moves the notes text placeholder and slide to a landscape orientation.

5 Click any placeholder border to select it.

6 Click the **Home** tab.

7 Click the **Italic** button (*I*).

8 Type a font size into the Font Size text box. This example uses a font size of 40.

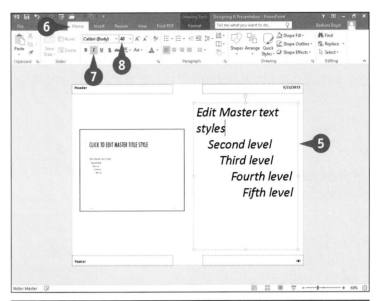

C You can select a bullet point to format an individual bullet.

D You can click the **Drawing Tools Format** tab to display other formatting options.

9 Click the **Notes Master** tab.

10 Click **Close Master View**.

Notes Master view closes.

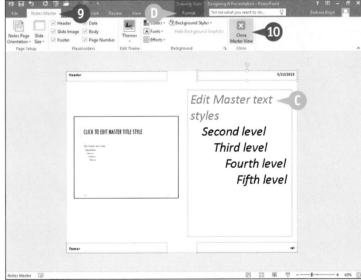

Is there a way to print just notes, and not slides?
Yes. If you remove the slide placeholder from the notes master, the slide images still appear on Notes Page view. You must display Notes Page view, go to each individual page, and delete the slide placeholder. Then the notes print without the slides.

Can I format the font for the header, footer, date, and page number?
Yes. You can format the header, footer, date, and page number placeholders just like any other placeholder. Click the border of the placeholder, and then use commands from the **Home** tab to format the text or the placeholder.

Create a Custom Slide Layout

There may be times when you need a slide with a unique layout. For example, you may want to compare three items, but there is no slide layout with three content placeholders. You can work in Slide Master view to add a new slide layout to the set of master slides. This saves time because you do not need to insert additional placeholders into individual slides. You create your custom slide layout with three content placeholders, then insert new slides with the custom layout, or apply the custom layout to existing slides in your presentation.

Create a Custom Slide Layout

1 Display Slide Master view.

Note: To display Slide Master view, see the section "Open and Close Slide Master View."

2 Click in between the thumbnails where you want to insert the new slide layout.

3 Click **Insert Layout**.

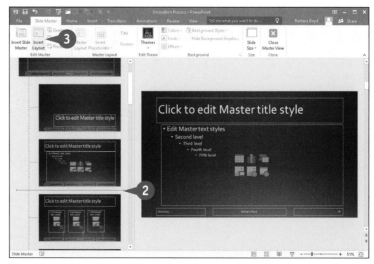

Ⓐ A new layout master appears as a thumbnail.

4 Click **Insert Placeholder**.

5 Click and drag across the slide where you want the placeholder.

Note: See "Insert a Placeholder" earlier in this chapter.

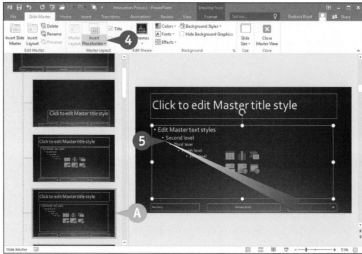

B The placeholder appears.

You can move, format, and resize the placeholder as needed.

You can then copy and paste the placeholder if you want to create more than one of the same.

6 Click **Rename**.

The Rename Layout dialog box appears.

7 Click the **Layout name** field and type a name for your new layout.

8 Click **Rename**.

9 Click **Close Master View** when finished.

Slide Master view closes.

10 Click the **Home** tab.

11 Click the **New Slide** down arrow (⯆).

The gallery of layouts appears.

C Your custom layout appears in the gallery.

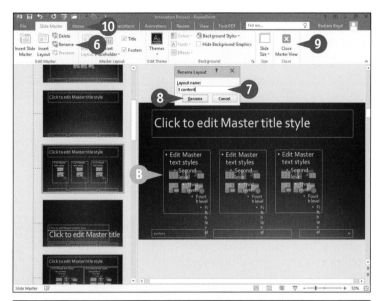

Can I assign a unique name to my custom layout master?

Yes. Your custom layout master works just like any other layout master. See "Rename Master Slides" earlier in this chapter to learn how to rename your custom layout master. Try to give it a name that uniquely identifies it so you can quickly find it when you insert a slide.

Can I change the background for my custom slide layout?

Yes. You cannot change the theme, but you can change the background. Click your custom layout master. You can click commands such as **Colors** and **Effects** in the Background group on the **Slide Master** tab to make background changes. See Chapter 7 for more on changing backgrounds of slides.

CHAPTER 12

Finalizing a Slide Show

After you add all your slide content, tweak your design, and add graphics, animations, and transitions, you are almost done. Now, to complete your presentation, you review and comment on it — and perhaps ask others to do the same; set the show parameters, rehearse, and possibly record a narration; and finally, present your slide show!

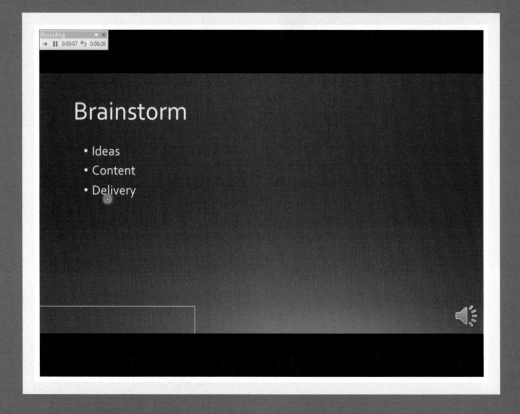

Save a Presentation to OneDrive

OneDrive is a cloud service provided by Microsoft for free. You can post a presentation to OneDrive and give permission to people to access it and work with it, which means several people can work on the same document. OneDrive is a cloud storage location available to anybody who has a Microsoft Live account, and most computers and tablets with an Internet connection can access the account. Storing files to OneDrive is also a convenient offsite place to back up important files.

Save a Presentation to OneDrive

Connect to a OneDrive Account

1 Click the **File** tab to show Backstage view.

2 Click **Save As**.

3 Click **Add a Place**.

4 Click **OneDrive**.

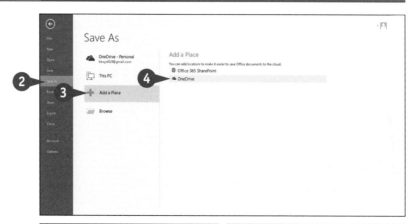

The Microsoft account Sign In dialog box appears.

5 Click the text box and type your username.

6 Click **Next**.

The second Microsoft account Sign In dialog box appears.

Ⓐ If you do not have a Microsoft account, click the **Sign up now** link.

7 Click the text box and type your password.

8 Click **Sign in**.

Microsoft creates a OneDrive account for you.

Save to OneDrive

1 Click the **File** tab to show Backstage view.

2 Click **Save As**.

3 Click your OneDrive.

4 Click **Browse**.

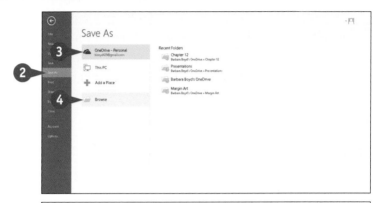

B The Save As dialog box appears with the OneDrive selected.

5 Scroll to the folder where you want to save the file.

6 Click the **File name** text box.

7 Type a name.

8 Click **Save**.

PowerPoint saves your presentation to OneDrive.

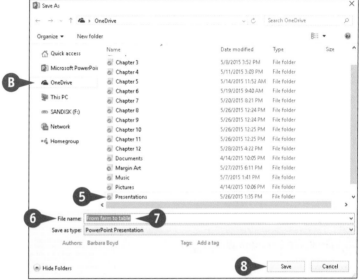

Now that I saved the presentation to OneDrive, how do I get to it?

OneDrive appears on your computer as another drive, the same as if you plugged a flash drive into the USB port or accessed a drive on a server on your network. Click your user folder icon on your desktop or the Windows taskbar, and then look in your user folder (the user folder in the example in this section is named Barbara Boyd). The folder is named OneDrive and the icon looks like two clouds. You can also click **OneDrive** on your Windows Start screen.

Send a Presentation for Review

Asking for feedback on your presentation before you give a slide show is a good idea. A second, or third, opinion helps because another viewer can spot errors you missed, point out confusing areas, or suggest improvements. A reviewer can check your facts, validate technical advice, or verify procedures. You can share your presentation on OneDrive so multiple reviewers can make comments on the same document, making it easier for you to incorporate them. You can also email your presentation to others for review, and the reviewers can add comments to the presentation and then email it back to you.

Send a Presentation for Review

Note: These steps assume that your OneDrive account is properly configured and you have an Internet connection.

1. Click the **File** tab to show Backstage view.

2. Click **Share**.

3. Click **Invite People**.

4. Click **Save to Cloud**.

The Save As window opens.

5. Double-click the OneDrive account you want to save the file to.

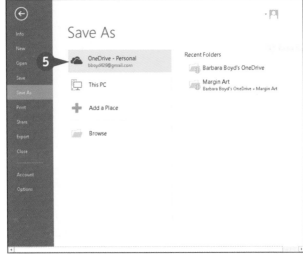

The Save As dialog opens.

6 Click the folder that you want to contain the file.

Ⓐ The folders you see are on your OneDrive.

Ⓑ If you want to change the name of the presentation, type a name in the **File name** text box.

7 Click **Save**.

The Share window opens.

8 Type the email address of the people you want to review your file in the name text box.

9 Click the permissions down arrow (▼) and choose **Can edit**.

10 Write a short message asking the recipients to review your presentation.

11 Click **Share**.

An email is sent to the people you shared the document with. A link in the email gives them access to your file on OneDrive, which they can comment on by choosing to edit the presentation in PowerPoint Online.

Note: You can open the file with the comments from OneDrive in the same manner that you open files from your computer, by clicking **Open in Backstage view**, and then clicking **OneDrive** instead of This PC.

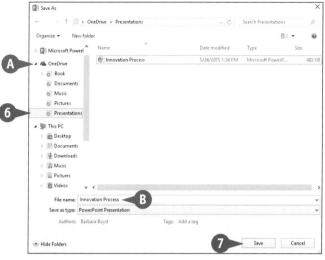

TIPS

I want some people to have permission to edit and others to only view my presentation. Can I do that?

Yes, but you must compose two different emails. Repeat the process, but change the recipients, the message, and the choice in Step **9** from Can Edit to **Can view**. Click **Share**, and PowerPoint gives those people viewing permission.

What do I do when a reviewer returns my presentation file?

Open the email and click the down arrow next to the file name. Click **Save As**, choose the folder to hold the file, and click **Save**. Rename the file to distinguish it from what you sent to the reviewers — for example, add the reviewer's initials to the name or "v2" for version 2.

Add and Delete Comments

If you have been asked to review a presentation or you want to mark up your own presentation, you can use the Comments feature to document your notations. PowerPoint identifies each comment with a marker, making it easy for the presentation designer to find and consider each comment. Each comment contains the name of the person making the comment and the date, and the comment can be attached to a slide or an object on the slide. After you add your comments, save the file and the presentation comments are ready for review.

Add and Delete Comments

1 Select a slide in Normal view.

2 Click the **Review** tab.

3 Click **New Comment**.

The Comments task pane appears.

Ⓐ A comment marker (💬) appears on the slide.

4 Type the comment text.

5 Press **Enter**.

Note: You can click and drag the comment marker to move it.

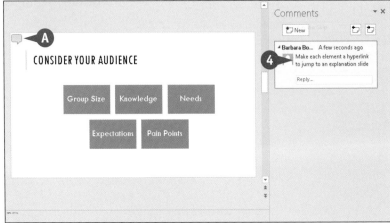

6 Click an object on the slide.

7 Click **New**.

B A comment marker appears on the object.

8 Type the comment text, and press Enter.

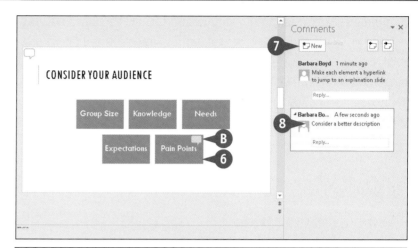

9 Position the mouse pointer over a comment and click the **Delete** icon (✗) that appears.

PowerPoint deletes the comment.

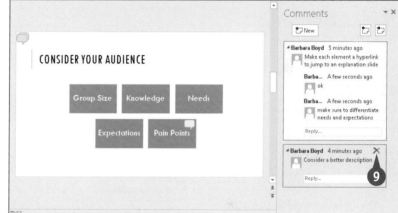

TIPS

I noticed some misspellings in the comments. How do I change them?

Select a comment by clicking either the comment marker or the comment in the Comments pane. Click the text once to select all the text, and click again to insert the insertion point in the text. Edit the text and press Enter.

Why do some comment markers overlap a little and others overlap almost completely?

Comment markers that overlap almost completely are comments and their replies, which are grouped tightly; clicking these markers selects them all. Comment markers grouped loosely and that barely overlap are different comments on the same slide or object — you can select them individually.

Review Comments

Comments are a great way to give and receive feedback without changing the presentation. After you receive feedback — or make a few notes on your own presentation — you can look through the presentation file, read the individual notes, and decide whether to make any changes based on them. You can then delete (throw away) individual comments as you review them, or delete all comments on a slide or in the presentation. You can also show or hide comments — that way, you can design your presentation without distractions but come back to comments at a later time if needed.

Review Comments

1. Select a slide with a comment in Normal view.

2. Click the **Review** tab.

3. Click **Show Comments**.

   Show Markup is checked by default.

4. Click **Comments Pane**.

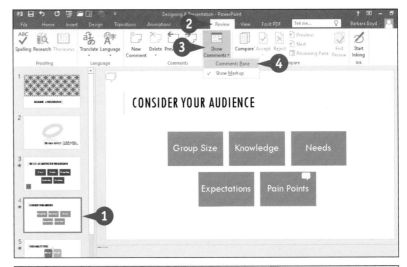

   The Comments pane and all comments appear.

5. Click a comment marker.

   The comment appears selected in the Comments pane.

6. Click a **Reply** text box.

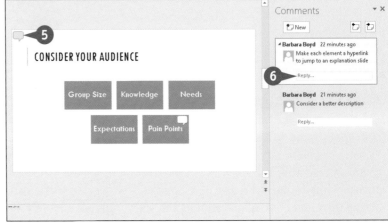

⑦ Type a reply.

⑧ Press `Enter`.

Ⓐ Note that the comment and its reply are grouped together.

⑨ Click the **Next Comment** button (🗗).

Note: You can use the Next Comment (🗗) and Previous Comment (🗗) buttons to move from one comment to another, as well as from slide to slide.

When you reach the last comment on a slide, PowerPoint moves to the next comment within the presentation, which may be on the next slide or another slide farther ahead.

Ⓑ You can click the **Expand** icon (▷) to see a collapsed comment and related replies.

Ⓒ You can click the **Collapse** icon (◢) to collapse a comment and its associated replies.

TIP

There are many comments on my presentation. Is there a way to delete all of them simultaneously instead of clicking the delete button for each one?

Yes. Follow these steps:

① Click the **Review** tab.

② Click the **Delete** down arrow (▼).

③ Click **Delete All Comments and Ink on This Slide** to delete the comments on the current slide or **Delete All Comments and Ink in This Presentation** to delete comments in the entire presentation.

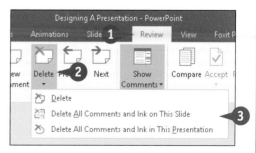

Compare Presentations

Comparing presentations is an alternative to sharing a file on OneDrive where everyone comments on the same file. PowerPoint enables you to compare a reviewed presentation with the original. You can email a copy of your presentation to peers, and allow them to review and edit it — no need to do anything special, just send it. After everyone makes changes, you can compare them all to the original, making it unnecessary to read the entire presentation thoroughly all over again — PowerPoint points out the changes for you. Then, you can accept or reject their changes.

Compare Presentations

1 Open the original presentation that you sent to others for review.

2 Click the **Review** tab while in Normal view.

3 Click **Compare**.

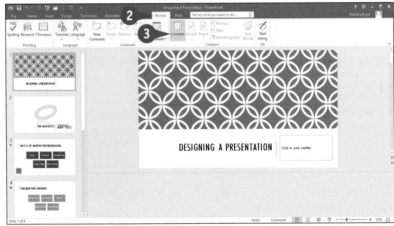

The Choose File to Merge with Current Presentation dialog box appears.

4 Click the folder that contains the edited presentation.

5 Click the presentation that others have edited.

Note: The name of the edited presentation does not need to be the same as the original. In fact, you probably want to give reviewed copies a different name to distinguish them from the original.

6 Click **Merge**.

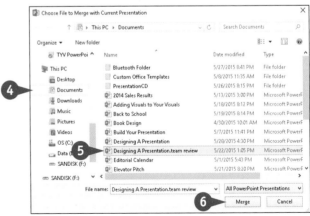

7 In the Reviewing pane, click a slide with changes, or click **Next** to go to the first change.

A Changes are marked with an icon (). Positioning the mouse pointer over a marker reveals change details.

B Comments and changes to slides appear here.

C Changes to the presentation appear here.

8 Click a marker ().

9 Click the **Accept** down arrow (▼).

10 Click a revision choice.

Accepted changes display check marks in both the change icon and the Revision pane.

11 Click **Previous** or **Next** to go to other changes.

12 Click **End Review**.

13 In the dialog box that appears, click Yes to end the review.

Note: PowerPoint rejects any unaccepted changes.

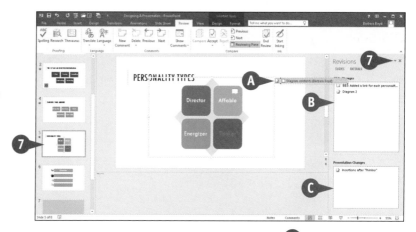

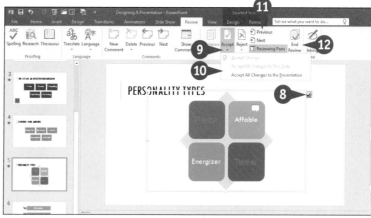

TIPS

Can I see the slides from the edited presentation?

Yes. The Reviewing pane automatically appears with the Details tab displayed. Click the **Slides** tab in the Reviewing pane, and PowerPoint shows you the slide from the edited presentation that correlates to the slide that you have selected in your presentation.

Can I reverse accepting a change?

Yes. Accepted changes display check marks. Click an accepted change and then click the **Reject** command button on the Review tab. Any changes that are not accepted are automatically rejected when you end the review; however, you can always run the comparison again.

Protect a Presentation

You may not want anybody else to present your slide show, or you may not want others to see how you designed it. Your presentation may have sensitive information that you do not want other people to access. PowerPoint enables you to password-protect your presentation so that only those with the proper credentials can open it. Remember to record the password, though — you will want to open it yourself!

Protect a Presentation

1 Click the **File** tab to show Backstage view.

2 Click **Info**.

3 Click **Protect Presentation**.

4 Click **Encrypt with Password**.

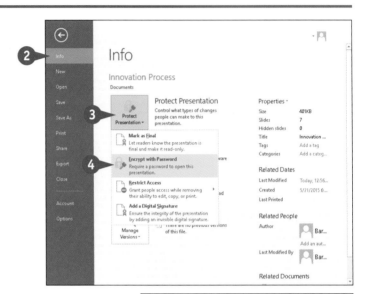

The Encrypt Document dialog box appears.

5 Type a password.

6 Click **OK**.

The Confirm Password dialog box appears.

7 Reenter the password typed in Step **5**.

8 Click **OK**.

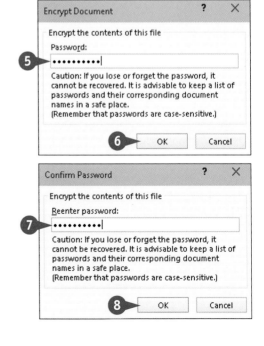

PowerPoint protects the presentation.

9 Click **Close**.

10 Open the presentation.

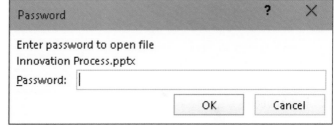

PowerPoint asks for the password.

TIPS

How can I remove the password?
You go through the same process as when you add a password. However, when the Encrypt Document dialog box appears, it displays an encoded password. Delete the encoded password and click **OK**. The presentation then becomes unprotected.

What is the Mark as Final item on the Protect Presentation menu?
The Mark as Final feature shows you and others that the presentation is finished and ready for presenting. The Save command is no longer available, and PowerPoint places a Marked as Final icon in the status bar. When you open a presentation with this status, a message appears, informing you of the status. You can click the **Edit Anyway** button to edit and save the presentation.

Select a Show Type and Show Options

PowerPoint offers options to best meet your needs depending on how and where you will give your presentation — for example, whether you will give it in person or let someone watch it alone and click through the slides at his own pace. Or you can choose the color of the on-screen laser so it contrasts with your slide background. You should check these settings so you know exactly what will happen when you run your presentation.

Select a Show Type and Show Options

1 In Normal view, click the **Slide Show** tab.

2 Click **Set Up Slide Show**.

The Set Up Show dialog box appears.

3 Click an option to select whether you want a speaker to present your slide show, a person to view it on a computer, or many people to view it at a kiosk (○ changes to ◉).

4 In the Show Slides section, click the **All** option to view your entire slide deck or click the **From** option (○ changes to ◉) and click the spinner icons (⬍) to choose the specific range of slides you want to include in your slide show.

5 Click the **Pen color** button (🖊▾) and select a color from the palette.

6 Click the **Laser pointer color** button (🖊▾) and select a color from the palette.

Note: See Chapter 13 to learn about Pen annotations and the Laser Pointer.

7 Click one or more options to select whether you want your show to loop continuously, run without narration, or run without animation (☐ changes to ☑).

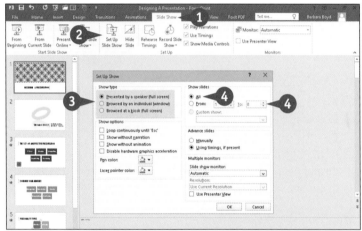

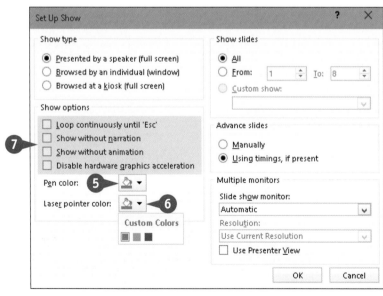

⑧ Click either the **Manually** option (slides advance with a mouse click) or click the **Using timings, if present** option (⚪ changes to ⦿).

Note: The **Using timings, if present** option has an effect only if you set any slide timings. Timings, such as setting a slide to advance automatically or after you rehearse timing the show, do not work if you set this option to **Manually**.

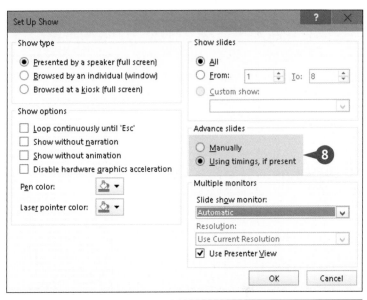

⑨ Click **Use Presenter View** (☐ changes to ☑) to take advantage of Presenter View tools during your presentation. See Chapter 13 to learn more.

⑩ Click **OK**.

PowerPoint applies your new settings and closes the dialog box.

⑪ Click the **Save** icon (💾) to save the settings.

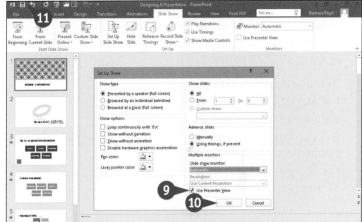

TIPS

Why would I want to show my presentation without animation?

Animations are fun, but on computers lacking adequate resources, they may run slowly and delay your show. If you are using an older computer to present your show, preview it to be sure that animations run smoothly. If they do not, change this setting to avoid any problems.

What is a loop and why would I use it?

Looping is a term for running media, such as songs or videos, over and over again from beginning to end. If you plan to show your presentation at an informational booth or kiosk, where people may stop, watch a bit, and then move on, you probably want the presentation to loop.

Specify Slides to Include

Although you can select a range of slides by using the Set Up Slide Show options as explained in the previous section, you may want to show only some non-sequential slides. For example, you may want to show only the beginning, summary, and conclusion of a long slide show to executives who do not need to see details, but show the entire presentation to middle management. To create two presentations from one slide deck, you can create a custom slide show that you can quickly and easily access and play.

Specify Slides to Include

1 In Normal view, click the **Slide Show** tab.

2 Click **Custom Slide Show**.

3 Click **Custom Shows**.

The Custom Shows dialog box appears.

4 Click **New**.

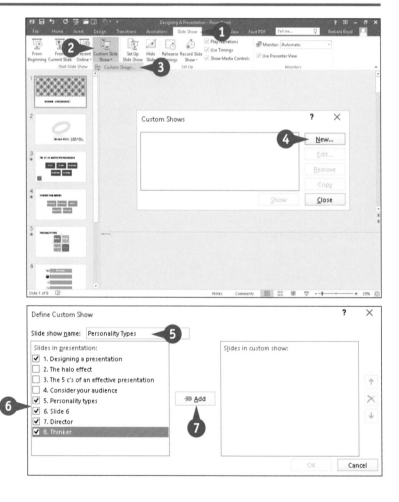

The Define Custom Show dialog box appears.

5 Type a name in the **Slide show name** text box.

6 Click the slides that you want in your custom slide show (☐ changes to ☑).

7 Click **Add**.

A PowerPoint adds the slides to the Slides in Custom Show list.

8 Click **OK**.

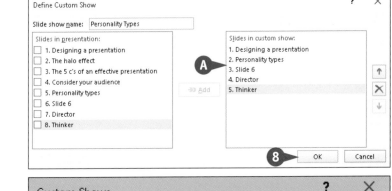

B PowerPoint adds the custom show to the list.

9 Click **Close**.

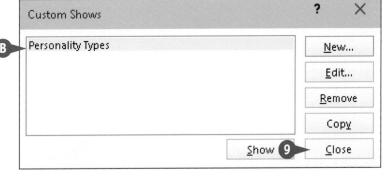

10 Click **Custom Slide Show**.

The menu lists all custom slide shows for this particular presentation.

11 Click the custom show you want to present.

PowerPoint starts your custom slide show.

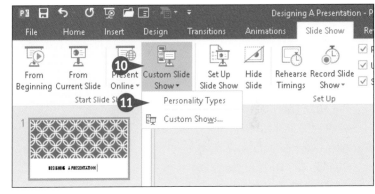

TIPS

Can I modify my custom show?

Yes. Repeat Steps **1** to **3**, click your custom show in the list, and then click **Edit.** Add slides by repeating Steps **6** and **7**; delete or move slides by clicking them and then pressing **Delete** (✕) or the **Move Up** (⬆) or **Move Down** (⬇) buttons. Click **OK** when you finish making changes.

What if I do not want to show a slide located in the middle of my presentation?

With a large presentation, it may be inconvenient to build a custom show that excludes only one slide. In this case, just hide the slide. Change to Slide Sorter view, right-click the slide, and then click **Hide Slide** on the shortcut menu.

Rehearse Timing

Rehearsal is a key component of presentation preparation, and saying all you want to say in your allotted time takes practice. You can use the Rehearse Timings feature during your rehearsals to ensure that your presentation takes the proper amount of time to deliver. If you set up slides to advance automatically during your slide show, Rehearse Timing is a good way to make sure you allow enough time for each slide.

Rehearse Timing

1 Click the **Slide Show** tab.

2 Click **Rehearse Timings**.

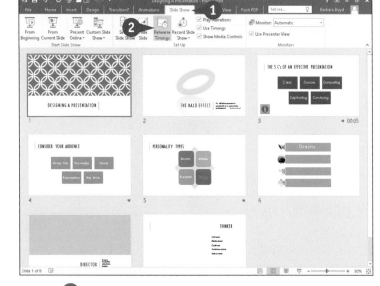

The slide show begins and the Recording toolbar appears.

3 Rehearse the slide narrative, clicking the **Next** button (→) to advance the slide.

A This shows the elapsed time of the current slide.

B This shows the elapsed time of the entire show.

C Click **Repeat** (↻) to start the timing over for the current slide.

D Click the **Close** button (✕) to exit the slide show early.

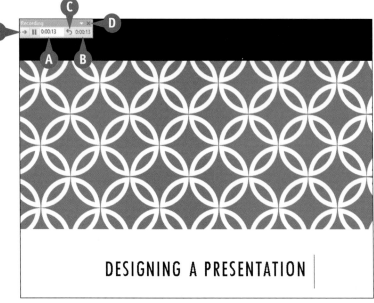

④ Click the **Pause** button (▮▮) to suspend the timing.

The Recording Paused dialog box appears.

⑤ Click **Resume Recording**.

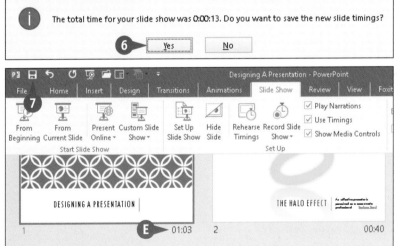

After the last slide — or if you press `Esc` — a message box asks if you want to save the timings.

⑥ Click **Yes** to save the timings, or click **No** to exit the rehearsal without saving the timings.

The presentation appears in Design view.

Ⓔ The timing applied to each slide appears below its thumbnail.

⑦ Click the **Save** icon (🖫) to save the timings.

TIP

Are rehearsing timings and recording a slide show basically the same thing?
No. Although you can have slides advance automatically through a slide show if you either rehearse timing or record a show, the similarities stop there. Rehearse timing records the timing of each slide as an evaluation and planning tool. You can record a narrative and the movements of the laser pointer only when you record the show. You usually record a show because you are absent when the slide show runs — an important difference. If the slide show runs on a kiosk or on someone's computer, you want to record a narration and the movements of the laser pointer.

Record a Narration

If you do intend to show your PowerPoint presentation at a kiosk or share it through email or a website, you can — and probably should — record a narration that talks the viewer through your key points. Recording a slide show also sets up your presentation to advance automatically at the end of each slide's narration. This nice feature gives you the option to present the show in person, or to personalize a presentation when you are not physically there. You do not necessarily need to record the entire presentation; you can record just a few slides if you choose.

Record a Narration

1 If your computer does not have a built-in microphone, plug a microphone into your computer.

2 Click the **Slide Show** tab.

3 Click **Record Slide Show**.

The Record Slide Show dialog box appears.

4 Click to enable (☑) both options.

5 Click **Start Recording**.

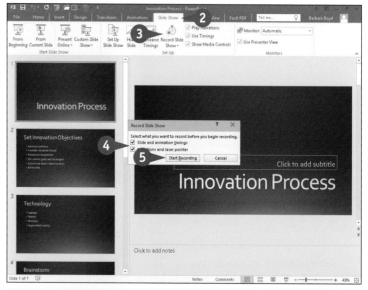

The slide show begins and the Recording toolbar appears.

6 Narrate the slide, speaking clearly into the microphone.

A Hover the mouse pointer in the lower-left corner to reveal on-screen controls that will be invisible during playback.

B Click the pen icon (▨) to switch between laser, pen, and highlighter, which enable you to write on the slide while presenting.

7 Click the **Next** button (▶) to advance the slide.

8 Press Ctrl while clicking the primary mouse button to display the laser pointer, and then drag it across the screen to show items of interest.

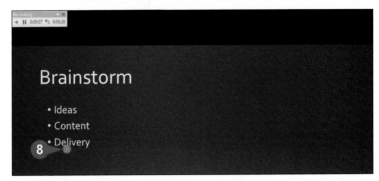

When the slide show ends, Design view reappears.

C The timing applied to each slide appears below its thumbnail.

D Slides with narration display a speaker icon (🔊).

9 Click to enable (✔) both **Play Narrations** and **Use Timings**.

10 Click the **Save** icon (🖫) to save the narration.

11 Click **From Beginning**, sit back, watch, and listen to the automated slide show.

TIP

Can I clear timings and narrations?

Yes. Follow these steps:

1 Click the **Slide Show** tab.

2 Click the **Record Slide Show** down arrow (▼).

3 Click **Clear**.

4 Click an item from the menu.

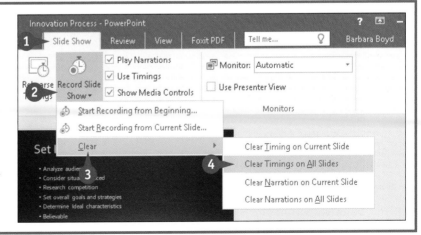

CHAPTER 13

Presenting a Slide Show

You have created an effective, informative slide show, but the real work is still to come — presenting. PowerPoint offers many tools to help you give a flawless presentation. Familiarity with them will enable you to choose those that best meet your needs and help you present the slide show smoothly.

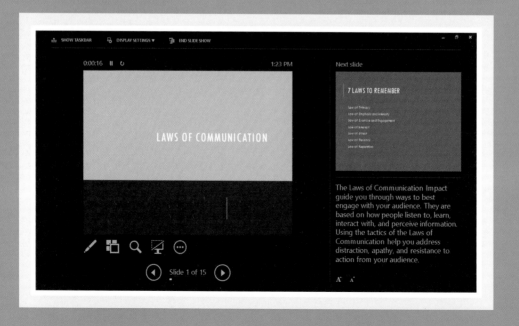

Prepare to Present

A successful presentation — live or recorded — requires solid content, good design, and a prepared presenter. Aside from making sure your presentation is error free, you want to know your material and presentation environment, and test the equipment you will use — ideally in the location where you will be presenting. The audience will assess your professionalism and the quality of your presentation as well as the ideas you are trying to convey. Rigorous practice and repetition will help you become familiar with the message of your presentation and the tools you use so you can give the best show possible.

Check Your Presentation for Errors

Checking your slides for details such as spelling, grammar, and typos can save you a lot of embarrassment at showtime. Use the presentation outline to review the text so you are not distracted by design elements, and take advantage of the PowerPoint tools mentioned in Chapter 4, such as the spelling and grammar checker, thesaurus, and research tool. In addition, ask a friend or colleague to proofread the presentation for textual errors and to provide feedback on the design and flow of your ideas.

Rehearse the Slide Show

Before you present it to an audience, rehearse your presentation many times — rehearse in front of a friend or record yourself. You may discover undesirable mannerisms or expressions that you want to avoid. Know your material so you can anticipate each slide, know what comes next, and be able to jump to another slide if the audience requests specifics. Avoid reading from the slide show, and use the Notes feature only to prompt your memory for specific details. Finishing your presentation in the allotted time is considered courteous. Use the Rehearse Timings feature in PowerPoint to check your timing, and make changes accordingly.

Know Your Presentation Space

To avoid problems during your presentation, test your equipment before the presentation, and visit the site if you can. Knowing the size of the room, the acoustics, and the layout of the stage and audience seating can help you prepare. Try to meet your audience before the presentation so you can collect preliminary questions and identify people who need extra attention.

Set Up Your Show

Be sure to check slide show settings explained in Chapter 16. Before the presentation, you should set up the format for the slide show, such as a live presentation versus one shown at a kiosk, which slides to include (see Chapter 9), monitors and resolution, and how you will control the advancement of the slides. Even if you are using your own laptop, it could crash, so bring a backup of your presentation. Package your presentation and associated files with the PowerPoint viewer, as explained in Chapter 14, in case you find yourself on a computer without PowerPoint.

Start and End a Show

You have researched, written, designed, and rehearsed. Now, the day has arrived — showtime! All you need is to start the slide show and navigate through it. You can pause or stop the show at any time, and restart to view all the remaining slides in your presentation. If you are presenting to a small group, you probably want to start the show and have the first slide or a black screen visible before the audience arrives. With a larger group, consider showing a video loop or contact information while the audience is settling in.

Start and End a Show

1 Click the **Slide Show** tab.

2 Ensure that **Show Media Controls** is enabled (☑).

3 Click **From Beginning**.

Note: You can also press F5 to begin the show.

The slide show begins.

When you move the mouse pointer, the on-screen toolbar appears faintly in the lower left corner.

4 To end the show before you reach the last slide, click the **Options** icon (⋯) on the on-screen toolbar.

5 Click **End Show**.

Note: You can also end the slide show by pressing Esc.

The slide show closes.

Navigate Among Slides

No slide show would be any good without the ability to move through the slides. You can use the shortcut menu or the Slide Show on-screen toolbar, or click the screen to move through a slide show. You can move back or forward one slide at a time, or you can pick a specific slide to show. You can also press the keyboard arrows to move forward and backward through the slide show. All these options are also available in Presenter view, which is covered later in this chapter.

Navigate Among Slides

1 With your presentation in Slide Show view, click the **Next** icon (▶) to advance the slide.

Note: You can also click the slide or press ➡ to advance the slide. Keep in mind clicking the slide also runs animations.

2 Click the **Previous** icon (◀) to move to the previous slide.

Note: You can also press ⬅ to move to the previous slide.

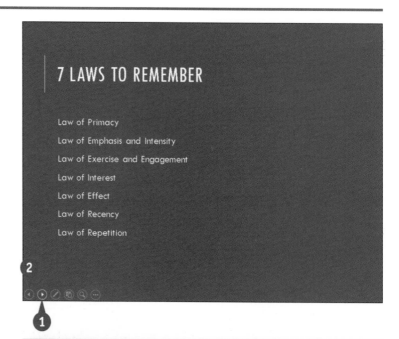

The slides advance.

3 Click the **All Slides** icon (▣).

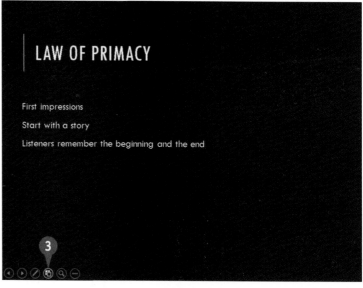

All slides appear.

Ⓐ Click the **Back** button (⬅) to return to the current slide.

Ⓑ Click and drag the slider to zoom in or out, resizing the thumbnails.

④ Click the slide you want to show.

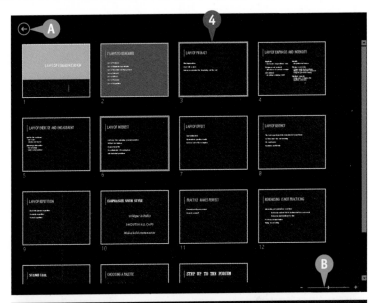

The selected slide appears.

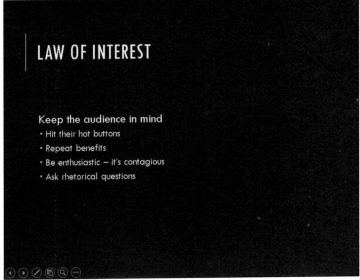

Can I use a tablet to run my presentation, and if so, are the commands the same?

Yes, you can install PowerPoint 2016 on your tablet and then access your presentations from your OneDrive account. Your tablet's portability means you have access to your slide shows anytime, anywhere. You can give your presentation to one or two people while looking at the slides on your tablet, or, with some technical assistance, connect it to a projector or monitor. The on-screen commands are similar to the computer version of PowerPoint, although you tap the screen rather than use the mouse or trackpad. Swipe left and right to move between slides.

Zoom In

Ideally, you want all the text and objects on a slide to be easily visible to your audience members without them having to strain to see. However, someone may ask to get a better look at the details of an image. If your audience has trouble seeing something on a slide, you can zoom in on the slide with a click of the on-screen toolbar during the slide show. After zooming, you can move the zoom area to any region of the slide with a simple click and drag of the mouse.

Zoom In

1 With your presentation in Slide Show view, click the **Zoom** icon (🔍) on the on-screen toolbar.

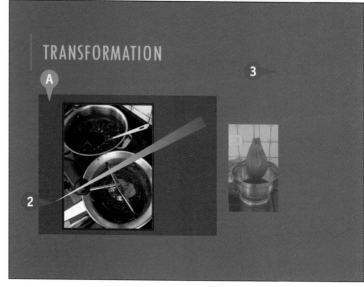

Ⓐ A marquee appears, showing the zoom area. The mouse pointer changes to a zoom magnifying glass.

2 Drag the marquee with the zoom magnifying glass to the area of interest.

3 Click the screen.

Ⓑ PowerPoint zooms in on the marquee area. The 🔍 changes to a hand icon.

④ Click and drag a hand icon to any area of the slide to move the zoom area.

Press `Esc` or right-click the mouse to return to the full-screen view.

TIPS

The slides seem to advance properly when I use the Next icon on the on-screen toolbar, but not when I click the slide. Why not?

You may have some animations on the slide that run when you click the slide instead of advancing the slide. Also make sure that you enable (☑) **On Mouse Click** on the Transitions tab.

I set up the slide show to advance slides automatically, but sometimes I want to advance faster. Can I change this setting?

Yes. Enable (☑) the **On Mouse Click** option on the Transitions tab. The slide will advance automatically and also when you click either the slide or the **Next** icon (▶) on the on-screen toolbar.

Use the Pointer

To present a truly professional slide show, you should use a laser pointer to emphasize a specific point or part of an image. PowerPoint enables you to turn the mouse pointer into an on-screen laser pointer when you are showing your slides. The laser pointer is a great way to draw your audience's attention to a particular spot on a slide. You can quickly and easily enable and use the laser pointer during your slide show to point out something with flair and style.

Use the Pointer

1 With your presentation in Slide Show view, click the **Options** icon (⬛) on the on-screen toolbar.

2 Click **Arrow Options**.

3 Click a setting from the menu.

Automatic shows the mouse pointer, but hides it when inactive; **Visible** shows the mouse pointer continuously; **Hidden** hides the mouse pointer continuously.

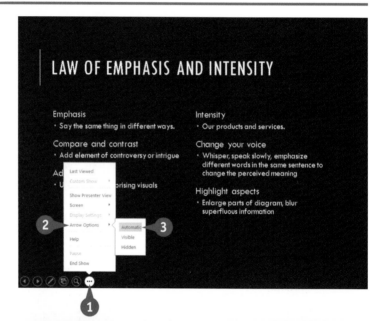

4 Click the **Pen** icon (✏) on the on-screen toolbar.

5 Click **Laser Pointer**.

The mouse pointer changes to the laser pointer, and the laser pointer appears continuously.

Note: You can change the laser pointer color by clicking **Set Up Slide Show** on the Slide Show tab, as explained in Chapter 12.

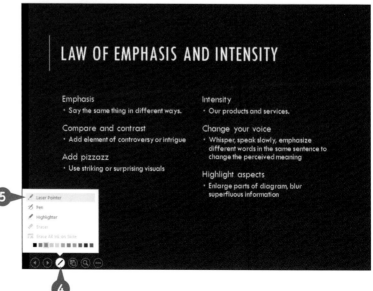

6 Drag the mouse around the area you want to identify on-screen.

7 Position the pointer over the on-screen toolbar.

The pointer temporarily changes back to the mouse pointer.

8 Click the **Next** icon (▶).

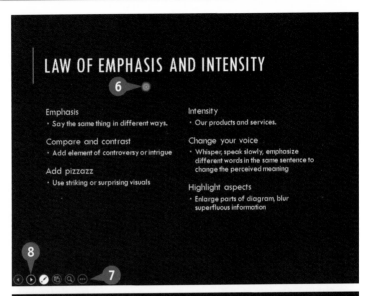

9 The slide advances and the pointer changes back to the laser pointer.

Note: Press Esc. The laser pointer changes to the mouse pointer.

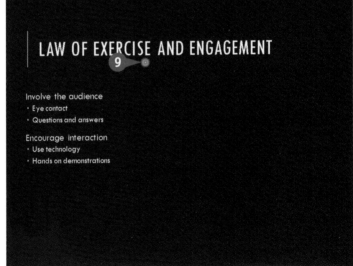

Is there an easier way to turn on the laser pointer?
Yes. There are two ways: Press Ctrl+L to switch to the laser pointer, then press Ctrl+A to return to the mouse pointer. To use the laser pointer briefly, press Ctrl, press the primary mouse button, and then drag the mouse to move it. When you release the mouse button or Ctrl, the mouse pointer comes back.

I hid the mouse pointer arrow and now cannot find the on-screen toolbar. What should I do?
Right-click anywhere on the screen to open a contextual menu. Click **Pointer Options**, then **Arrow Options**, and then **Automatic** or **Visible**. The mouse pointer reappears.

Mark Up with Pen and Highlighter

With the pen tool, PowerPoint enables you to highlight or annotate important points in the slide show during your presentation. You can choose Pen for a thin, opaque line, or Highlighter, which gives you a thicker, translucent line. You can also choose a color for both. You can save annotations so they appear the next time you present your slide show — if that option is enabled in PowerPoint Options (see Chapter 16). If you present with a tablet, consider using a stylus, which is often easier to use than your finger for writing.

Mark Up with Pen and Highlighter

1 With your presentation in Slide Show view, click the **Pen** icon (▨) on the on-screen toolbar.

2 Click **Pen**.

The pointer changes to a point of color on the screen.

A You can click to change the color of the Pen or Highlighter.

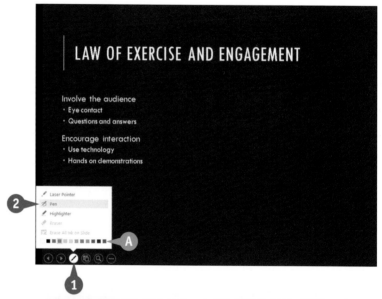

3 Click and drag on the screen around the area you want to identify.

A line appears where you dragged the mouse.

Press Esc to turn off the Pen.

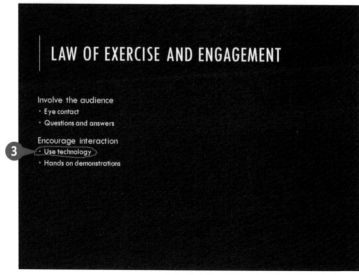

4 Click the **Pen** icon () on the on-screen toolbar.

5 Click **Highlighter**.

The pointer changes to a rectangular patch of color on the screen.

6 Click and drag on the screen over the area you want to highlight.

A thick, translucent line appears where you dragged the mouse.

7 Press Esc to turn off the Highlighter.

8 Press Esc to exit the slide show.

PowerPoint asks if you want to save your annotations.

9 Click **Keep** or **Discard**.

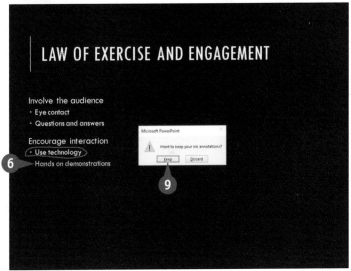

TIPS

Why can I not seem to erase my annotations?

You can erase annotations only during the current session of your slide show. If you exited the slide show and saved the annotations when prompted, they are permanent and you cannot erase them the next time you view the slide show.

Why does PowerPoint exit the slide show when I press Esc to clear the Pen?

You may have pressed Esc a second time, which exits the slide show. Be patient; it sometimes takes a few seconds for the Pen or Highlighter to change back to the mouse pointer. You may need to move the mouse to see the pointer if your on-screen arrow option is set to Automatic, which hides the pointer when inactive.

Erase Annotations

When you work with the Pen and Highlighter tools to mark up a slide, in essence the slide becomes a whiteboard or blackboard. These tools enable you to circle or highlight many things in your slide show. However, you may want to remove some markings from a slide if you want to use the slide show for another presentation, or if you need more room on a slide where there are too many markings. You can remove annotations from the slide using a tool in the on-screen toolbar.

Erase Annotations

1 With your presentation in Slide Show view, click the **Pen** icon (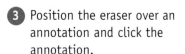) on the on-screen toolbar.

2 Click **Eraser**.

The Pen icon changes to an Eraser icon (⬤) and the mouse pointer changes to an eraser.

A You can click **Erase All Ink on Slide** to remove all annotations from the current slide.

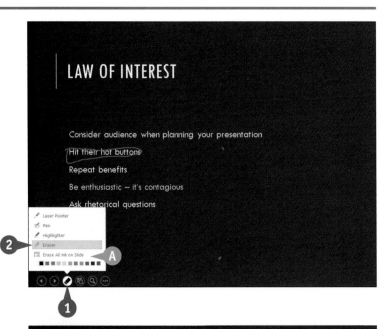

3 Position the eraser over an annotation and click the annotation.

The annotation disappears.

4 Press Esc to clear the eraser.

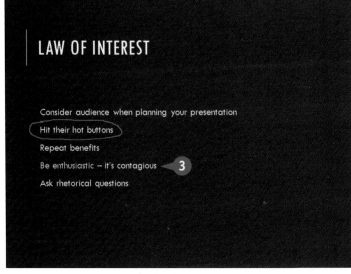

Display Slide Show Help

Even with multiple rehearsals and equipment checks, problems may arise during your presentation, and you may not know how to repair them. If you need help running your show after starting it, you do not need to stop the show to open PowerPoint Help. The slide show on-screen help shows shortcuts for running the show and managing presentation features such as pointer options. If you are using Presenter view, you can open the on-screen help for the slide show on the Presenter view screen on your laptop without the audience ever seeing it.

Display Slide Show Help

1 With your presentation in Slide Show view, click the **Options** icon (⬤) on the toolbar.

Note: You can also right-click the screen to display the shortcut menu.

2 Click **Help**.

Note: You can also press F1 during the slide show to see Help.

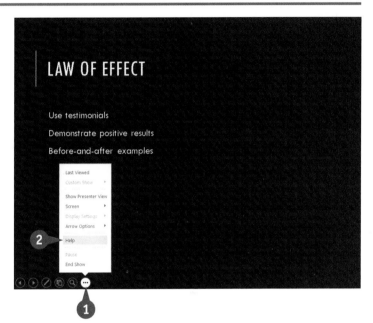

The Slide Show Help window appears.

A PowerPoint groups the shortcuts with a tab for each category.

3 Look up the shortcut to perform the procedure you want.

The shortcut appears in the left column and the description in the right.

4 When you finish, click **OK**.

The Help window closes.

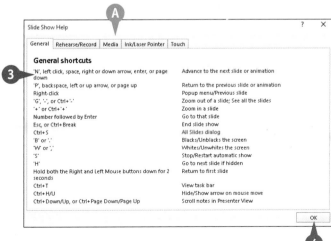

Enable Presenter View

Presenter view enables you to view your presentation complete with speaker notes and timer on your computer, while the audience sees only the slide show on the main screen. With Presenter view, the slide show controls are continuously visible and accessible, and PowerPoint Help shows only on your monitor. If you need to go to the All Slides view to go to a particular slide, only you see it. A timer shows the elapsed time, and you can see both the current and the next slide.

Enable Presenter View

1 Click the **Slide Show** tab.

2 Click **Use Presenter View**
(☐ changes to ☑).

3 Click **From Beginning** to begin
the slide show.

Your laptop shows Presenter view.

Note: If you want to see Presenter view without connecting your computer to a monitor or projector, press **Alt** + **Shift** + **F5**.

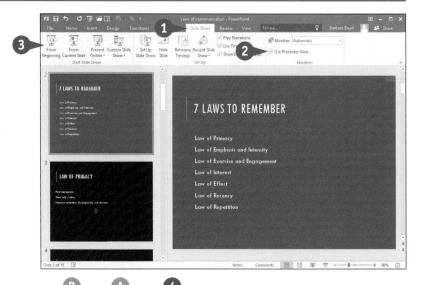

Ⓐ You can click **Display Settings** to specify which screen shows the main show and which screen shows Presenter view.

Ⓑ You can click **Show Taskbar** to switch to a different program.

Ⓒ You can click **Black Screen** (⬛) to display a black screen.

4 Click **End Slide Show**.

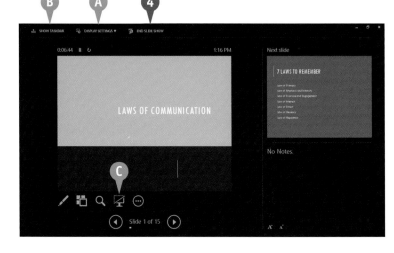

Use Presenter View

During a live presentation, you want to give the audience your full attention, which means facing the audience and not looking at the projector screen. If you connect your laptop to a projector or monitor, you can use Presenter view. With Presenter view, you see the slide currently being viewed by the audience, the next slide, any notes you made, and a suite of tools specifically designed to help you give a professional presentation. There is no need to search for tools on the main screen or have the audience watch you search for another slide. Everything is visible and available in Presenter view.

Ⓐ Toolbar

The toolbar is nearly identical to the on-screen toolbar and is always visible in Presenter view.

Ⓑ Command Buttons

These commands are conveniently visible in Presenter view, but hidden on the main screen.

Ⓒ Timer

The timer shows the elapsed time of the show, and you can pause and restart it.

Ⓓ Notes

Notes are visible and you can change their font size.

Ⓔ Slide Preview

You can see the next slide and collect your thoughts in preparation.

Ⓕ Advance Slides

You can advance slides with confidence by clicking buttons rather than slides.

Switch to a Different Program

You can switch to a different program and work with it during a slide show. For example, if you are giving a presentation on Microsoft Word, you may need to go to Word to demonstrate a feature that you are showing in your slide show. Perhaps someone asks to see the data for a chart and you want to show it during the slide show. You can quickly and easily switch to that other program, work with it, and then return to your slide show. To return to your slide show, you can minimize or close the other program.

Switch to a Different Program

1 With your presentation in Slide Show view, click the **Options** icon (⬚).

2 Click **Screen**.

3 Click **Show Taskbar**.

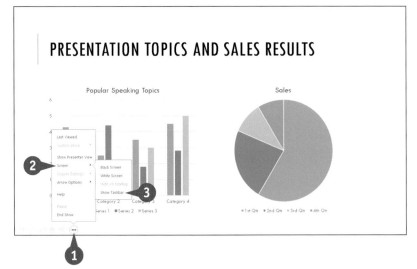

The Windows taskbar appears.

4 Click an open program on the taskbar.

This example clicks Excel.

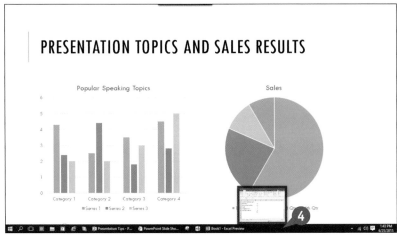

The program you clicked appears on the screen.

5 To return to your slide show, find the slide show on the taskbar and click it.

A You can also click the **Close** button (✕) to close the program, Excel in this example, or the **Minimize** button (—) to minimize the program.

The slide show reappears.

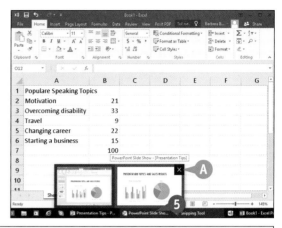

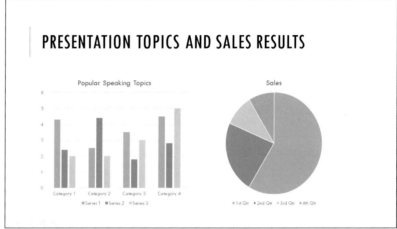

PRESENTATION TOPICS AND SALES RESULTS

TIPS

Can I open a program during a slide show?
Yes. When the taskbar appears, you can use it in any way that you normally would, including to go to the Windows Start screen to open a program. You can also press ⊞ to switch between the Windows Start screen and the slide show.

Is there another way to switch to a different program?
Yes. If you are using a laptop and the audience is watching on a projector screen or monitor, you can use Presenter view. Presenter view has a command button for this very purpose. You can switch to another program with one click of the mouse.

CHAPTER 14

Sharing a Presentation

PowerPoint enables you to share your presentation in varied formats and across diverse venues. You can save your slide show in different file formats, such as a PDF, Word document, or video file. You can also publish slides as JPEG or TIFF graphics. You can share them via email or on a cloud-based website.

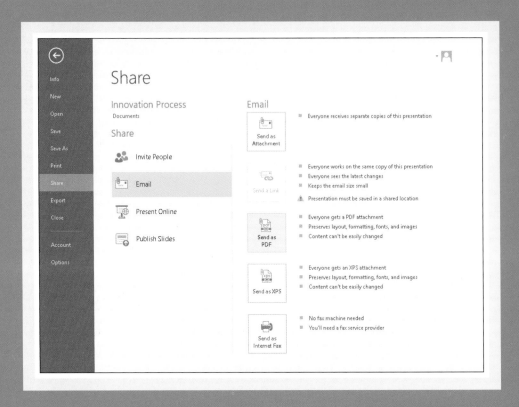

Make a PDF Document from a Presentation

You can make a PDF (portable document format) file from your presentation so that anyone with a PDF reader can view it — but not make changes. Because a PDF file is an image of your slide show, it can be viewed on virtually any computer, regardless of its operating system, and on most tablets and smartphones. Another benefit of a PDF file is that you can print it on paper. By saving a presentation as a PDF file, you preserve your presentation's fonts, formatting, and images.

Make a PDF Document from a Presentation

1 Click the **File** tab to show Backstage view.

2 Click **Export**.

3 Click **Create PDF/XPS Document**.

4 Click **Create PDF/XPS**.

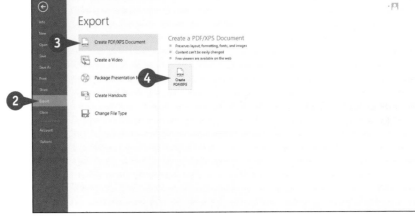

The Publish as PDF or XPS dialog box appears.

5 Click the folder where you want to save your file.

6 Click the **File name** text box.

7 Type a name.

8 Click **Options**.

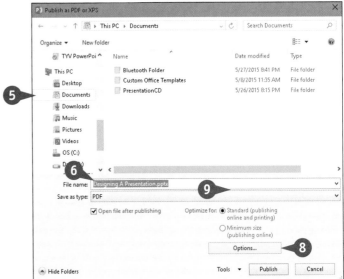

Ⓐ You can output any of the four types of printouts (see Chapter 15).

Ⓑ If you choose Handouts, you can specify the number of slides per page.

Ⓒ You can select a range of slides to print.

9 Click **OK**.

10 Click **Publish**.

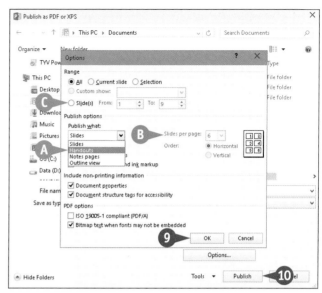

PowerPoint creates the PDF file in the specified folder and shows the status.

PowerPoint opens the file with your PDF reader.

TIPS

I do not have a PDF reader on my computer. Where can I find one?

PDF viewers are free, and most computers already have a PDF reader installed at the time of purchase. However, if you do not have one, you can go to the Adobe website, www.adobe.com, and download its Acrobat Reader.

What is the advantage to preserving the fonts, formatting, and images of my presentation?

Computers can have different sets of fonts loaded with their software. It is possible that a computer viewing your presentation does not have the font you used. Preserving the fonts, formatting, and images carries that information along with the presentation so it looks the same on any computer.

Create a Video of a Presentation

You can create a video of your presentation, which enables you to share your message even when you cannot give it in person. Almost anybody can view it because PowerPoint saves it in either a Windows Media Video (WMV) or MPEG-4 format, which can be viewed on most computers and handheld devices. A video that you make from a presentation is secure because no one can change it after the conversion process is complete; and it is a great way to present a slide show from a kiosk where you start it and let it continually loop, or on your website where visitors can watch it on demand.

Create a Video of a Presentation

1 Click the **File** tab to show Backstage view.

2 Click **Export**.

3 Click **Create a Video**.

4 Click the **Resolution** down arrow (▼).

5 Click a resolution suited to your needs.

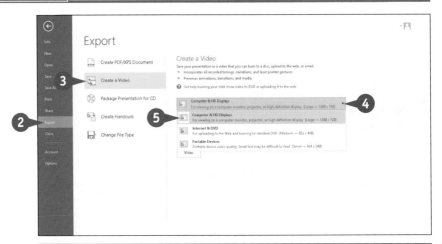

6 Click the **Timings and Narrations** down arrow (▼):

A You can click **Don't Use Recorded Timings and Narrations** if you recorded them, but do not want to use them.

B You can click **Use Recorded Timings and Narrations** if you recorded them and want to use them.

C You can click **Record Timings and Narrations** if you want to record them at this time.

Note: See Chapter 12 to learn about recording timings and narrations.

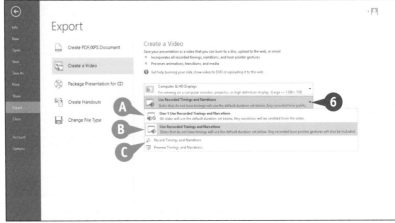

⑦ Click the text box and type a default time or use the spinner (⊕) to set it.

The default time refers to how long a slide appears if it has no timings associated with it or you chose not to use timings.

Ⓓ You can click this link for online help.

⑧ Click **Create Video**.

The Save As dialog box appears.

⑨ Click the folder where you want to save the video.

⑩ Click the **File name** text box to select it, and then type a filename.

Ⓔ You can click the drop-down arrow (▾) to change the file type.

⑪ Click **Save**.

The dialog box closes and PowerPoint creates the video in the specified folder.

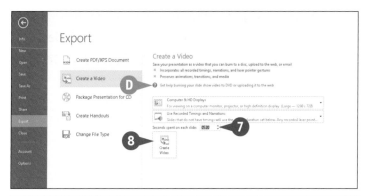

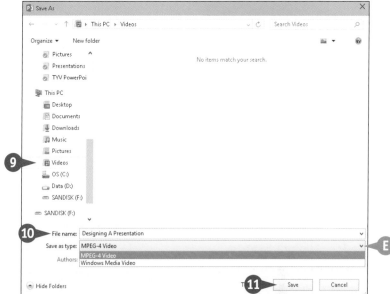

TIPS

Why does nothing seem to happen when I click Save?

PowerPoint takes a long time to make the video and does not notify you when it is done. However, while it is working, you see a status meter and Cancel button at the bottom in the status bar. When the status meter disappears, the video is done.

Why would I want to change the resolution?

The higher the resolution of your video, the bigger the file, and the more memory it takes to store it. This affects load times and sometimes the quality of playback if computer resources are limited. The Resolution drop-down list has settings for the Internet and for portable devices. You can change the resolution for your target audience.

Save a Presentation as a Slide Show

You can arrive early and set up your computer, open PowerPoint, search for your slide show, and then — finally — begin the presentation, or you can save the presentation so that it opens automatically in Slide Show view. To open it, you navigate to it with Windows Explorer, double-click it, and it opens directly to your first slide as a slide show. This is particularly convenient if you are not familiar with PowerPoint but want to present a slide show.

Save a Presentation as a Slide Show

1. Click the **File** tab to show Backstage view.

2. Click **Export**.

3. Click **Change File Type**.

4. Click **PowerPoint Show**.

5. Click **Save As**.

The Save As dialog box appears.

6. Click the folder where you want to save your file.

7. Type a filename in the **File name** text box.

8. Click **Save**.

The dialog box closes and PowerPoint creates the PowerPoint Show file in the specified folder.

9 Open File Explorer and double-click the file in the specified folder.

The file opens as a slide show.

DESIGNING A PRESENTATION

What do the different PowerPoint extensions mean?	
Extension	**Description**
PPSX	PowerPoint slide show
PPTX	PowerPoint presentation
PPTM	PowerPoint presentation with macros
POTX	PowerPoint template
PPT	PowerPoint 97-2003 format
ODP	Open Document Presentation

Are there other advantages to sending a PowerPoint Show (PPSX) to someone instead of a standard presentation (PPTX)?

Yes. If you send this format to others instead of the standard presentation format, they will not be able to see or change the details of your design. They will also not be able to copy any part of your presentation.

Package a Presentation

You can share your presentation on OneDrive or another slide-sharing website (see Chapter 12), or you can save a presentation in a format that includes a PowerPoint viewer plus any files needed to view your presentation and distribute it on a CD or flash drive. This viewer enables the presentation to be viewed on a computer that does not have PowerPoint installed on it. You probably want to record a narration for this type of presentation. The package includes both embedded and linked files, as well as embedded fonts so your presentation can be viewed as you originally intended.

Package a Presentation

1 Click the **File** tab to show Backstage view.

2 Click **Export**.

3 Click **Package Presentation for CD**.

4 Click **Package for CD**.

Note: Choose this option even if you want to put the file on a flash drive or in a folder on your computer.

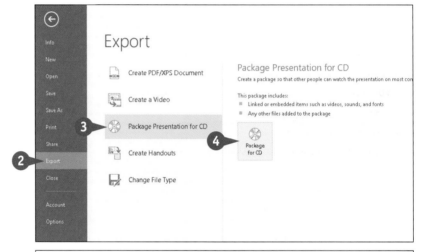

The Package for CD dialog box appears.

5 Click **Copy to Folder**.

Ⓐ You can also insert a CD in your CD drive and then click **Copy to CD** — PowerPoint burns the presentation files directly to the CD.

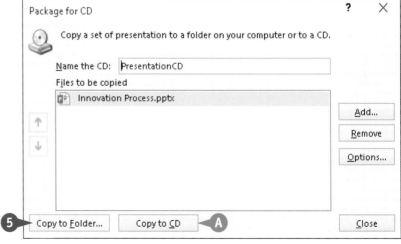

The Copy to Folder dialog box appears.

6 Type a name in the **Folder name** text box.

B Note the folder location where the presentation package will be saved. You can click **Browse** to change the location to an external drive.

7 Click **OK**.

8 Click **Yes** in reply to the message that asks, "Do you want to include linked files in your package?"

C PowerPoint creates a presentation package and saves it in the location that you specified.

Note: If you want to distribute the presentation via email, send the entire folder to your intended viewers.

D To view the slide show, double-click the presentation.

Note: If the computer does not have PowerPoint, this action opens a web page to download the PowerPoint viewer.

9 Click the **Close** button (✕) to exit.

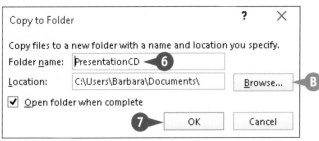

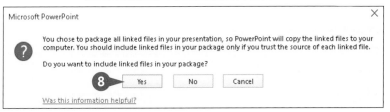

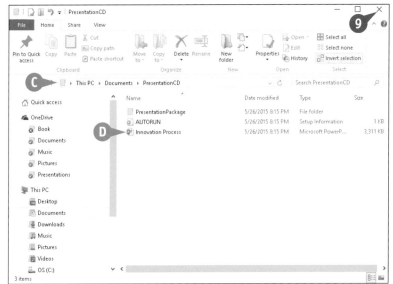

TIPS

What does the Options button do?
You can click the **Options** button to open the Options dialog box. This displays the options Linked Files and Embedded TrueType Fonts — always keep these enabled (☑). This ensures that your presentation looks the way you intended. You can also set a password to open the presentation and check for personal data that may be in the presentation.

What is the Add button for?
You can include more than one presentation in a package. Click the **Add** button and the Add File dialog box appears — use it to browse to another presentation. When you find the presentation file you want to add, click it and then click **OK**. PowerPoint adds it to the list.

Publish Slides as Graphics

You can create a graphic of one or more slides in your presentation so that you can use them for different purposes. You may want to post them on a website, use one as the cover photo of your social network profile, or make high-quality postcards to hand out at a tradeshow. You can create either PNG images or JPEG images. PNG are print quality, and JPEG are Internet or database quality. There is no need to create a new folder to hold the graphic files because PowerPoint creates a new folder during this process.

Publish Slides as Graphics

1 Click the **File** tab to show Backstage view.

2 Click **Export**.

3 Click **Change File Type**.

4 Click an image file type.

This example selects PNG Portable Network Graphics.

5 Click **Save As**.

The Save As dialog box appears.

6 Click the folder where you want to save your file.

7 Type a filename in the **File name** text box.

This example uses the filename Presentation Graphics.

8 Click **Save**.

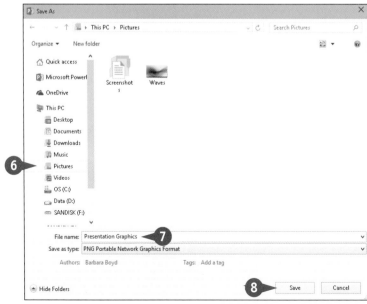

A dialog box appears.

9 Click **All Slides**, or click **Just This One** to save only the current slide.

A dialog box appears.

10 Click **OK**.

PowerPoint creates the graphics for each slide in the folder you specified.

In this example, PowerPoint created a folder called Presentation Graphics in the specified folder, and it contains the PNG graphics.

11 Navigate to the folder with File Explorer.

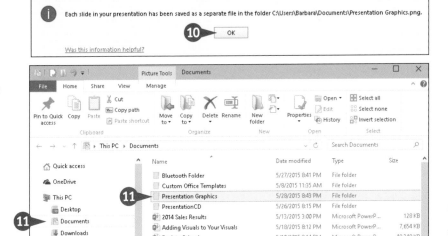

TIPS

How does the PNG image file type differ from JPEG?

A JPEG is a compressed picture type and trades image quality for smaller file size. The PNG format uses a compression format that does not trade image quality for file size. PNG produces better results for certain applications, such as printing.

I saved the graphics to the My Documents folder, but I cannot find them. Where are the files?

PowerPoint creates a folder for you, and places all the graphics in it. You will find this folder in the folder you specified (My Documents, in this case), having the same name as your presentation and containing PNG files named Slide1, Slide2, and so on.

Share the Presentation via Email

If you want someone to review your presentation and add comments or make changes, you probably want to share it on OneDrive as explained in Chapter 12. If you simply want someone to view your presentation — for example, you want to send it to a client as a follow-up to the in-person presentation you made — sending by email is a good choice. You can also create a link to the presentation manually so you can copy and paste the link in an email or other electronic document.

Share the Presentation via Email

Share via Email

Note: See Chapter 12 to learn how to share a file on OneDrive.

1 Click the **File** tab to show Backstage view.

2 Click **Share**.

3 Click **Email**.

4 Click **Send as PDF**, which preserves the fonts and design of your presentation and sends a file that cannot be easily changed.

Note: You can click **Send as Attachment**, but your presentation is sent as a PowerPoint file that can be edited.

PowerPoint converts your file to a PDF document and attaches it to a blank email message.

6 Click the **To** text box and type the email addresses of your recipients.

7 Click the message text box and type a message to the recipients.

8 Click **Send**.

The message with the attached PDF file is sent to your recipients.

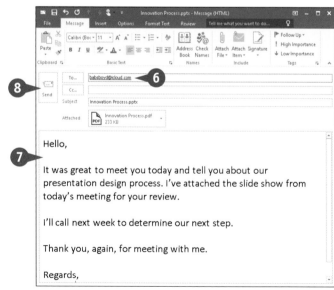

Share via a Link

Note: You must save the presentation to OneDrive before creating a link. See Chapter 12.

1 Click the **File** tab to show Backstage view.

2 Click **Share**.

3 Click **Get a Sharing Link**.

4 Click **Create Link** next to View Link to let people only look at your file, or **Edit Link** to let people make changes to your file.

A PowerPoint creates a link to the presentation on OneDrive. You can copy and paste this link into a web browser to access the presentation.

B Click **Disable Link** to make it inactive.

Note: You can paste this link to a Word or Notepad document and put it on a network drive for people to access, or you can send it to someone in an instant message.

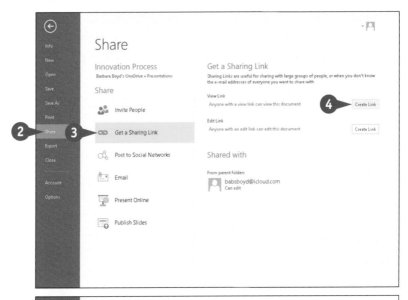

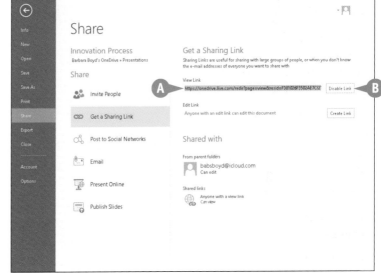

When I click Share, Get a Sharing Link is not an option. What does this mean?
You have not yet saved the presentation to OneDrive. Click **Save to Cloud** to open the Save As screen. Then save the presentation to OneDrive (for more information, see Chapter 12).

Can I create both a View Link and an Edit Link?
Yes. Click both **Create Link** buttons to create two types of links. Paste the appropriate link in the message or document where you want to share the presentation. For example, you could send an Edit Link to people whom you want to review the presentation and paste a View Link on your website.

Broadcast a Presentation

In today's business world, it is common for people to communicate using the Internet. Many business people now join a meeting remotely instead of flying or driving to the meeting. You can broadcast your slide show so anyone who has an Internet connection can watch the show live, and without the expense of a webcast service. PowerPoint creates a link to the broadcast to share with audience members. All your audience needs is a web browser and the link to join the slide show! You must have a Microsoft account, which is free, to broadcast a slide show.

Broadcast a Presentation

1 Click the **File** tab to show Backstage view.

2 Click **Share**.

3 Click **Present Online**.

4 Click **Present Online**.

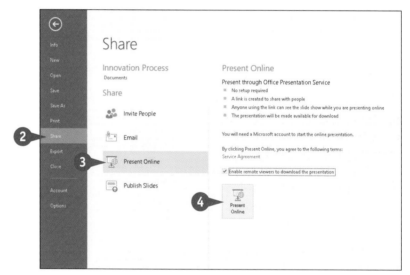

The Sign In dialog box appears. If you are already signed in to your Microsoft Live account, you do not receive this dialog box.

5 Click the text box and type your username.

6 Click **Next**.

The second Microsoft account Sign In dialog box appears.

A If you do not have a Microsoft account, click the **Sign up now** link.

7 Click the password text box and type your password.

8 Click **Sign in**.

The Present Online dialog box appears.

You are connected and can start presenting at any time.

9 Click **Send in Email**.

A blank message appears with the link pasted in the message text box.

10 Address and send the message.

The message window closes and you see the Present Online dialog box again.

Note: Audience members can click the link from their email into a web browser.

11 Click **Start Presentation**.

Note: You may need to wait for all audience members to join the slide show. If the slide show has begun when they join the web session, it appears in their web browser. If the slide show has not yet started, a message appears telling them to wait for it to begin.

12 Present the slide show to your audience.

13 When the slide show ends, click **End Online Presentation**.

14 In the dialog box that appears, click **End Online Presentation**.

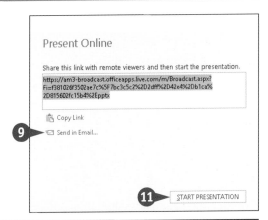

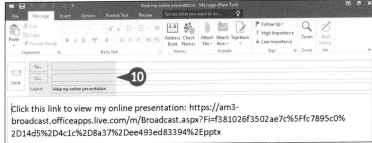

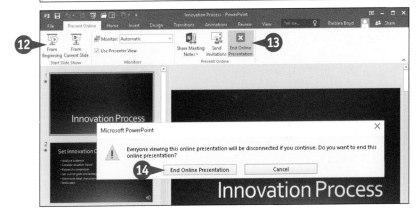

TIPS

What is Copy Link in the Present Online dialog box?

If you want to send an instant message, use an email program other than Microsoft Outlook, or perhaps send a Tweet about your imminent presentation, you can click **Copy Link**, which pastes the link into the Clipboard so you can then paste it where you want.

Can I send more invitations after closing the Present Online dialog box or after starting the show?

Yes. If you started the slide show, press Esc to stop it and display Normal view. Click the **Present Online** tab, and then click **Send Invitations**. The Present Online dialog box appears and you can send more invitations to join the show. Click **From Beginning** to restart the show.

CHAPTER 15

Printing Presentations

Although most of the time you will distribute copies of your presentation electronically, there may be times you want to print a presentation. You may want a hard copy of your slides to review away from your computer, or you might want to print slide handouts for your audience to follow during your live presentation or as notes for them to take away after.

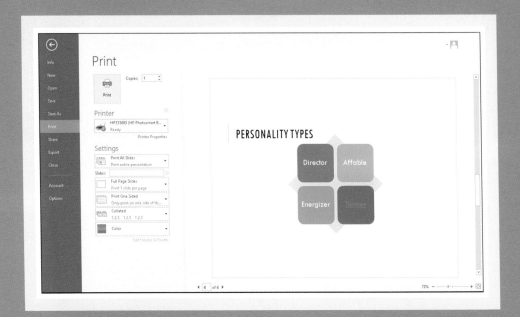

Using Print Preview

It is a good practice to see what your slides look like before you use resources for printing. Slides with colorful or dark backgrounds can use a lot of printer ink, and color printers are expensive to operate. You can use the Print Preview feature to see what your printout looks like before printing so that you do not waste these resources. You can print your presentation in different formats, and Print Preview has options that enable you to see what your printout will look like: slides, black-and-white slides, notes, outline, and so on.

Using Print Preview

1 Click the **File** tab to show Backstage view.

2 Click **Print**.

PowerPoint displays the slide show in the Print Preview view.

Ⓐ Click ◀ or ▶ to navigate through the pages.

Ⓑ Click ➕ or ➖ to zoom in and out.

3 Click **Edit Header & Footer**.

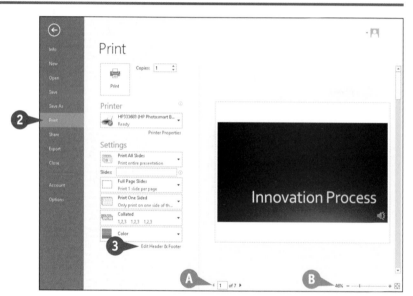

The Header and Footer dialog box appears.

4 Click the **Date and time**, **Slide number**, and **Footer** options to enable settings (☐ changes to ☑).

Note: See Chapter 11 to learn more about header and footer settings.

5 Click **Apply to All**.

Ⓒ Alternatively, you can click **Apply** to apply the setting to only the currently visible page.

PowerPoint applies your new settings and closes the Header and Footer dialog box.

Ⓓ The date and slide number appear in the Print Preview.

❻ To change printers, click the **Printer** down arrow (▼).

❼ Click a printer.

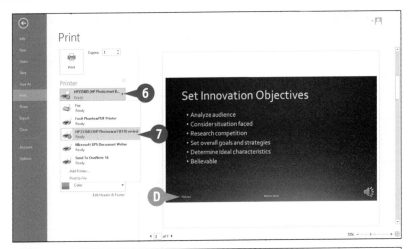

PowerPoint changes the printer.

❽ Click the **Copies** spinner (⬍) or type a number into the text box to change the number of copies to print.

Ⓔ If you print multiple copies, click **Collated** to choose how you want the pages to print: collated or uncollated.

❾ Click **Print**.

PowerPoint prints the presentation.

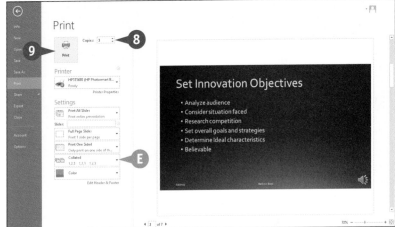

Why is my Print Preview black and white when I have it set up for color?

PowerPoint knows if a black-and-white printer is selected for printing, so it automatically shows the Print Preview in black and white. Select your color printer from the Printer list to change the Print Preview to color.

I want to save paper. Can I print on both sides?

Yes, if your printer has two-sided printing capabilities. Click the down arrow (▼) next to Print One Sided, and click **Print on Both Sides**. PowerPoint will print all the odd pages first, then you take the printed pages and place them in the paper tray again, face-up or face-down depending on your printer.

Print Slides

PowerPoint enables you to print a single slide, your entire presentation, or selected slides. You can print slides in black and white, grayscale, or in color (if you have access to a color printer). Other options are available, such as printing multiple slides per page, printing your notes with slides, or even framing slides with a border so that you can more easily see light-colored slides against the white, printed pages.

Print Slides

1 Click the **File** tab to show Backstage view.

2 Click **Print**.

PowerPoint displays the slide show in Print Preview view.

3 Click the **Slides** down arrow (⏷).

4 Click **Custom Range**.

A You can click **Print Selection** to print the slides currently selected in Normal view.

B You can click **Print Current Slide** to print the visible slide.

C You can print a range or specific slides by selecting them here.

5 Type the slide numbers you want to print in the **Slides** text box, separated by commas.

D Click the **Information** icon (ⓘ) for more information.

This example types **2,5-6**, which will print slide numbers 2, 5, and 6.

6 Click **Print**.

PowerPoint prints your selection of slides.

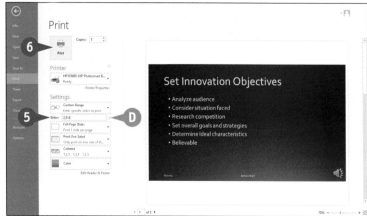

Print Hidden Slides

You may decide not to show every slide in a presentation, but you want to print the entire presentation for someone to review. Although you may hide specific slides during your presentation, as explained in Chapter 9, you can print the hidden slides without revealing them in your slide show. By default, PowerPoint prints hidden slides, but you can easily adjust print settings to exclude hidden slides from printing.

Print Hidden Slides

① Click the **File** tab to show Backstage view.

② Click **Print**.

The Print Preview appears.

Ⓐ In this example, 8 pages are scheduled to print.

③ Click the **Slides** down arrow (▼).

④ Click **Print Hidden Slides** (✔ disappears from the menu).

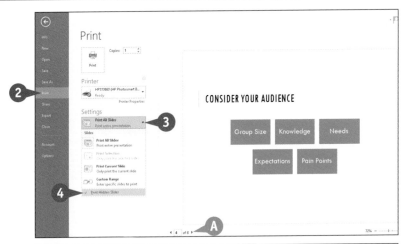

Ⓑ PowerPoint changes the number of pages now scheduled to print.

⑤ Click **Print**.

PowerPoint prints the presentation without the hidden slides.

Note: The Print Hidden Slides option is disabled if there are no hidden slides in the presentation.

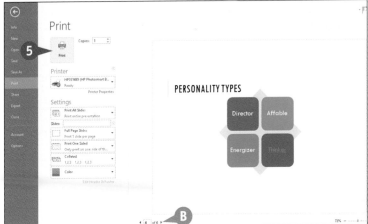

Print Handouts

A presentation handout helps audience members follow along and gives them a place where they can write notes for future reference. You can view presentation handouts in Print Preview and easily print them from that view. You can print anywhere from one to nine slides on a handout page, in landscape or portrait orientation. Printing several slides per page can save paper when you want to print handouts for a lengthy presentation, but make sure your audience can read the slides when there are several per page.

Print Handouts

1 Click the **File** tab to show Backstage view.

2 Click **Print**.

PowerPoint displays the slide show in Print Preview view.

3 Click the **Print Layout** down arrow (▼).

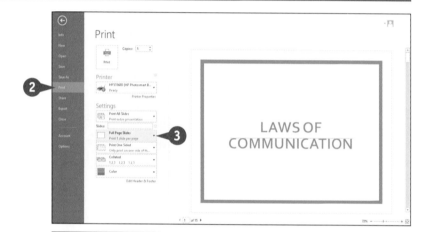

The gallery of print layouts appears.

4 Click a layout under the Handouts heading.

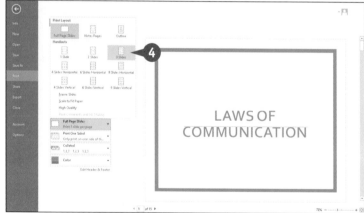

The slide layout changes in Print Preview, and the orientation drop-down list appears under the Settings heading.

5 Click the **Orientation** down arrow ( ).

6 Click an orientation.

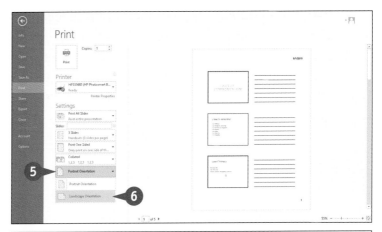

The page orientation changes in Print Preview.

7 Click **Print**.

PowerPoint prints the presentation in the layout you specified.

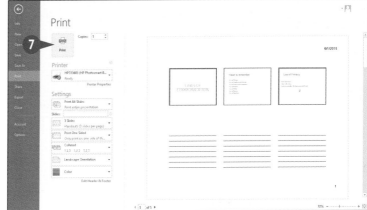

Can I add a background color to the handout page, or hide information such as the page number?

Yes. Click the **View** tab and then click **Handout Master** (see Chapter 11). You can enable (☑) or disable (☐) page information by clicking the check boxes in the Placeholders group on the Handout Master tab. Click **Background Styles** and click a background from the gallery. Click **Close Master View** when you finish.

How many slides should I include per page in a handout?

Two slides per page ensures that your audience can read the handout and leaves plenty of space for notes. If you have only a few bullet points per slide, you may be able to read the handout with four slides per page.

Print Handouts with Microsoft Word

Handouts in PowerPoint are structured and somewhat limited. For example, you cannot change the size of slides on the handout printout and you cannot edit notes in Print Preview. Exporting printouts to Microsoft Word gives you the versatility that PowerPoint lacks. For example, you can create a worksheet that the audience completes while listening to your presentation. Exporting to Word enables you to take advantage of all the capabilities of a robust word processing program. Just remember to save your Word file after you make changes.

Print Handouts with Microsoft Word

1 Click the **File** tab to show Backstage view.

2 Click **Export**.

3 Click **Create Handouts**.

4 Click **Create Handouts**.

The Send to Microsoft Word dialog box appears.

5 Click an option under the **Page layout in Microsoft Word** heading (⊙ changes to ⊙).

6 Click an option to paste or link the slide images in Word (⊙ changes to ⊙).

7 Click **OK**.

A document with the layout you chose appears in Microsoft Word.

Note: The Word document may appear only as a blinking task on the Windows taskbar. Click the icon to see the Word document.

Note: Word does not save the document automatically. If you are keeping the handouts, save it now.

⑧ Edit the Word document just like any other Word document.

Ⓐ You can add, edit, and format any text.

Ⓑ You can delete slides and add graphics.

Note: Remember to save your document after you make changes.

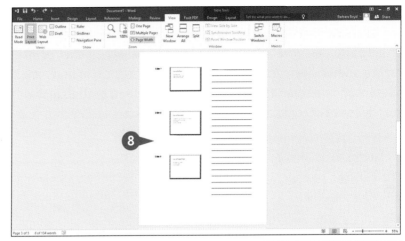

Why does my computer seem to lock up when I create handouts with Word?

The process takes a while, and the Word document may open minimized, which means it appears only on the Windows taskbar. Go to the Windows taskbar and click the Word document (it should be blinking) to make it appear.

What is the difference between Paste and Paste Link?

If you choose Paste, PowerPoint pastes images into the Word document. If you select Paste Link, the images in Word are linked to the presentation, and you can double-click the images to edit the presentation slides. Choosing Paste Link creates a smaller Word document, but the presentation must accompany it. Choosing Paste makes the Word document independent, but bigger.

Print the Outline Only

Sometimes you want to focus only on the presentation text and not the graphics. For example, you may want to give a copy of the outline to colleagues to use as an agenda at a staff meeting. It may also be convenient for you to have only the bullet points on paper so you can look down at the podium instead of looking at the projector screen during the slide show. You can print the presentation outline to do just that. The printed outline includes titles, subtitles, and bullet points, but does not include any text entered in footers or inserted text boxes.

Print the Outline Only

1 Click the **File** tab to show Backstage view.

2 Click **Print**.

PowerPoint displays the slide show in Print Preview view.

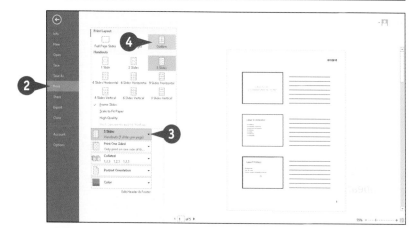

3 Click the **Print Layout** down arrow (⬇).

The gallery of print layouts appears.

4 Click **Outline**.

Print Preview changes to Outline view, and the orientation drop-down list appears under the Settings heading.

A You can click here to change the orientation of the page.

5 Click **Print**.

PowerPoint prints the outline.

Print Notes

If you are presenting a slide show, you may want a cheat sheet with additional facts or answers to possible audience questions. You can print each slide with its associated notes — the notes that were typed in the Notes pane of Normal view. The Notes printout shows one slide per page and includes the notes under the slide. You can resize and move the slide and format the notes font in the Notes Master view (see Chapter 11).

Print Notes

1 Click the **File** tab to show Backstage view.

2 Click **Print**.

PowerPoint displays the slide show in Print Preview view.

3 Click the **Print Layout** down arrow (▼).

The gallery of print layouts appears.

4 Click **Notes Pages**.

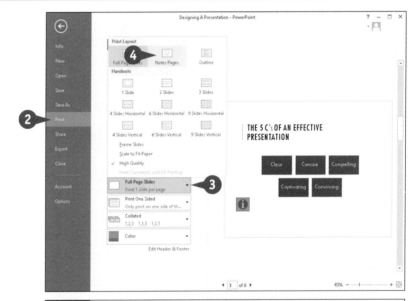

5 Click **Print**.

PowerPoint prints the Notes pages.

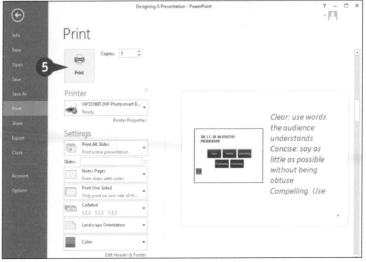

Print in Black and White or Grayscale

You can print a presentation in color, black and white, or grayscale. Grayscale provides some shading to help you see graphics and background elements. Black and white removes all shading, and this can significantly reduce your ability to see background and graphics details. Printing in color is expensive compared to black-and-white printing and it can also be slower, depending on the printer. You can provide a link to see your slides in color online but distribute a more eco-friendly grayscale printout.

Print in Black and White or Grayscale

1 Click the **File** tab to show Backstage view.

2 Click **Print**.

PowerPoint displays the slide show in Print Preview view.

3 Click the **Color** down arrow (⯆).

4 Click **Grayscale**.

Ⓐ You can click **Pure Black and White** to print in black and white with no shading.

The Print Preview appears in grayscale.

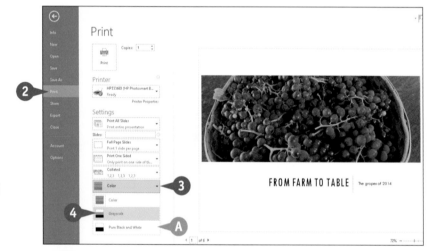

5 Click **Print**.

PowerPoint prints the presentation in grayscale.

Create Frame Slides

You can make your presentation handouts look crisp and professional by framing the slides. When you print slides with a frame, PowerPoint places a neat borderline around the edge of the slides that defines them on the printed page. Having a frame around slides in a printout is particularly nice when the slides of your presentation are white or a light color. The frame sets the slides apart from the white, printed page and improves the appearance of the printout by defining the edge of the slides.

Create Frame Slides

① Click the **File** tab to show Backstage view.

② Click **Print**.

PowerPoint displays the slide show in Print Preview view.

③ Click the **Slide Layout** down arrow (▼).

The gallery of print layouts appears.

④ Click **Frame Slides**.

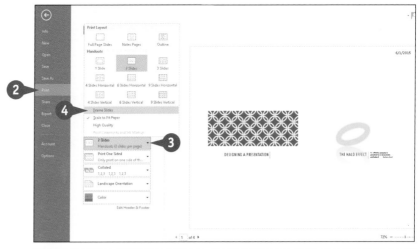

Ⓐ Print Preview shows a border around the slides.

⑤ Click **Print**.

PowerPoint prints the presentation.

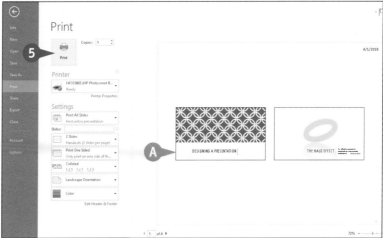

CHAPTER 16

Changing PowerPoint Options

PowerPoint is a powerful tool that becomes even more powerful when you customize it the way you want it to perform. You can adjust various settings to personalize PowerPoint, so you can use it more efficiently and effectively.

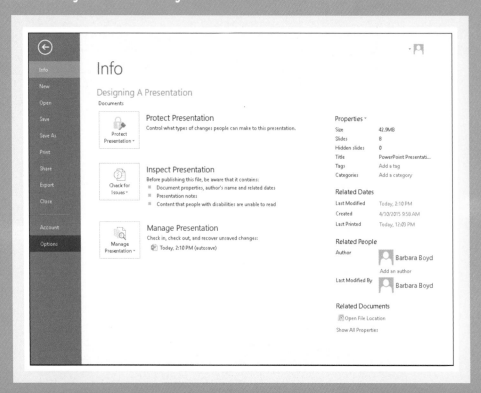

Introducing PowerPoint Options

Powerful provides a wide variety of option settings for customizing how you work with it. The options are grouped on tabs in the PowerPoint Options dialog box, and then further grouped into categories. You can change these settings to control the behavior of certain features in PowerPoint, and optimize less noticeable settings such as the default save location. Settings that are more visible include customizing the Quick Access Toolbar and the Ribbon so that your favorite and most commonly used commands are at your fingertips. Changing the options makes PowerPoint your personal presentation design tool.

General Options

In the General options, you can enable or disable the Mini Toolbar and Live Preview. The Mini Toolbar is a floating contextual toolbar that gives you quick access to formatting commands when you select text. Live Preview shows how a feature affects your slide when you position the mouse pointer over a choice in a gallery. You can enable or disable ScreenTips, which is the feature that gives you pop-up descriptions of command buttons when you position the mouse pointer over a command button on the Ribbon. You can also change the username, which appears in the properties of presentations.

Proofing Options

This tab affects the way that Microsoft Office checks for spelling and grammar errors in PowerPoint. Changes to these settings also affect the settings in the other Microsoft Office programs. You can add words to the custom dictionary and make exceptions to spelling rules. You can customize the powerful AutoCorrect and AutoFormat tools. While you type, AutoCorrect detects possible spelling errors and AutoFormat adjusts formatting to the surrounding slide elements. You can control settings such as whether PowerPoint automatically capitalizes the first words of sentences and whether it checks the spelling of words that are in all uppercase.

Save Options

You can adjust the way PowerPoint saves presentations with the Save options. This tab controls the default file location for saving documents, and enables you to choose the default file format. AutoRecovery automatically saves your PowerPoint presentation at regular intervals so that if PowerPoint unexpectedly closes, it can recover your work. You can disable AutoRecovery or adjust how often AutoRecovery automatically saves presentations. You can even save the fonts you use in your presentation to guarantee that the presentation looks good even on a computer that does not recognize the fonts you use.

Language Options

With this tab, you can choose the language used for the Ribbon, tabs, ScreenTips, and Help. You can include additional editing languages, which affect dictionaries, grammar checking, and sorting. This is useful if you use languages other than English in your presentations, such as when your organization has divisions or departments overseas. If you use languages other than English, setting up and using these options can make your experience with PowerPoint 2016 easier.

Advanced Options

Advanced options enable you to customize settings for printing, some editing, and slide show features. Some settings, such as print options, apply only to individual PowerPoint presentations. Advanced options control what you see on the screen during slide show presentations. For example, you can control whether you see the pop-up toolbar during presentations, which allows you to perform various tasks during a slide show presentation. Cut, copy, paste, and display options are also found here.

Ribbon and Quick Access Toolbar Options

Although you can add a limited number of commands to the Quick Access Toolbar from the toolbar itself, you can add any command to it from the Quick Access Toolbar tab in the Options dialog box. Besides adding commands to the Ribbon, you can add tabs and groups, as well as rename existing tabs and groups. This feature is excellent for creating a Ribbon tab containing your most commonly used commands.

Add-ins

Add-ins are small chunks of programming that enhance the functionality of PowerPoint. These are either developed specifically for PowerPoint, or are Component Object Model (COM), which use the functionality of another program in PowerPoint, such as a PDF writer or screen-capture program. You can download or create add-ins that give you special tools to design presentations or that add special functionality to your slide shows. Add-ins are available through third parties, or you can create them if you have programming experience.

Trust Center

In the Trust Center, you can read the Microsoft privacy statements and learn about security. Although malicious programs attach to documents in various ways, you can customize settings to control the behavior of safeguards used against them. If you open only presentations that you trust, you can minimize security so there is no need to respond to security messages. If you open presentations of unknown origin, you can heighten the security so that malicious programs cannot affect your computer through a PowerPoint presentation.

Modify General Options

PowerPoint provides a wide variety of options that enable you to customize how it works. User interface options, such as seeing Live Preview, ScreenTips, and the Mini Toolbar, are found in General options. You can change the username, which PowerPoint records in the properties of each presentation to identify who creates it. You find settings that control whether PowerPoint opens to the Start screen and which file extensions PowerPoint will open. You can change these options in the General tab of the PowerPoint Options dialog box.

Modify General Options

1 Click the **File** tab to show Backstage view.

2 Click **Options**.

The PowerPoint Options dialog box appears.

3 Click **General**.

4 Click to enable (☑) or disable (☐) options under the User Interface Options heading.

Ⓐ You can position your mouse pointer over the Information icon (ⓘ) to see a brief description of an option.

Ⓑ You can click the **ScreenTip style** drop-down arrow (▾) and select a ScreenTip style to display when you position the mouse pointer over a command.

5 Type your username and initials in the text boxes.

Ⓒ You can click the **Office Background** and **Office Theme** drop-down arrows (▾) and select a background pattern and color scheme for the PowerPoint window.

6 Click **Default Programs**.

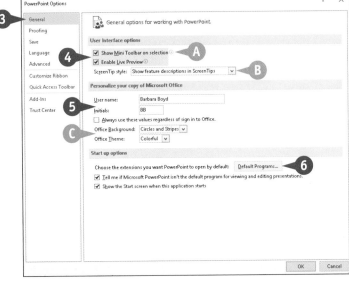

The Set Program Associations
dialog box appears.

7 Click to enable (☑) or disable
(☐) files whose extensions you
want PowerPoint to open by
default.

8 Click **Save**.

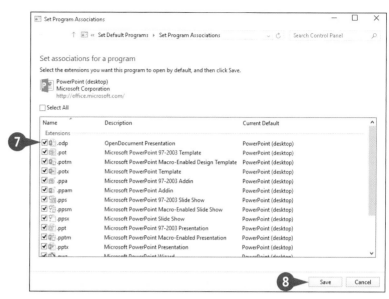

PowerPoint saves your changes
and the dialog box closes.

9 Click **Show the Start screen
when this application starts**
(☑ changes to ☐) to disable
the Start screen page when
PowerPoint starts.

When disabled and you open
PowerPoint, a new blank
presentation opens that uses
your default template.

10 Click **OK**.

PowerPoint applies your
new settings and closes the
PowerPoint Options dialog box.

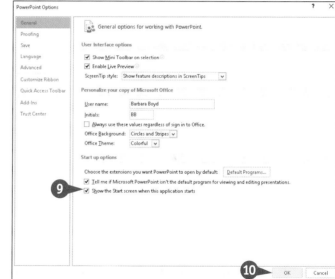

What is the Mini Toolbar?
The Mini Toolbar is a floating, contextual formatting toolbar that appears when you right-click an object to
use the submenu. The Mini Toolbar contains the most commonly used formatting commands for the object
that you select. For example, it shows the formatting commands from
the Font group of the Home tab when you select text. If you enable the
Mini Toolbar in the General options, the Mini Toolbar automatically
appears when you click and drag across text in a placeholder.

Change Spelling Options

Misspellings in presentations are never good. The powerful spell-checker in Microsoft Office automatically and continually checks spelling in PowerPoint as you type. The spell-checker identifies possible misspellings by underlining them with a red, wavy line. To review a word, you can simply right-click it. You can use this tool to check spelling as you type text, or you can disable the tool. When you need to check spelling, you can always use the spell-checker manually. You can add words that the spell-checker does not know in the PowerPoint Options dialog box.

Change Spelling Options

1 Click the **File** tab to show Backstage view.

2 Click **Options**.

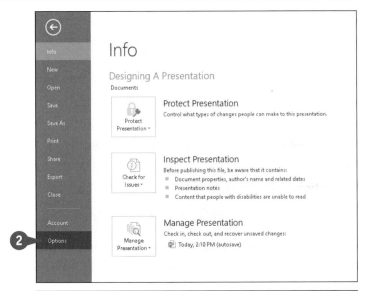

The PowerPoint Options dialog box appears.

3 Click **Proofing**.

4 Click to enable (☑) or disable (☐) options that determine how the spell-checker flags certain errors.

Note: Changes that you make here also affect the spell-checker in the other Microsoft Office programs.

5 Click **Custom Dictionaries**.

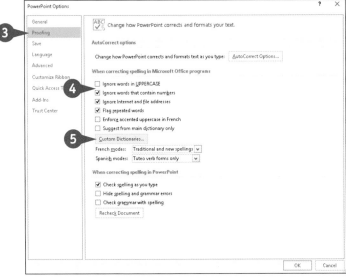

PowerPoint displays the Custom Dictionaries dialog box. PowerPoint automatically creates a custom dictionary (CUSTOM.DIC) when you add words during a spelling check. You can manually add words to your custom dictionary.

6 Click **CUSTOM.DIC** (☐ changes to ✔).

7 Click **Edit Word List**.

The CUSTOM.DIC dialog box appears.

8 Type the desired word in the **Word(s):** text box.

9 Click **Add**.

PowerPoint adds the word to the Dictionary list.

10 Click **OK**.

The CUSTOM.DIC dialog box closes.

11 Click **OK** to close the Custom Dictionaries dialog box.

12 Click to enable (✔) or disable (☐) spell-checker options in PowerPoint.

Ⓐ If you disable the **Check spelling as you type** option, you can run the spell-checker manually by clicking the **Spelling** command on the Review tab of the Ribbon.

13 Click **OK**.

PowerPoint applies your new settings and closes the PowerPoint Options dialog box.

TIP

Can I delete words from the custom dictionary?
Yes. You can delete words from the custom dictionary by following these steps:

1 Follow Steps 1 to 7 in this section.

2 Click the word you want to delete.

3 Click **Delete**.

4 Click **OK** in each of the three open dialog boxes.

Change AutoCorrect Settings

AutoCorrect can be a blessing or a curse. By adjusting the AutoCorrect options, you can add words to a list of common misspellings, empowering AutoCorrect to automatically correct words that you routinely misspell. For example, you can tell it to change "actino" to the word "action" automatically. You can also delete corrections that already exist on the list that do not help you. For example, you can delete the automatic correction of changing (c) to ©. You can also make exceptions of words that you do not want to be marked as misspelled.

Change AutoCorrect Settings

1 Click the **File** tab to show Backstage view.

2 Click **Options**.

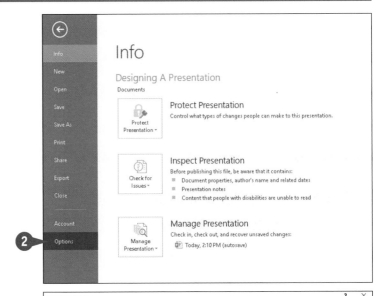

The PowerPoint Options dialog box appears.

3 Click **Proofing**.

4 Click **AutoCorrect Options**.

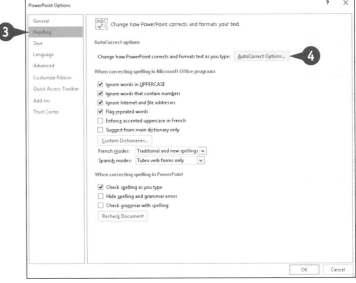

The AutoCorrect dialog box appears.

5 Click the **AutoCorrect** tab.

6 Click to enable (☑) or disable (☐) any of the standard AutoCorrect options.

A To disable the misspelling correction feature, click the **Replace text as you type** option (☑ changes to ☐).

7 To add a word to the list, type the misspelled version of the word in the **Replace:** text box.

8 Type the correct spelling of the word in the **With:** text box.

9 Click **Add**.

B You can delete a word from the list by clicking it and then clicking **Delete**.

10 Click **OK** in each of the two open dialog boxes.

PowerPoint applies your new settings.

TIP

AutoCorrect thinks the word "TO." is the end of a sentence and capitalizes the next letter. How can I prevent this?

You can add the word to a list of exceptions by following these steps:

1 Follow Steps **1** to **5** in this section, clicking the **Exceptions** button on the right side of the dialog box.

2 Click the **First Letter** tab.

3 Type your exception in the Don't capitalize after: text box.

4 Click **Add**.

5 Click **OK**.

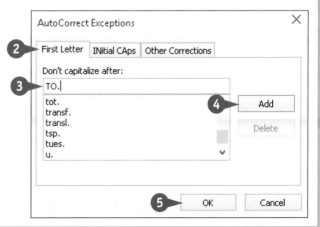

Change AutoFormat Settings

AutoCorrect has a feature called AutoFormat, which speeds up certain formatting that is cumbersome to perform. Examples include changing straight quotes to smart quotes, replacing ordinals (1st) with superscript (1st), and changing Internet paths to hyperlinks (www.test.com). AutoCorrect also automates bulleted and numbered lists. You can also choose to automatically fit text to placeholders, but remember that this will change the font size, so you may want to disable this feature. You can customize these settings to suit your particular needs.

Change AutoFormat Settings

1 Click the **File** tab to show Backstage view.

2 Click **Options**.

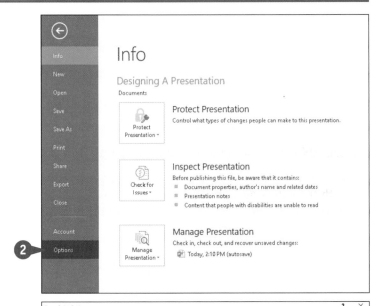

The PowerPoint Options dialog box appears.

3 Click **Proofing**.

4 Click **AutoCorrect Options**.

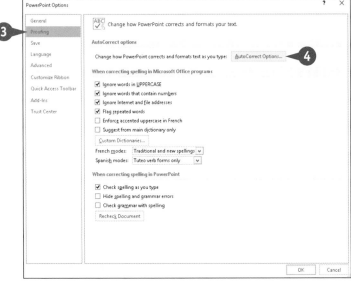

The AutoCorrect dialog box appears.

⑤ Click the **AutoFormat As You Type** tab.

⑥ Click to enable (☑) or disable (☐) any of the options under **Replace as you type**.

⑦ Click to enable (☑) or disable (☐) any of the options under **Apply as you type**.

These settings control whether text automatically sizes in the placeholders.

⑧ Click **OK** in each of the two open dialog boxes.

PowerPoint applies your new settings and closes both the AutoCorrect and PowerPoint Options dialog boxes.

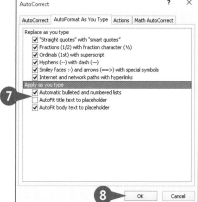

TIP

Why does PowerPoint change words that I type in all caps to lowercase?

AutoCorrect has a setting that corrects the accidental use of ⎩Caps lock⎭. To disable this option:

① Follow Steps 1 to 4 in this section.

② Click the **Correct accidental use of cAPS LOCK key** option (☑ changes to ☐).

③ Click **OK** to close each of the open dialog boxes.

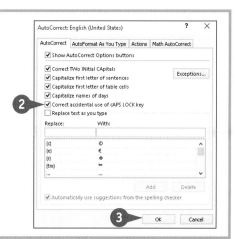

Customize Save Options

By default, PowerPoint saves a presentation in your user Documents folder with the PowerPoint 2016 format. For example, if your username is Barbara and you save a presentation for the first time, the Save As dialog box uses the folder c:\Users\Barbara\Documents\ as the default. If you share your presentations with colleagues who use an older PowerPoint version, you may want to change the settings so the default file format is the PowerPoint 2013 format because PowerPoint 2013 cannot open a file format later than that. You can also embed fonts in the saved presentation to preserve its look on any computer.

Customize Save Options

1 Click the **File** tab to show Backstage view.

2 Click **Options**.

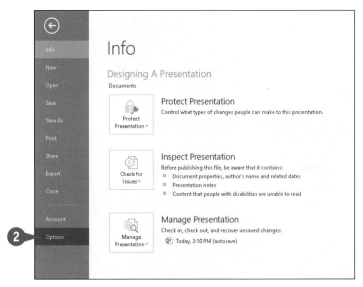

The PowerPoint Options dialog box appears.

3 Click **Save**.

4 Click the **Save files in this format** drop-down arrow (⌄).

5 Click a file format.

Note: The file type for PowerPoint 2016 is PowerPoint Presentation.

The next time you save a new file, the file type you specify here will appear as the file type in the Save As dialog box. You can choose a different file type during the save.

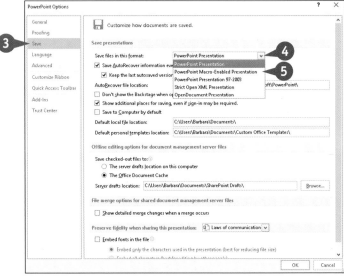

6 Click to enable (☑) or disable (☐) options under the **Save presentations** heading.

Ⓐ Make sure the **Save AutoRecover information every** option is enabled (☑) to take advantage of the automatic saving feature.

Ⓑ If desired, click the spinner box (🔁) to change the number of minutes between AutoRecover saves.

Ⓒ AutoRecover files are discarded when you close PowerPoint. Click to enable (☑) this option to retain the last file if you close without saving the file.

Ⓓ To change the default save location, type a new default location.

7 Click the **Embed fonts in the file** option (☐ changes to ☑).

Ⓔ The fonts for this particular presentation are saved with it, so it will not appear differently when viewed on a system without those fonts.

Ⓕ You can further specify whether to embed all characters or only those in use.

8 Click **OK**.

PowerPoint applies your new settings and closes the PowerPoint Options dialog box.

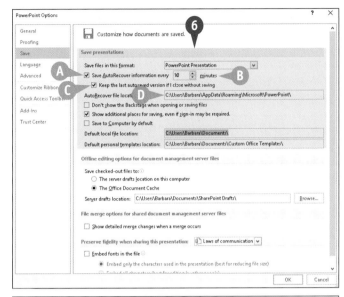

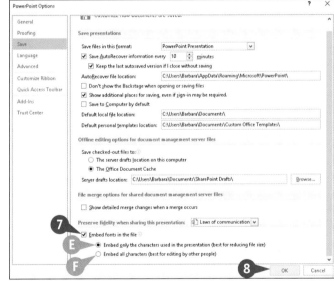

TIPS

What are the pros and cons of having the AutoRecover feature save frequently?
AutoRecover automatically saves your work at regular intervals in case PowerPoint closes unexpectedly. However, the pause you experience during the save might be lengthy if your presentation is large. You can disable AutoRecover if you do not want to be inconvenienced with this pause.

Why would I want to embed fonts in a presentation?
Some fonts are not available on every computer. If you view your presentation on a computer that is missing the fonts you used to design it, PowerPoint replaces the fonts with standard fonts from that computer. Embedded fonts travel with the presentation to ensure they are always in the presentation.

Modify View and Slide Show Options

You can change what features are available in the various PowerPoint views — for example, how many recent presentations you see on the Open screen of Backstage view and which menus are available during a slide show. The availability of these features may be determined by the option settings or by the type of presentation. In the Advanced Display and Slide Show options, you can also select which view PowerPoint uses by default, such as Normal view or Slide Sorter view.

Modify View and Slide Show Options

1 Click the **File** tab to show Backstage view.

2 Click **Options**.

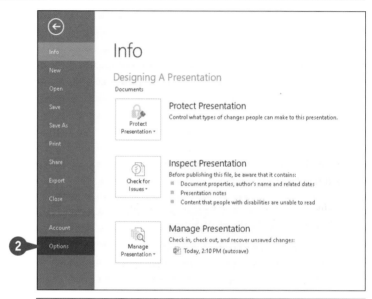

The PowerPoint Options dialog box appears.

3 Click **Advanced**.

4 Click and drag the scroll bar to locate the Display and Slide Show headings.

5 Click to enable (✔) or disable (☐) options under the Display heading.

6 Click the spinner box (⬆⬇) to change the number of files displayed in the Recent list on the File tab.

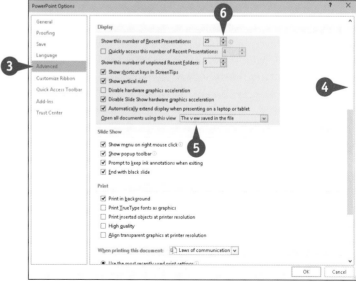

7 Click the **Open all documents using this view** drop-down arrow (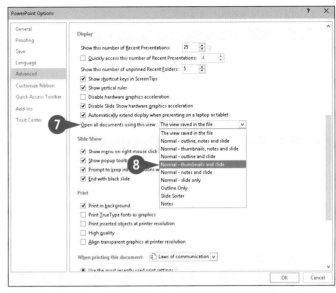).

8 Click a viewing choice.

PowerPoint uses the specified view when opening presentations.

9 Click to enable (☑) or disable (☐) options affecting behavior during a slide show.

Ⓐ Determines whether you can use the shortcut menu.

Ⓑ Controls the toolbar that faintly appears at the bottom left corner of slides.

Ⓒ Determines whether you can save annotations you made on the slides upon exiting the slide show.

Ⓓ Determines whether the slide show ends with a blank, black slide.

10 Click **OK**.

PowerPoint applies your new settings and closes the PowerPoint Options dialog box.

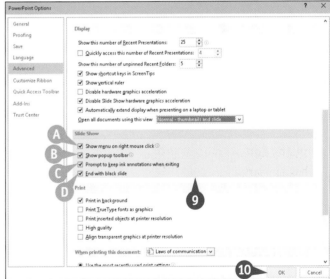

TIPS

What is the benefit of opening the presentation in Outline view?

If you start viewing the outline alone, you can concentrate on building the text for the presentation. This can be particularly helpful when you need a clean slate on which to organize your thoughts. The graphics of a slide can distract you from your outline because you may start thinking about the slide design.

Can I save annotations if I disable the Prompt to Keep Ink Annotations when Exiting option?

No. You can only save annotations by using the dialog box that prompts you to save them at the end of the slide show presentation. The prompt does not appear if you disable this option.

Change Editing Settings

You can change how certain editing tools work. For example, you may find it annoying when PowerPoint automatically selects an entire word when you click text, so you can disable that function; or you can reduce the number of undos, which consumes memory. You can also control the use of features such as the Paste Options button. This button appears when you paste a cut or copied object or text. It offers convenient options for pasting, and you can click it to see commands for working with a pasted selection.

Change Editing Settings

1. Click the **File** tab to show Backstage view.

2. Click **Options**.

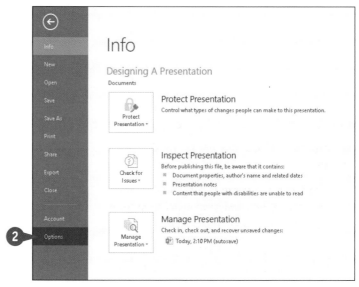

The PowerPoint Options dialog box appears.

3. Click **Advanced** and scroll to the Editing Options section.

4. Click to enable (☑) or disable (☐) options under **Editing options**.

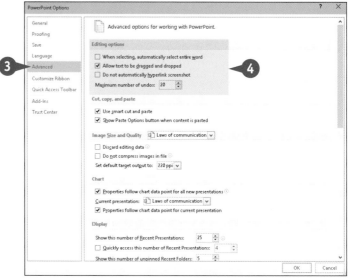

⑤ Click the spinner box (⬍) to change the number of undo edits you can perform with the Undo button (↩) on the Quick Access Toolbar.

This feature consumes considerable system memory, so if PowerPoint performs slowly, you should lower this number.

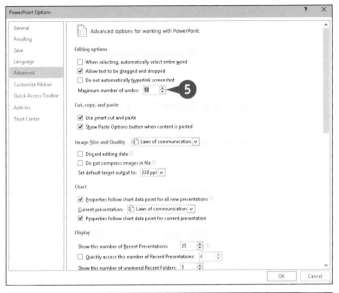

⑥ Click the check boxes to enable (☑) or disable (☐) options under the **Cut, copy, and paste** heading.

Ⓐ Smart cut and paste is a feature where PowerPoint adds missing spacing around pasted text or objects.

Ⓑ Click to disable the **Paste Options** button (🗐 (Ctrl)▾) that appears when you perform a copy-and-paste operation (☑ changes to ☐).

⑦ Click **OK**.

PowerPoint applies your new settings and closes the PowerPoint Options dialog box.

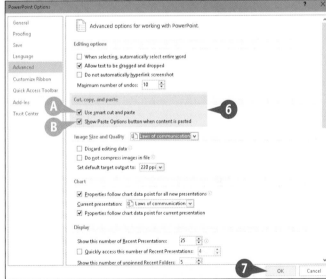

TIPS

What is the difference between the options in the Cut, Copy, and Paste section?

Selecting the **Show Paste Options button when content is pasted** option (☑) displays formatting options under where you paste. Selecting the **Use smart cut and paste** option (☑) eliminates errors by placing spacing between words if you do not select space around copied text.

What number should I use for the maximum number of undos?

The default undo value is 20 and is probably about right. If you need to undo more than 20 actions, it might be faster to reconstruct a slide from scratch. You can also close the file without saving, and then open it again to get back where you started.

Work with Print Options

You find print options when you click Print in Backstage view, but also when you click Options. The PowerPoint Options dialog box makes it easy to control presentation printing. For example, you can modify the way your printer handles fonts and the resolution of inserted graphics. You can also specify that a particular presentation always be printed with a particular printer and settings, saving you the trouble of choosing those settings every time you print that particular file. These settings can save time when printing presentations.

Work with Print Options

1 Click the **File** tab to show Backstage view.

2 Click **Options**.

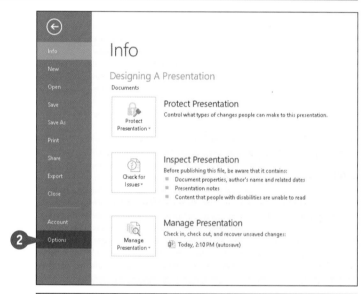

The PowerPoint Options dialog box appears.

3 Click **Advanced**.

4 Click and drag the scroll bar to the bottom of the PowerPoint Options dialog box.

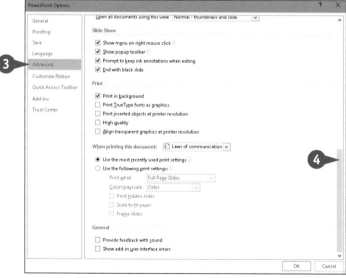

5 Click the check boxes to enable (☑) or disable
(☐) options under the **Print** heading.

🅐 **Print in background** enables you to work in
PowerPoint while printing.

🅑 **Print TrueType fonts as graphics** prevents
distortion of fonts.

🅒 Enable this setting to use the printer's resolution
settings to ensure quality printing of graphics.

🅓 **High quality** increases the resolution of
graphics, but can slow printing.

6 The next options apply to a single presentation;
click the drop-down arrow (▼) to select which
presentation these options will affect. You can
also set these options in the Print dialog box
accessed from Backstage view.

Note: The list shows open presentations; if only one
is open, you see only that one.

7 Click the presentation to which you want to
apply the settings.

8 Click the **Use the following print settings**
option (◯ changes to ◉).

The related settings become available.

9 Click to select print settings.

10 Click **OK**.

PowerPoint applies your new settings and closes
the PowerPoint Options dialog box.

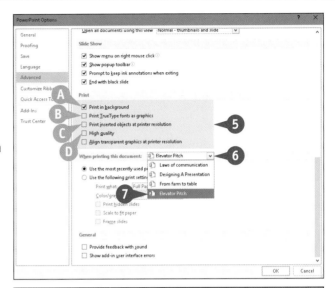

TIPS

**How can I change print settings for a presentation
that is not in the When Printing This Document
drop-down list?**

Only open presentations appear in this list; the current
presentation is the default. Click Cancel to close the
PowerPoint Options dialog box. Open the presentation
file, and then reopen the PowerPoint Options dialog box.
That presentation now appears in the list.

My printer prints slowly. How can I fix this?

You can try a couple of things. Enabling the
Print in Background option can slow down your
printer, so try disabling this feature. Also,
deselect Print inserted objects at printer
resolution (☐). This option can slow printing
because it may change the resolution of
graphics, which can take considerable time.

Customize the Quick Access Toolbar

The Quick Access Toolbar appears above the Ribbon in the upper left corner of the PowerPoint window. You can move it below the Ribbon if you want. PowerPoint sets up this toolbar with the most common frequently used commands, but you can customize it to reflect the commands you use most frequently, and you can remove buttons that you do not use. This enables you to reduce the number of clicks needed to run commonly used commands, thus streamlining your design work.

Customize the Quick Access Toolbar

1 Click the **Quick Access Toolbar** down arrow (⟱).

2 Click **More Commands**.

Ⓐ You can click **Show Below the Ribbon** to move the Quick Access Toolbar to that location.

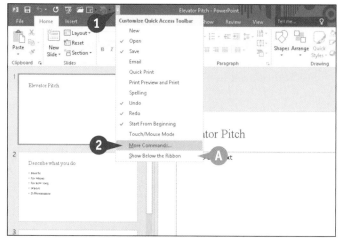

The PowerPoint Options dialog box appears, with Quick Access Toolbar displayed.

3 Click the drop-down arrow (⟱) and select the category or tab that holds the command button you want to add to the Quick Access Toolbar.

4 Find your desired command on the list and click it.

Ⓑ To add a command to the toolbar of a particular presentation, click the drop-down arrow (⟱) and select that presentation from the Customize Quick Access Toolbar list.

5 Click **Add**.

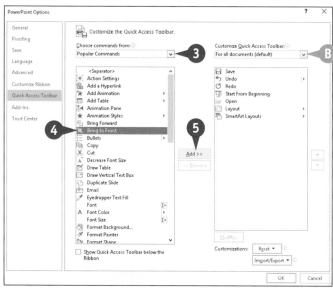

C The command appears on the list of commands under Customize Quick Access Toolbar.

D Click these arrows to change a command's position.

E Click **Remove** to remove a command from the toolbar.

6 Click **OK**.

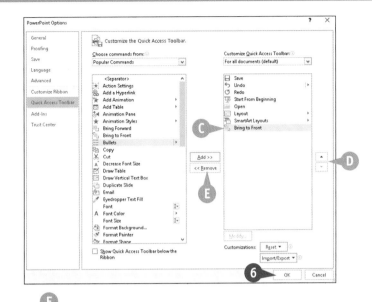

F The PowerPoint Options dialog box closes, and the Quick Access Toolbar reflects the changes you made.

TIP

How do I change the Quick Access Toolbar so it looks like it did when I first installed PowerPoint?
Follow these steps to reset the Quick Access Toolbar:

1 Follow Steps **1** and **2** in this section.

2 In the PowerPoint Options dialog box, click the **Reset** button.

3 Click **Reset only Quick Access Toolbar**.

4 Click **Yes** in the dialog that appears, and then click **OK**.

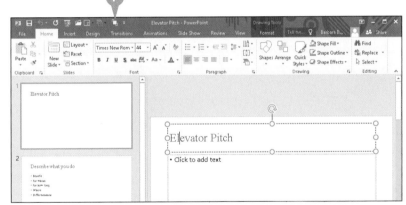

Customize the Ribbon

PowerPoint gives you full flexibility in customizing the Ribbon. You can add commands, tabs, and groups to the PowerPoint Ribbon, enabling you to have maximum proficiency in the way you handle tasks and commands. An excellent use of this feature is creating a Ribbon tab with your most commonly used commands so they are at your fingertips on a single tab, thereby making design work efficient and effective. You can add commands to existing tabs and rename existing tabs and groups.

Customize the Ribbon

Tour the Ribbon Tab Outline

1 Click the **File** tab to show Backstage view.

2 Click **Options**.

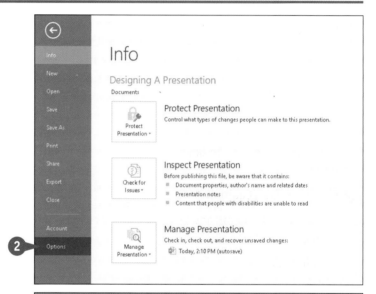

The PowerPoint Options dialog box appears.

3 Click **Customize Ribbon**.

4 Click the plus sign (⊞) to expand a level (⊞ changes to ⊟).

A The first level of names on the list shows Ribbon tabs.

B The second level shows Ribbon groups.

C The third level shows Ribbon commands, or Ribbon menus and galleries.

D The fourth level shows commands of Ribbon menus and galleries that are on the third level.

5 Click the minus sign (⊟) to collapse the **Home** tab (⊟ changes to ⊞).

Add a Custom Tab to the Ribbon

1 Click the check box to disable a tab and remove it from the Ribbon (☑ changes to ☐).

2 Click a tab name from the list — your custom tab will be inserted below it.

3 Click **New Tab**.

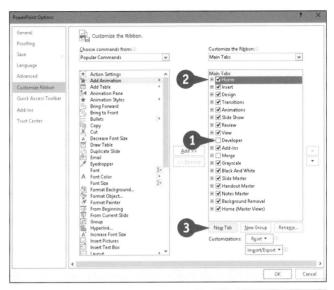

Ⓔ A new tab appears with one new group.

4 Click **New Tab (Custom)**.

Ⓕ You can use these buttons to change the position of the tab.

5 Click **Rename**.

The Rename dialog box appears.

6 Type a name in the text box.

7 Click **OK**.

The tab name changes to MyTab.

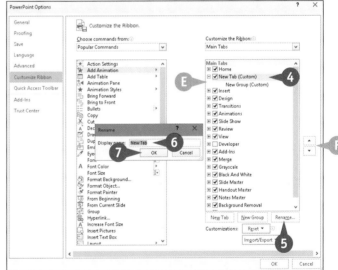

TIP

How do I make the Ribbon look like it did when I first installed PowerPoint?

To reset the Ribbon, follow these steps:

1 Follow Steps 1 to 3 in this section.

2 Click the **Reset** button.

3 Click **Reset all customizations**.

4 Click **OK**.

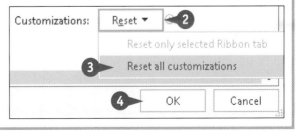

How people use Ribbon commands depends upon how they work with PowerPoint. In fact, PowerPoint users often have a group of commands that they frequently use, and many advanced users create a single tab with all their favorite commands on it. You can group commonly used commands on a custom tab to make it easier than ever to design your presentation. Regardless of the presentation that is open when you set up these options, the changes are reflected on all your present and future PowerPoint files.

Customize the Ribbon (continued)

Add a Group

1. Click the plus sign (⊞) to expand the **Insert** tab (⊞ changes to ⊟).

2. Click a group name from the list; your custom group will be inserted below it.

3. Click **New Group**.

   A new group level appears.

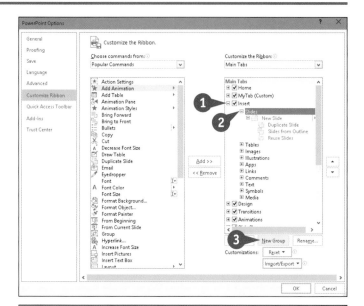

Add a Command

1. Click **New Group (Custom)**.

2. Click a command from the list.

3. Click **Add**.

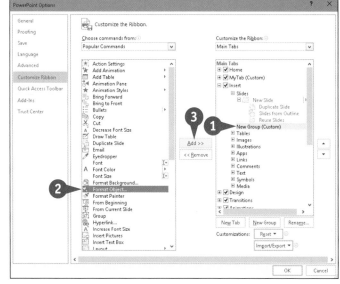

④ Repeat Steps **2** and **3** for any commands you want in any group, including existing groups.

Ⓐ PowerPoint adds your commands to New Group (Custom).

⑤ Click **NewGroup (Custom)**.

⑥ Click **Rename**.

The Rename dialog box appears.

⑦ Type a name in the text box.

⑧ Click **OK** to close the Rename dialog box.

⑨ Click **OK** to close the PowerPoint Options dialog box.

The PowerPoint Options dialog box closes, and the Ribbon reflects the changes you made.

Ⓑ PowerPoint adds MyTab to the Ribbon.

Ⓒ PowerPoint adds the group, renamed Group Objects, to MyTab.

Ⓓ PowerPoint adds the selected commands to New Group.

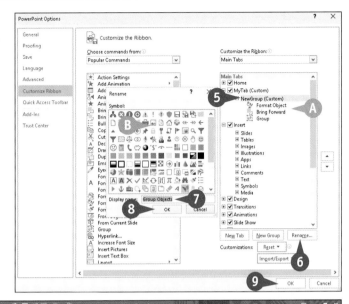

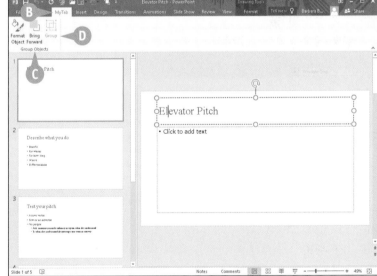

Why do some of the commands that I added to my custom group not work?

Some commands require you to select an object or text before you can use them. Select an object or text, and then try using the commands — they should now be available to use.

On the left side of the Options dialog box, I cannot find the command I want in the selected category. Is there another place to look?

Yes. Click the drop-down arrow (▾) on Choose commands from text box, and then click All Commands. If the command is currently available, it appears in the list of all commands. Keep in mind that PowerPoint 2016 may have removed some commands.

CHAPTER 17

Planning Your Presentation

The technical features of PowerPoint 2016 explained in the previous chapters are only a piece of the presentation puzzle. An effective presentation considers the audience's interests and uses PowerPoint slides to support and deliver the message that addresses their needs. A bit of forethought about your audience and message can make creating your presentation visuals easier.

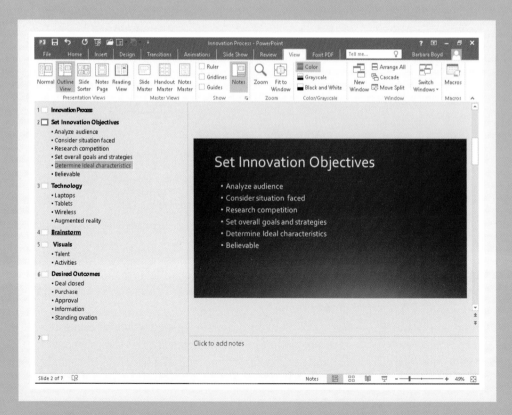

Understanding Presentation Types

There are many types of presentations but in their simplest form, all presentations have two parties: the presenter and the audience, each with a need or desire. The presenter wants to convey an idea, product, or service and seeks agreement from the audience. The audience wants to solve a problem or learn something new. The presentation is the point where the two meet. When you put your audience first and think about their needs, you become a more effective communicator.

Internal Meeting

PowerPoint slides may not be appropriate, or necessary, at every staff meeting, but when you have important news to share or many details to review, visuals can help your colleagues remember what you talk about or persuade them to agree to your idea. Slides can be particularly helpful during planning meetings, where you want to state the current situation and discuss the steps needed to move to the next stage. Although you can often be informal in language or dress when presenting to colleagues and co-workers, this does not mean you should be unprepared or sloppy; take the time to clarify your ideas and create professional slides.

Boardroom

When you present to executives (CEOs, CFOs, and the like) or venture capitalists, you want to limit your presentation to top-level information and cover the salient points, providing the information that enables them to understand the situation and make a decision. Be prepared, however, if they ask for details. You can provide details verbally, or use PowerPoint's hyperlink feature (see Chapter 7) to jump to a pre-prepared slide that shows the in-depth data supporting the top-level point on your main slide. It goes without saying: rehearse, rehearse, and rehearse again until the presentation is spontaneous and you are prepared for eventual questions; a competent presenter is perceived as and presumed to be a competent professional.

Sales

Decades ago, traditional sales presentations demonstrated a widget's features and closed with a question of how many did the customer want to buy. Today, a salesperson must demonstrate knowledge of the customer's dilemma and offer a solution. Rather than present a widget's features, you present the results and benefits the widget brings to the customer. Often sales presentations are made via video calls or webinars, which may mean the salesperson is not present during the sales presentation. Again, hyperlinks can help you customize a presentation to the audience, and if viewers are watching the presentation alone, hyperlinks let them jump to sections that most interest them.

Motivational

If you are an entrepreneur, author, or artist, motivational presentations are one of your key marketing tools. These presentations are often recorded, and the most popular spread virally online. You inspire and motivate people by telling your story (think TED talks, Wanderlust, and other venues like them) and the most effective slides show an image, a word, or a phrase related to that moment in your presentation. Your gestures, stance, and volume and tone of voice convey your enthusiasm or concern for your topic and pull the audience along with you.

Instructional

Slides are indispensable tools when teaching a concept or task-based lesson. You can refer to a simple list of steps as you go through a task or create a SmartArt diagram to illustrate the process. If students will be learning independently online, you can insert a video in your presentation that shows the task. Keep in mind the audience's knowledge and experience so that your instructional presentation is neither too simplistic nor too advanced. Rehearse in front of someone with experience similar to that of your audience to help you spot areas that are confusing or trite.

Keynote or Commencement

The honor of being asked to give a keynote or commencement speech goes to celebrities and experts. These speeches are the cornerstones of an event or graduation, and your message informs and inspires the audience. During a keynote speech you may present to an audience unfamiliar with, yet interested in, your field; for example, a keynote speech at a medical conference may be given by an architect and focus on the structural features of a new hospital. Commencement speeches tend to combine personal anecdotes and learned lessons to accompany young graduates into the world beyond university.

Scientific Conference

Professionals often find presenting research or scientific findings a daunting, yet necessary, task. Technical data must be presented in an unbiased, informative manner, yet you want the data to be compelling for your audience. Presenters often rely on charts and graphs to convey data. Instead of placing all your data on one chart, try to put only key data, highlighting the most important results with a different color or typeface, and then speak about the trials and data that led to those pertinent results; or use the *assertion-evidence presentation structure*, which presents the conclusion (the assertion) of your research at the top of each slide and subsequently takes the audience through the evidence that supports it.

Elevator Pitch

Chances are, slides will not accompany your elevator pitch, but you should be familiar with this type of presentation because it can lead to other, longer presentation opportunities. When someone asks, "What do you do?" you respond with your elevator pitch — the 118-second description of you, your business, or your product that leads the other person to say, "Tell me more." Create an elevator pitch that uses clever language to emphasize what you do for others, for whom you do it, how you help clients, and in what ways you solve problems. A concise, compelling elevator pitch can open the door to new contacts and clients.

Analyze Your Audience

The audience and their needs should influence the message you convey and is key to obtaining a *call to action* — what you want the audience to do after hearing your presentation to help solve a problem or fulfill a need. Through analysis, you can match audience needs and your call to action. This may be material, as in the purchasing of your product, or it may be figurative, as informing potential clients of your services.

Research

With Internet research, targeting your audience has never been easier. You can seek specifics about their size, expectations, experience, and influence. For a corporate sales call, use your favorite search engine to look up company and employee information. You can also research your competition to see how your offer stacks up against theirs. Visit online forums with an audience similar to yours to note the most common questions. Review previous conference programs for topics. As you research, you can gain a picture of your audience and how best to communicate with them.

Needs and Expectations

First and foremost, your presentation must respond to audience needs and expectations. Use social media or an online survey tool to gather basic information. What problems keep them up at night? What makes their lives easier? What tools do they lack? And do they expect to gain information, solutions, or assurances from your presentation? Also, how do they feel about your topic? If they have positive feelings, simply affirm those sentiments; if they have a negative viewpoint, you must first overcome that.

Knowledge Base

Whether you give a technical presentation at a conference or teach new clients how to use your software, consider how much they know about your topic. If you start with overly elementary information, you bore your audience; including excessively advanced and technical facts can confuse them. Ask your main contact about the audience's knowledge level. If possible, ask the audience a few probing questions before the presentation. Their knowledge level will dictate the language you use and the amount of time you spend giving them enough information to respond to the call to action.

Decision-Making Level

When making a sales call, or a *solutions offer*, ask ahead if the audience includes someone who can make a decision about your product or service, or if it just contains influencers who make recommendations to the decision makers. Both have their place in the corporate hierarchy, but you can tailor your presentation appropriately. For example, influencers, especially those with technical or financial expertise, will want details about how your product works and specifics on the return on investment; an executive-level decision maker may be more interested in the final outcome you offer, and not details.

Consider Design Options

Most companies hire experts to design products, logos, and brand images to elicit a desired customer reaction. Likewise, choosing the right presentation design elements engages your audience's visual and auditory senses and, through those senses, triggers an emotion. Triggering excitement and interest rather than boredom or agitation is more likely to create a lasting audience connection. If your company has a brand style guide, you may be required to use specific colors and typefaces for company presentations.

Images

When selecting images, choose something your audience has not seen before to grab their attention and create an affirmation with the words you speak. Alternatively, use images so heart-wrenchingly familiar that you are 99 percent sure to elicit the desired emotional response. Do not choose images that are familiar to the point of repeating what every other presenter on your topic has done. Rather, use images that enhance your message, and explore unique ways to represent your concepts, making sure your images are large enough to be seen from the back of the room.

Color

Studies show that colors impact the decisions we make and how we feel. Likewise, the colors you use in your presentation affect audience reaction. Pastels and *cool* colors — blues, greens, purples — tend to calm, whereas *hot* colors — reds, yellows, oranges — tend to excite. Many PowerPoint themes use a palette of complementary contrasting colors; others use hues from the same family; and some use only two: one light and one dark. When choosing colors, consider your presentation location: Use a dark background in a dark room, such as a theater setting. Use a light background in a light room, such as a conference room.

Typeface

With thousands of typefaces to choose from, you may be surprised that many presentations use the same ones: Arial, Times, Comic Sans. So, have fun experimenting with different typefaces, size, upper- and lowercase, and color as well as PowerPoint's WordArt effects. Notice how different typefaces change your message's tone: Script font recalls midcentury print ads; bold stencil resembles a poison warning.

Video and Animation

Video and animation add variety to your presentation and keep the audience interested. To mirror how our brains work, the most effective presentations introduce something different at 10-minute intervals; a new speaker, an interactive task, or a video or animation at the 10-minute mark compels your audience to pay attention. Your video can be shorter than 10 minutes, and you can intersperse more than one video in your presentation. Video or animation — such as a customer testimonial, a brief tour of your company's headquarters, or a product demonstration — can enhance your message.

Understanding Presentation Parts

Much like a business plan or a sales and marketing campaign, your presentation needs a strategy to meet identified goals and obtain the results you want. Thinking about and writing down your plan before you even open PowerPoint will make the time you spend using PowerPoint more efficient — you can concentrate on the design that supports the message you have already developed instead of designing and strategizing simultaneously. Consider the data you gathered when researching your audience and think about the best way to communicate your message, meet the needs and expectations of the audience, and guide them to take the call to action. Also, make sure you prepare for your allotted time so you do not find yourself rushing to finish your presentation.

Introduction

To begin, greet your audience and thank them for coming to the presentation. In a group that does not know you, introduce yourself (at a conference, the moderator will probably introduce you). Your chance to make a good first impression comes during the introduction, which sets the tone for the rest of the presentation. Open your presentation with a brief story related to your topic and a slide that shows an image or quote that supports your story. During a keynote or conference, you might tell a personal story, whereas in a boardroom or staff meeting, the most appropriate story may be one that describes the current situation that you want to discuss. Stories connect you and your audience.

Audience Identification

The audience attends your presentation to learn something new or discover a way to solve a problem and make their lives or business better. Following your introduction, summarize the audience's situation, demonstrate that you understand their concerns, and highlight your presentation points that will offer help or solutions. And, tell them what you want to happen by the end of the presentation. Transition into the core of your presentation by asking a rhetorical question that piques their curiosity about the rest of your presentation, use a metaphor, or cite a startling fact or statistic about their business.

Problem or Situation

Describe the problem or situation as you understand it. In a small group, you can ask for confirmation or feedback to both engage the audience and make sure your presentation and proposed solution will respond to their needs. Not all situations are problems. For example, if you want to persuade new clients to leave an existing vendor with whom they are satisfied and use your services, you need to demonstrate that you can improve an already good situation. Your slides may show images of the troublesome situation or statistics that demonstrate the current negative state of affairs.

Experience and Knowledge

Tell the audience about similar situations where your solution solved the problem. Cite other clients and highlight the positive outcome that came from working with you. Insert a video at this point with a client testimonial. In a scientific presentation, review the results of your research or trials. Each slide should show one fact or data point. If you use a chart or graph, emphasize the most important data point using a larger or different typeface or color.

Solution or Benefit

Describe the services, products, or information that you offer to solve the problem or improve your audience's situation. In a boardroom or staff meeting, describe the benefits that will occur if your idea is implemented. Guide the audience to imagine the outcome by storytelling. Be enthusiastic and positive in your speech and stance; if you are enthusiastic, your audience will be, too. Instead of a bulleted list of benefits, use slides with images that show the positive results of your solution and talk about the benefits with your spoken words.

Call to Action

You mentioned the call to action at the beginning of your presentation. Now you ask specifically for what you want. Remember, by agreeing to what you want, the audience also gets what it want. Your presentation should lead to a win-win outcome. Be clear in your request — vague requests lead to vague actions. If you are open to negotiation, then by all means negotiate, but after you have clearly stated what you want the audience to do. Restate the benefit that the audience receives when it agree to your request.

Using Props

You want the audience to pay attention while you make your presentation; in addition to eye-catching slides and compelling language, props can help keep the audience involved. With a small group, you can use interactive props that you give to the audience. If you have a physical product, showing a sample or a model version can help the audience understand, and remember, what you offer. Some props add humor or surprise to your presentation, such as fake dynamite to represent your "explosive ideas." The possibilities are limited only by your imagination.

Conclusion

Transition to your conclusion with a phrase such as, "As I finish up . . ." or "I'll close with three recommendations . . ." and then make a concise, direct conclusion. End with a strong, memorable statement that could be a brief story, a thought-provoking question or challenge, a quote, or a remarkable fact. You've already made your first impression, but the audience will remember your last, closing words. Your closing slide may read "thank you" but make sure you verbally thank your audience as well.

Give Your Presentation

How you give your presentation can be as important as what you say. Your posture, gestures, language, and voice engage your audience and affect how they perceive and react to your message.

Eye Contact

If you are engaging, your audience becomes engaged. Look audience members in the eye, moving from one person to another. Even in a large, theater-style setting, choose a few people at the front of the room to make eye contact with and gaze at one person in the back of the room.

Posture

As your mother said, "Stand up straight!" Standing with an erect spine, shoulders held back and down — not next to your ears — and your chin parallel to the floor conveys an open, relaxed, confident demeanor. It also makes breathing, and therefore speaking, easier. Keep your feet a comfortable distance apart with one slightly in front of the other, face the audience, and, if the setting permits, walk around without pacing. To stress a point, move to the center of the room, as close to the audience as possible, and speak louder.

Gesture

If you have no podium to grip — just kidding — you may wonder what to do with your hands. Depending on your topic, use them to indicate width, height, thickness, shape, or direction of an object or topic. You can also emphasize an on-screen data point or image using a handheld pointer, or PowerPoint's on-screen laser pointer. A raised fist or a chopping motion combined with facial expressions can stress statements you make with strong emotion. Although you want to appear spontaneous, practice gestures and facial expressions during presentation rehearsal and vary them to reinforce your message.

Language

When presenting to colleagues and peers, you use terminology everyone knows. However, when presenting to clients or people outside your field, you use layman's terms. Speak clearly and articulate your words. Speak more slowly to sustain a point, or accelerate slightly to show enthusiasm. Varying your speaking speed makes your presentation come across as natural and keeps your audience interested.

Voice

Your voice is your number one presentation tool. Good volume adds energy and intensity to your words. Poor volume renders your presentation worthless. You want to project your voice with your breathing and diaphragm without yelling, which only results in a sore throat. As you vary your speaking speed, you should also vary your volume level; if you use a monotone voice, you come across as bored with your topic and you will bore your audience. When you rehearse, vary voice speeds and volume in different parts of your presentation to determine what seems most natural and effective. Even the words you choose to stress in a single sentence can affect the audience's perception.

Respond to Questions

Questions from the audience give you an opportunity to learn if they understood your message, to clarify any points of confusion, and to identify topics and concerns that are a priority for your audience. Answering questions also gives you an opportunity to demonstrate your knowledge and professional demeanor in the face of potential conflict.

Prepare

Like a good scout, a good presenter prepares for potential questions, demands, objections, or feedback that may arise. List facts that might be challenged and prepare your answers from different perspectives. Think about how to respond to difficult or awkward questions: Do you want to be direct or subtle, disagree in the absolute or consider a different point of view, persuade or agree to disagree? Ask colleagues to listen to you rehearse and have them to ask questions for practice.

Encourage Participation

A calm voice, open stance, and friendly facial expression encourage audience comments and questions. At the start of your presentation, mention you have time allotted at the end for questions and explain how you will handle them. For example, you can pass around a microphone, have an assistant collect written questions, or have them sent via an electronic device. In a classroom, encourage questions during your presentation so students can grasp sequential material. In a boardroom, the audience will likely ask questions during your presentation. If your audience is reluctant to ask questions, consider making a statement to get them started; for example, "People often ask me . . . ."

Give Clear Answers

When someone asks a question, follow some simple steps to ensure a satisfactory answer. First, listen to the entire question without interrupting. Second, mentally analyze the motive for the question, such as the desire for information, clarification, or simply attention. Next, repeat the question in your own words to confirm what the inquirer wants. Finally, answer the question succinctly and completely — sometimes a yes or no is enough. Make eye contact with the inquirer and then look at the rest of the audience. End by asking if your response answered the question.

Dealing with Hecklers

When someone asks a question in an aggressive tone or begins yelling, as difficult as it may be, remain calm and respectful. Respond to the question — not the emotion. Try one of the following ways to maintain your professionalism: Use humor by smiling while saying something like, "That sounds like a trap"; ask the audience for a show of hands of who feels the same way. If no one does, suggest speaking alone afterward and move on to the next question; or rephrase the question from a neutral point of view and respond. If the confrontation is legitimate, acknowledge it with a phrase such as, "I understand your frustration" or "We messed up. Let me explain."

Index

A

Index

Index

Index